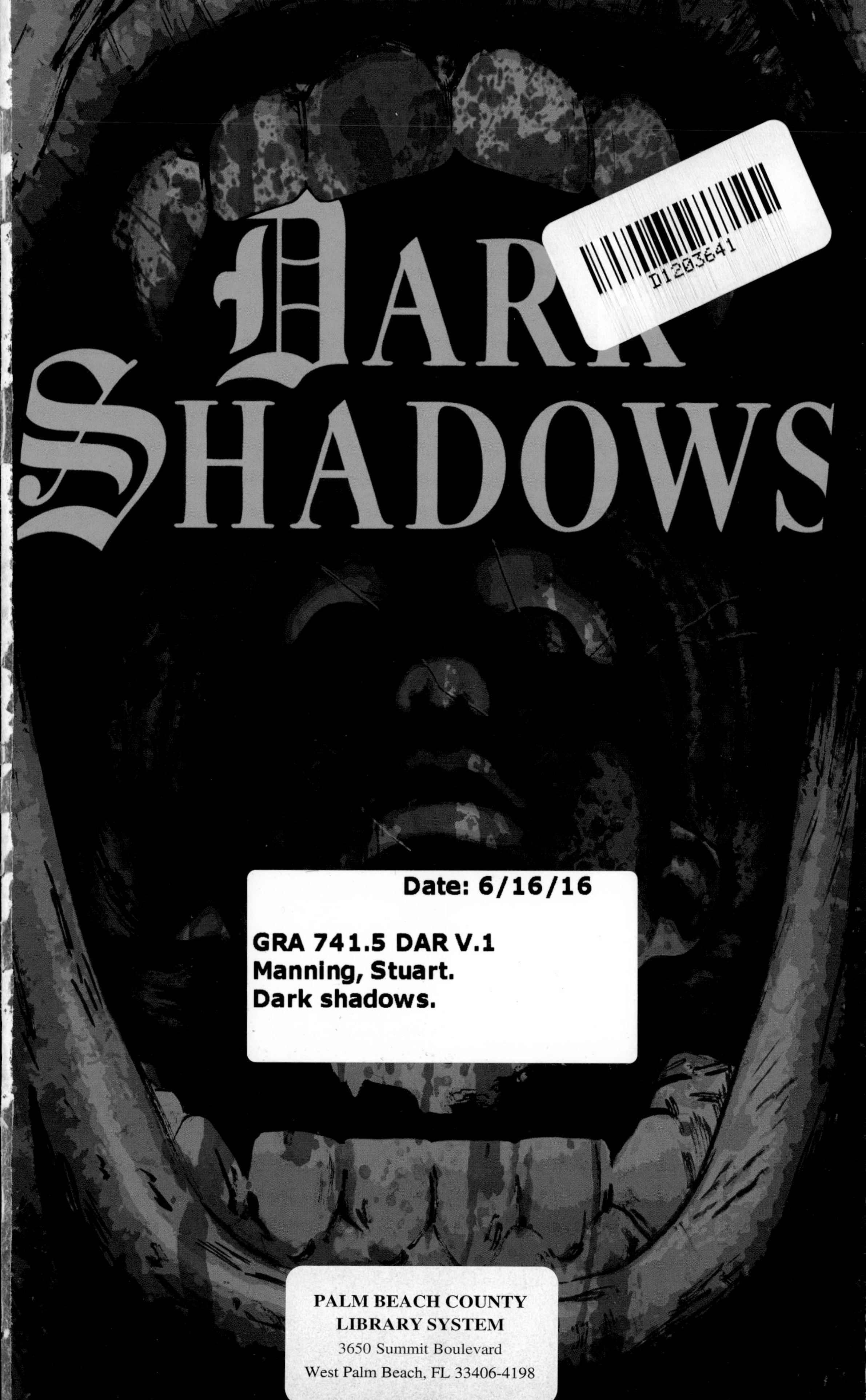
DAR
SHADOWS

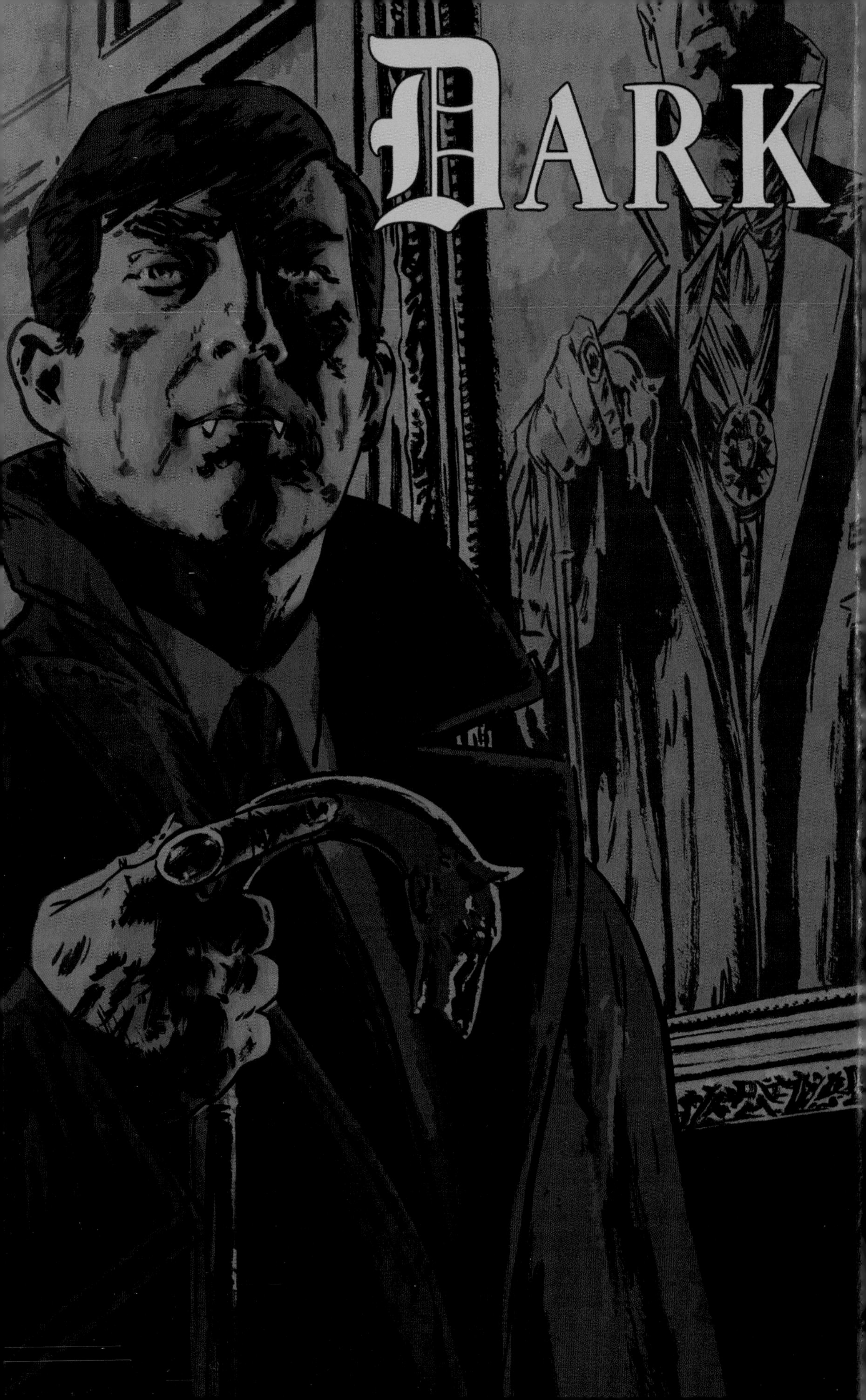
DARK

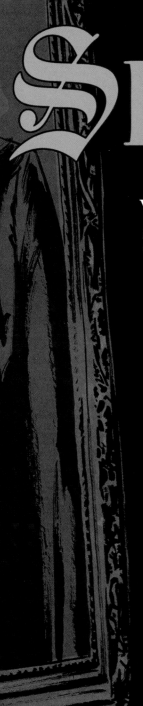

SHADOWS™

Written by
STUART MANNING

Illustrated by
AARON CAMPBELL (issues 1-3)
GUIU VILANOVA (issue 4)

Colored by
CARLOS LOPEZ

Lettered by
TROY PETERI

Collection cover by
FRANCESCO FRANCAVILLA

Collection design by JASON ULLMEYER
Special thanks to JIM PIERSON

This volume collects issues 1-4 of
Dark Shadows by Dynamite Entertainment.

DYNAMITE® ENTERTAINMENT
www.DYNAMITE.net
Follow us on Twitter @dynamitecomics

Nick Barrucci, President
Juan Collado, Chief Operating Officer
Joe Rybandt, Editor
Josh Johnson, Creative Director
Rich Young, Director Business Development
Jason Ullmeyer, Senior Designer
Josh Green, Traffic Coordinator
Chris Caniano, Production Assistant

COMIC SHOP LOCATOR SERVICE
888-COMIC-BOOK
comicshoplocator.com

First Printing
ISBN-10: 1-60690-275-X
ISBN-13: 978-1-60690-275-2
10 9 8 7 6 5 4 3 2 1

The year is 1971. The place, Collinsport, a remote fishing village on the Maine coastline. At its heart lies the ancestral Collinwood mansion, home to the wealthy Collins family, a dynasty living in the shadows of a troubled past. At the Old House on the estate lies the Collins family's darkest secret - Barnabas Collins, a man two centuries out his time, condemned by the witch Angelique to live for eternity as a vampire. As Barnabas struggles to keep his vampiric existence a secret, he faces an uncertain future living in fear of the supernatural forces that curse the Collins family across history.

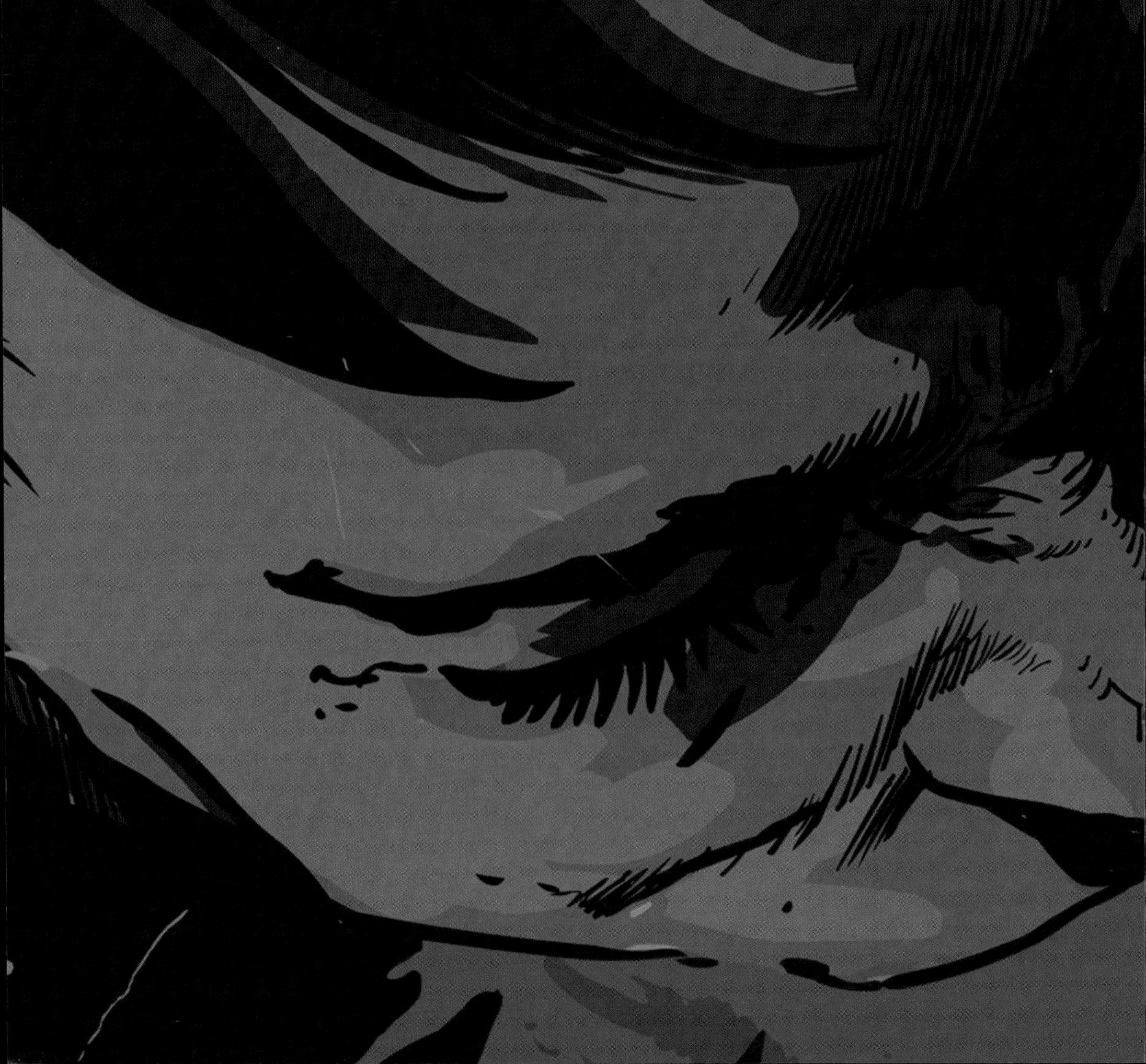

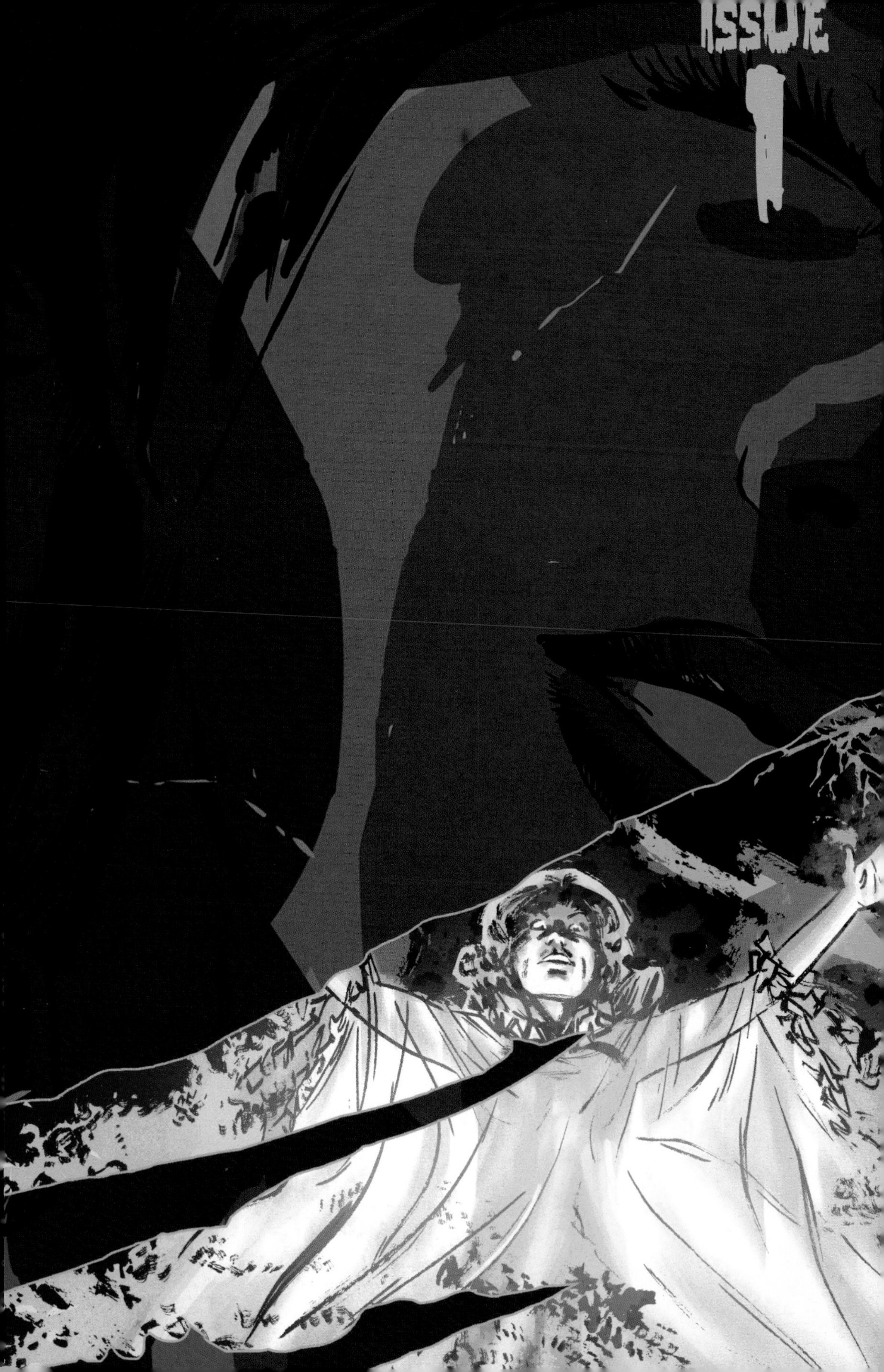
ISSUE
1

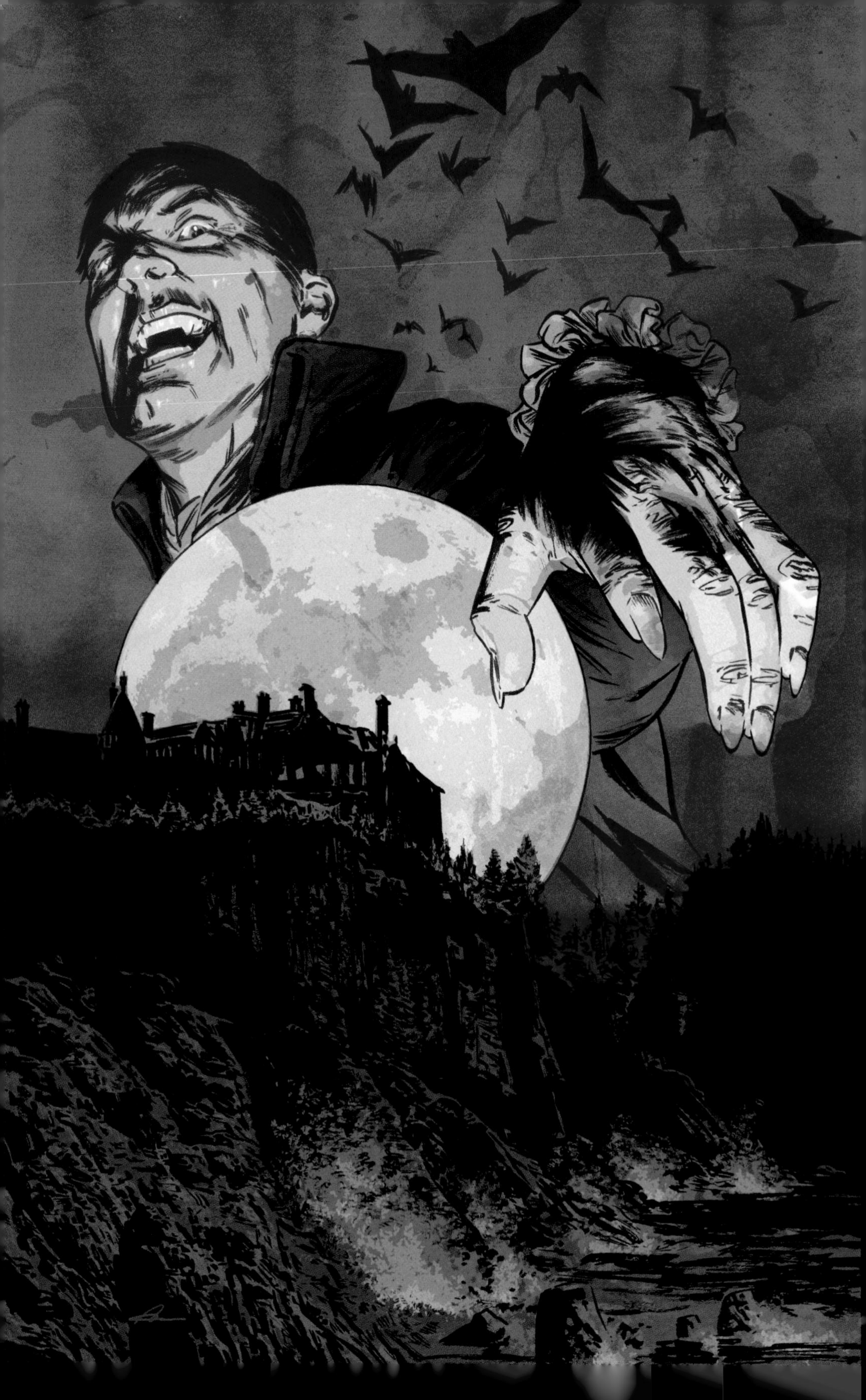

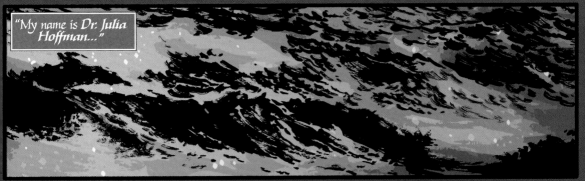

"My name is *Dr. Julia Hoffman...*"

"*Evening at Collinwood...* the house on Widow's Hill, and home of the *Collins family.*"

"It is a house of *secrets.* A place where I first arrived as a *stranger.*"

"Now *I know* so many of the Collins family's secrets..."

"The *secrets* they keep from *one another...* and secrets I keep from *them.*"

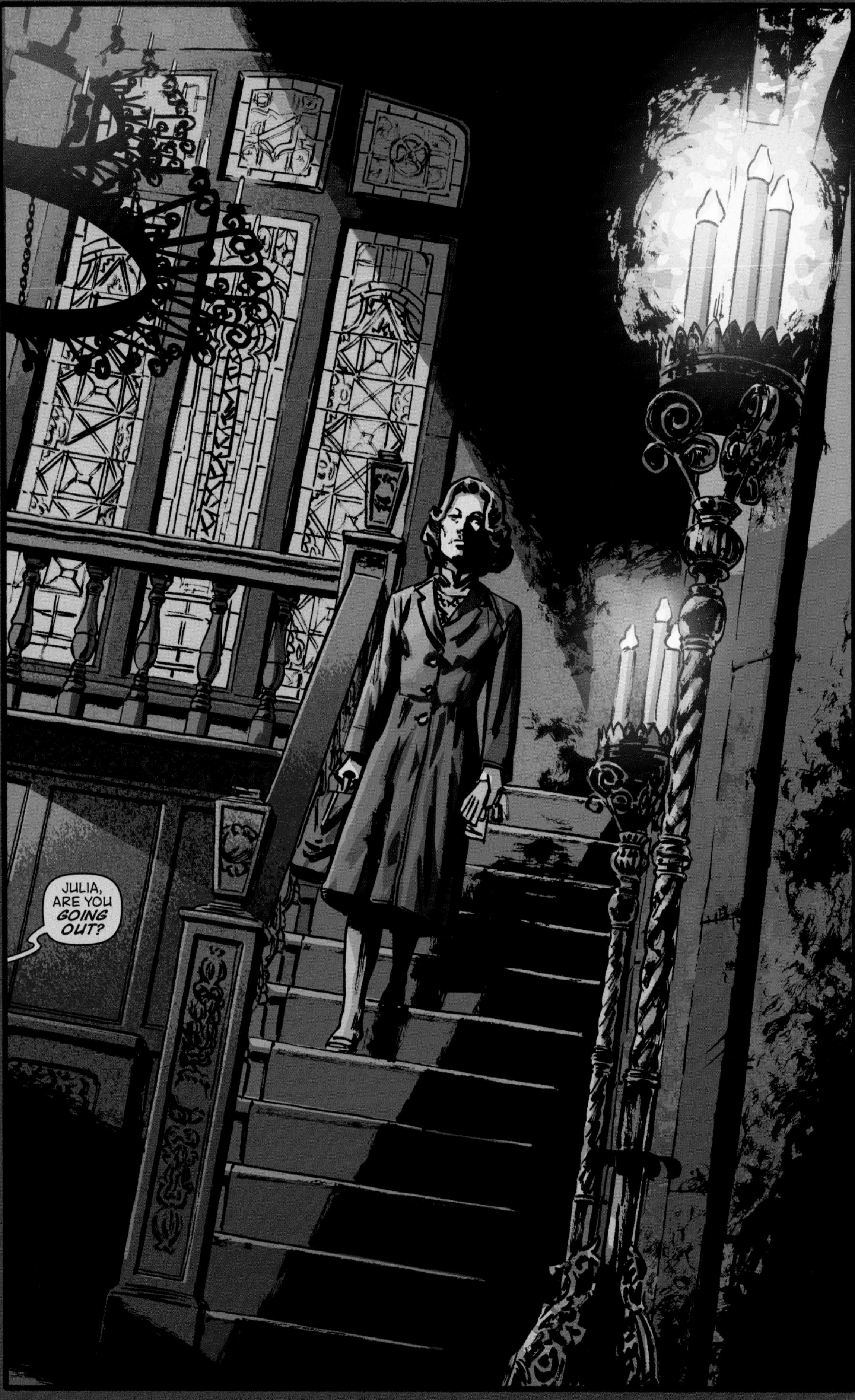
JULIA, ARE YOU *GOING OUT?*

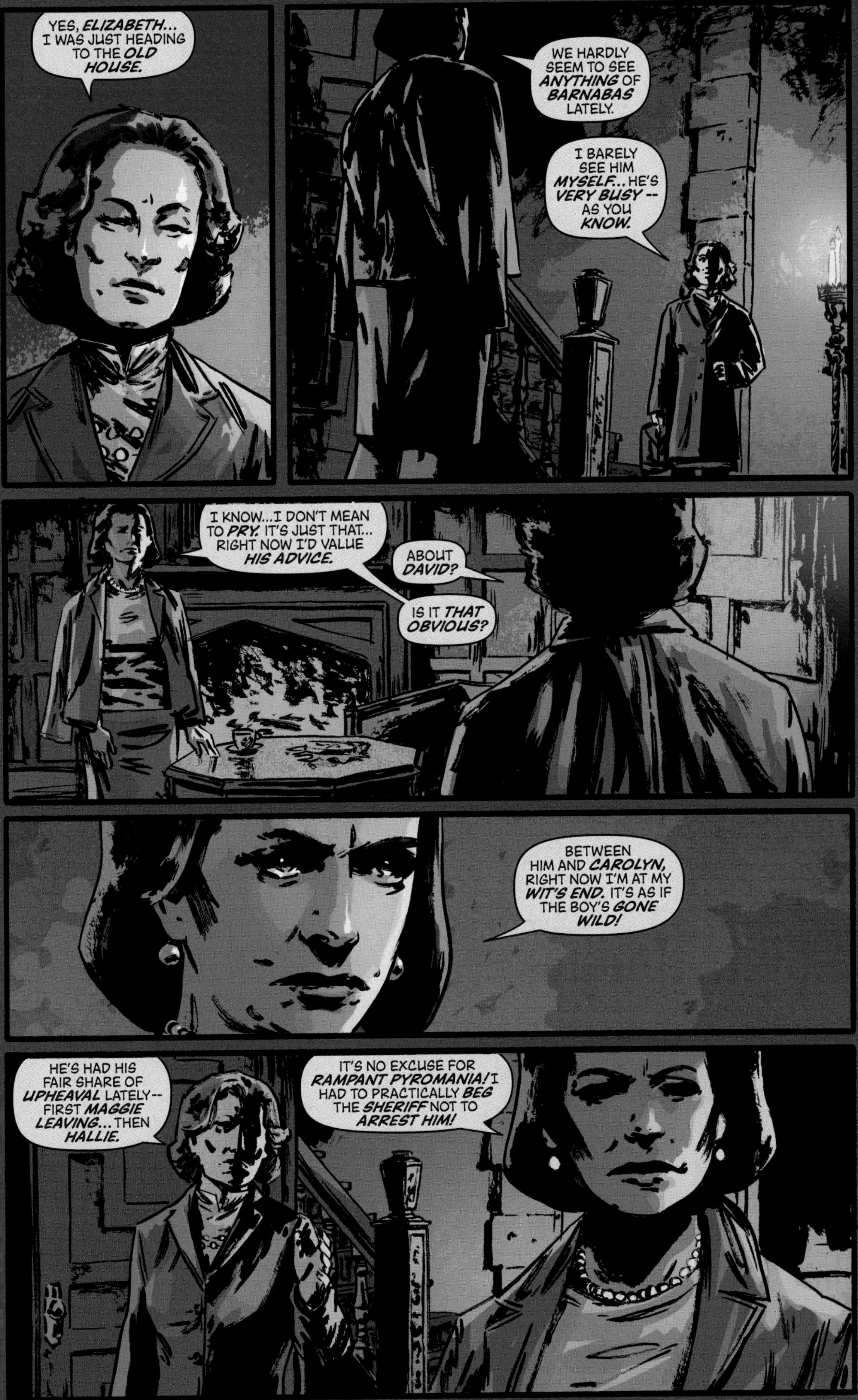
YES, ELIZABETH... I WAS JUST HEADING TO THE OLD HOUSE.
WE HARDLY SEEM TO SEE ANYTHING OF BARNABAS LATELY.
I BARELY SEE HIM MYSELF... HE'S VERY BUSY -- AS YOU KNOW.
I KNOW...I DON'T MEAN TO PRY. IT'S JUST THAT... RIGHT NOW I'D VALUE HIS ADVICE.
ABOUT DAVID?
IS IT THAT OBVIOUS?
BETWEEN HIM AND CAROLYN, RIGHT NOW I'M AT MY WIT'S END. IT'S AS IF THE BOY'S GONE WILD!
HE'S HAD HIS FAIR SHARE OF UPHEAVAL LATELY-- FIRST MAGGIE LEAVING... THEN HALLIE.
IT'S NO EXCUSE FOR RAMPANT PYROMANIA! I HAD TO PRACTICALLY BEG THE SHERIFF NOT TO ARREST HIM!

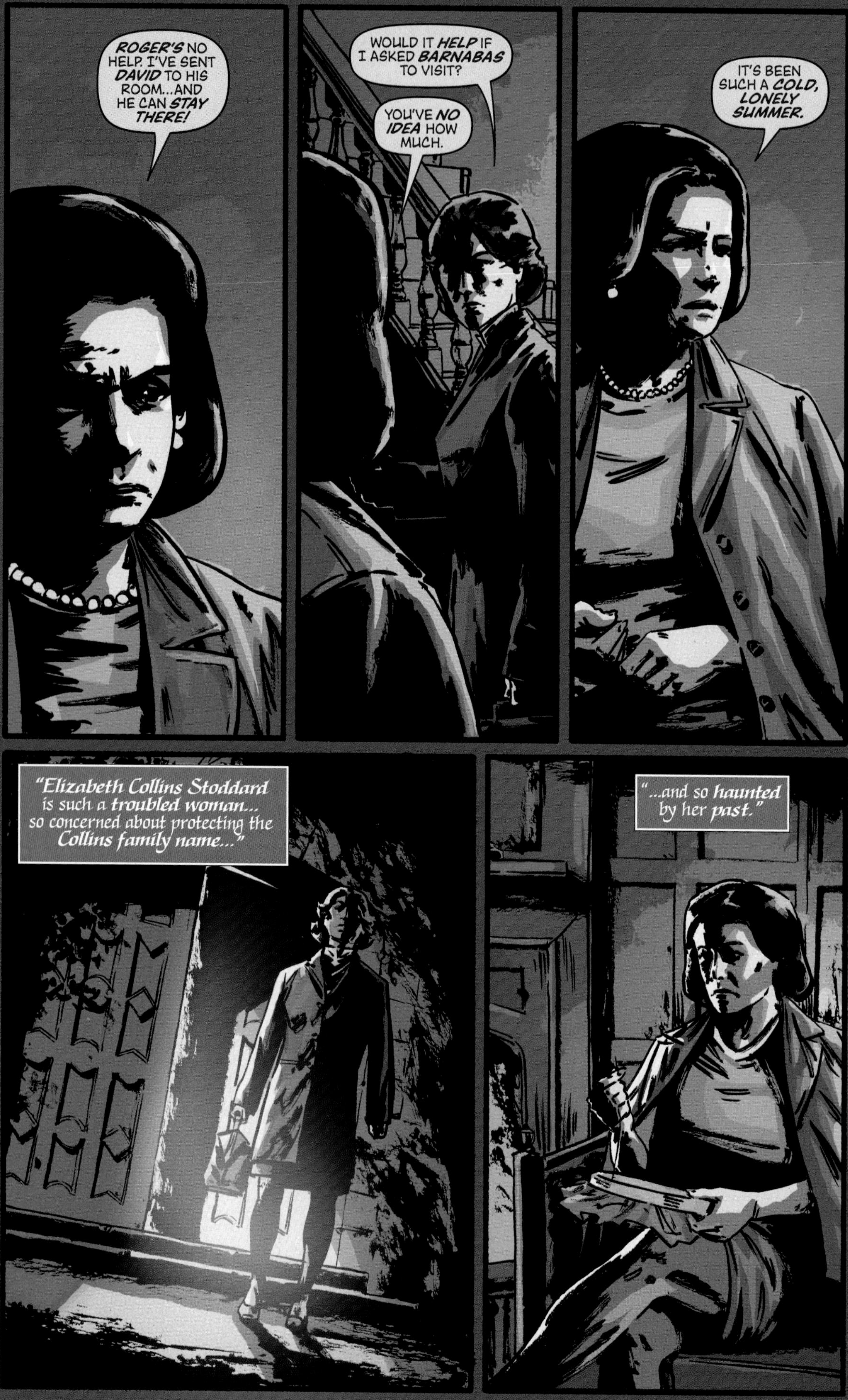
ROGER'S NO HELP. I'VE SENT DAVID TO HIS ROOM...AND HE CAN STAY THERE!
WOULD IT HELP IF I ASKED BARNABAS TO VISIT?
YOU'VE NO IDEA HOW MUCH.
IT'S BEEN SUCH A COLD, LONELY SUMMER.
"Elizabeth Collins Stoddard is such a troubled woman... so concerned about protecting the Collins family name..."
"...and so haunted by her past."

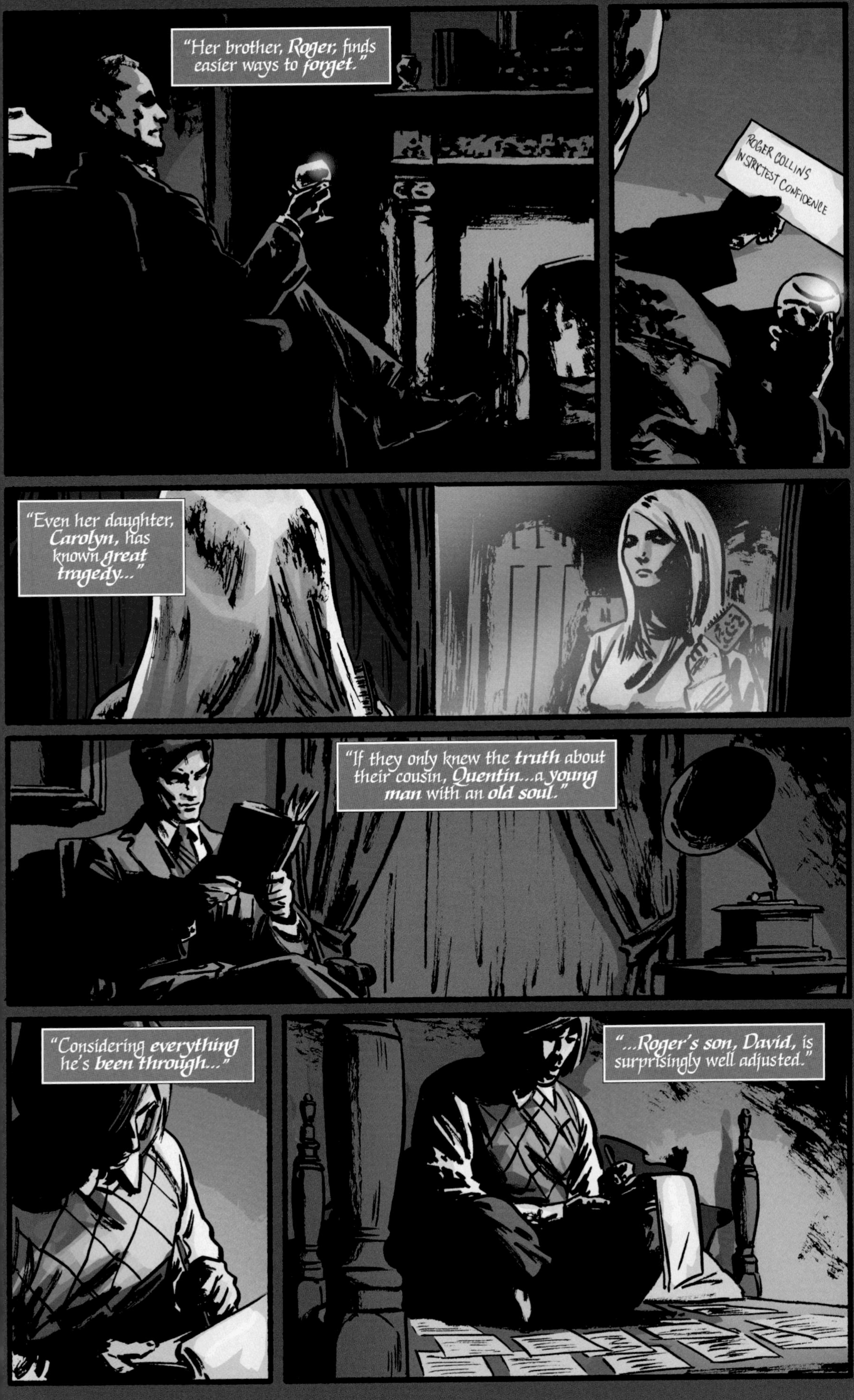
"Her brother, Roger, finds easier ways to forget."
ROGER COLLINS IN STRICTEST CONFIDENCE
"Even her daughter, Carolyn, has known great tragedy..."
"If they only knew the truth about their cousin, Quentin...a young man with an old soul."
"Considering everything he's been through..."
"...Roger's son, David, is surprisingly well adjusted."

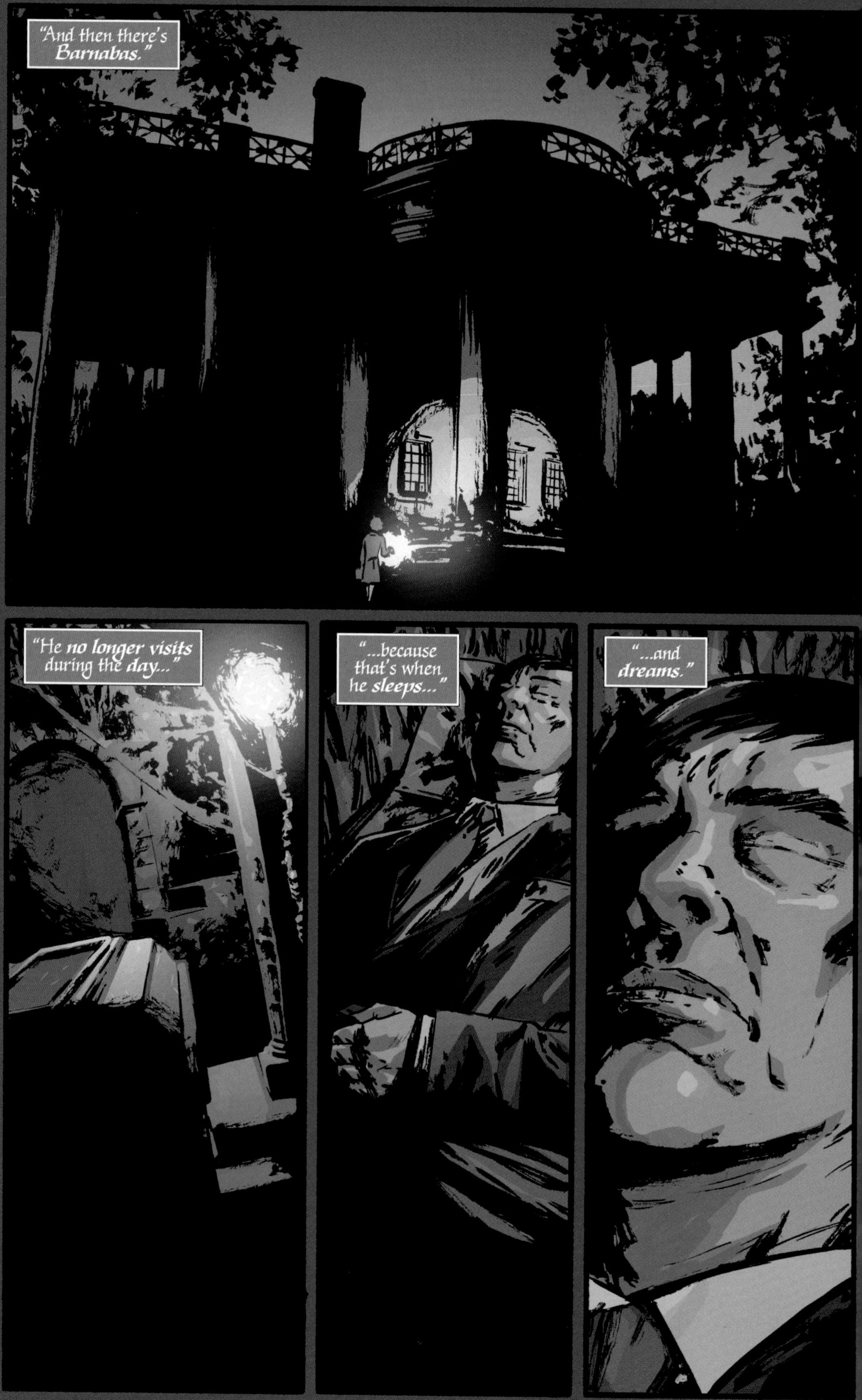
"And then there's Barnabas."
"He no longer visits during the day..."
"...because that's when he sleeps..."
"...and dreams."

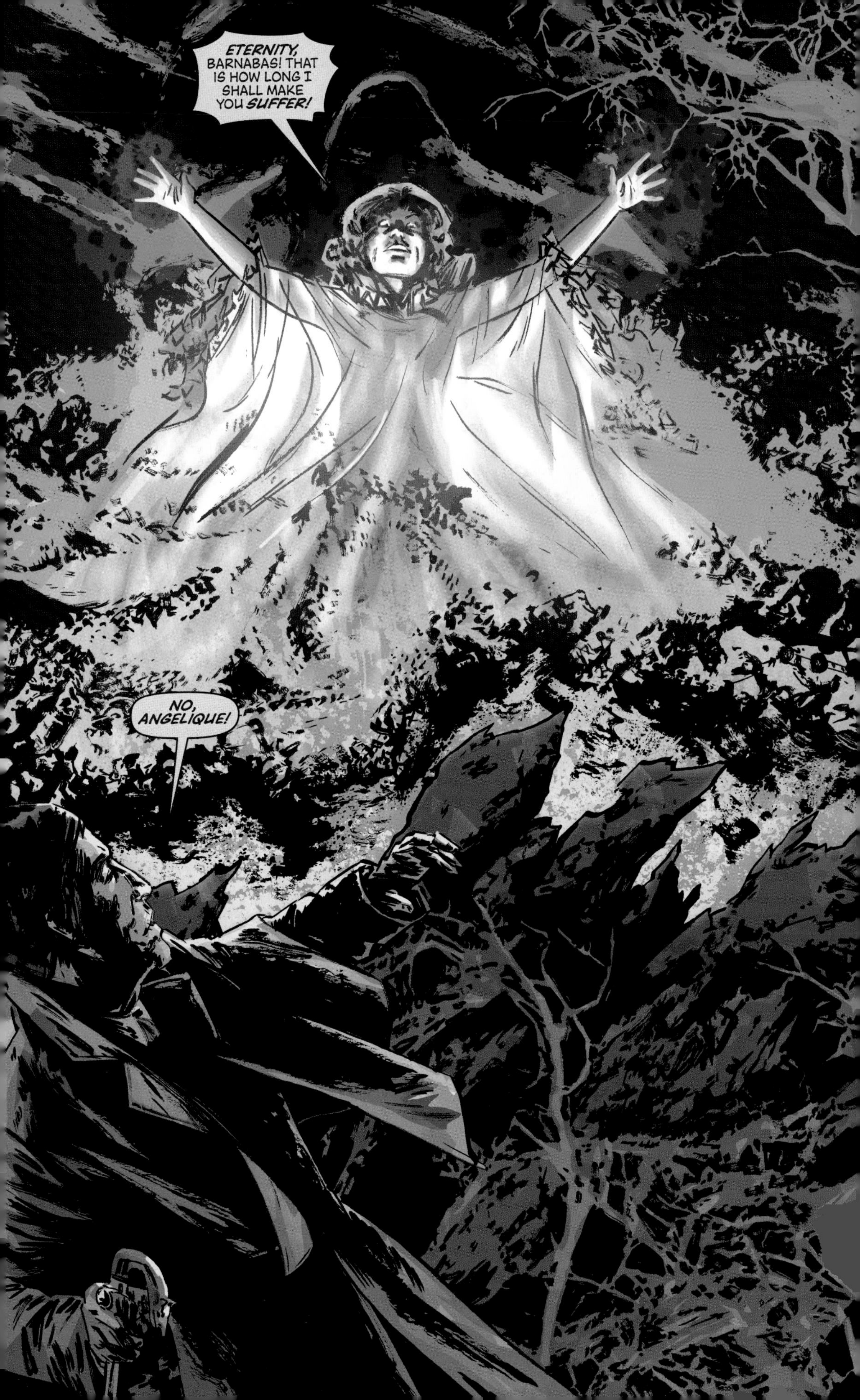
ETERNITY, BARNABAS! THAT IS HOW LONG I SHALL MAKE YOU SUFFER!
NO, ANGELIQUE!

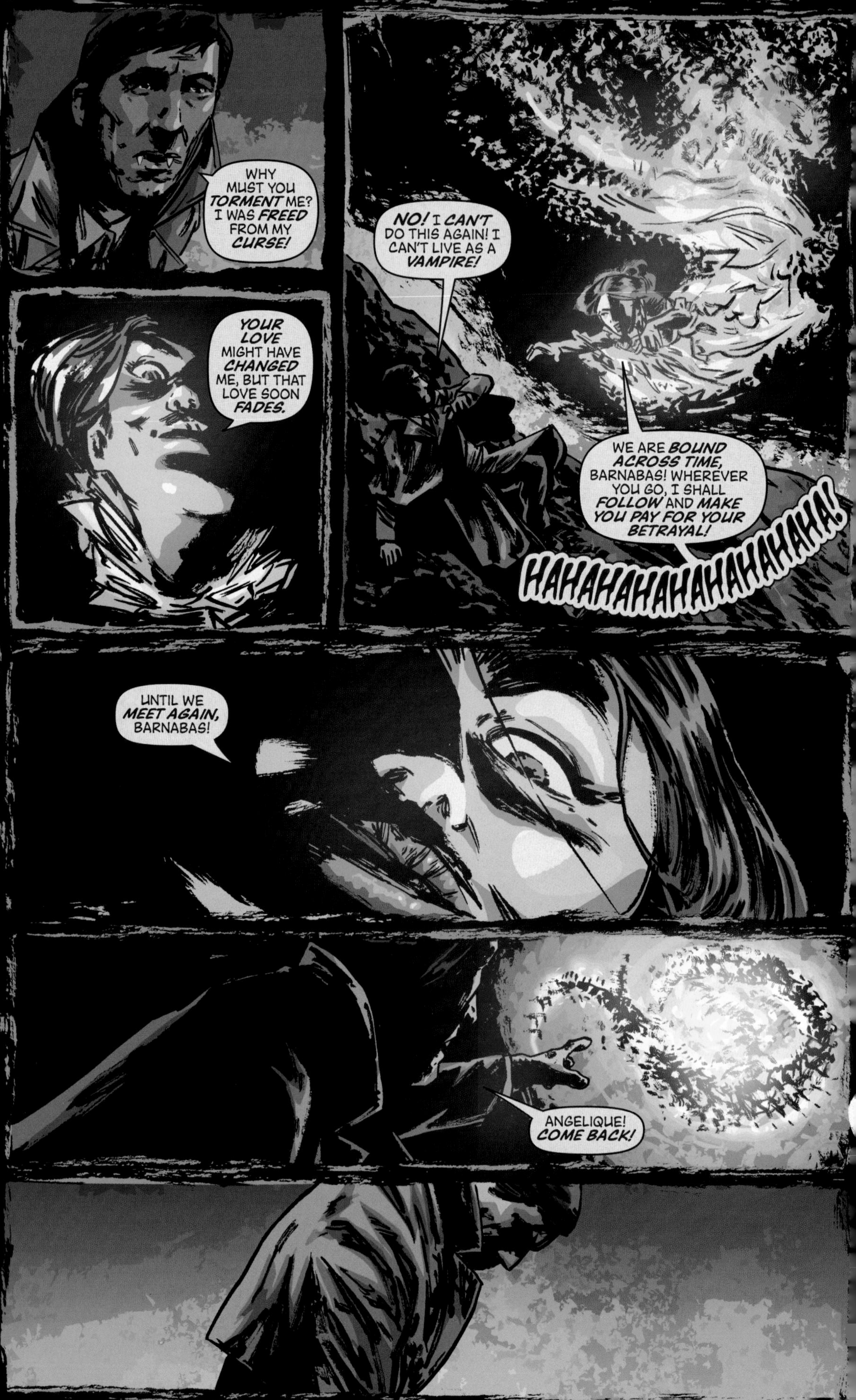
WHY MUST YOU TORMENT ME? I WAS FREED FROM MY CURSE!
YOUR LOVE MIGHT HAVE CHANGED ME, BUT THAT LOVE SOON FADES.
NO! I CAN'T DO THIS AGAIN! I CAN'T LIVE AS A VAMPIRE!
WE ARE BOUND ACROSS TIME, BARNABAS! WHEREVER YOU GO, I SHALL FOLLOW AND MAKE YOU PAY FOR YOUR BETRAYAL!
HAHAHAHAHAHAHAHAHAHA!
UNTIL WE MEET AGAIN, BARNABAS!
ANGELIQUE! COME BACK!

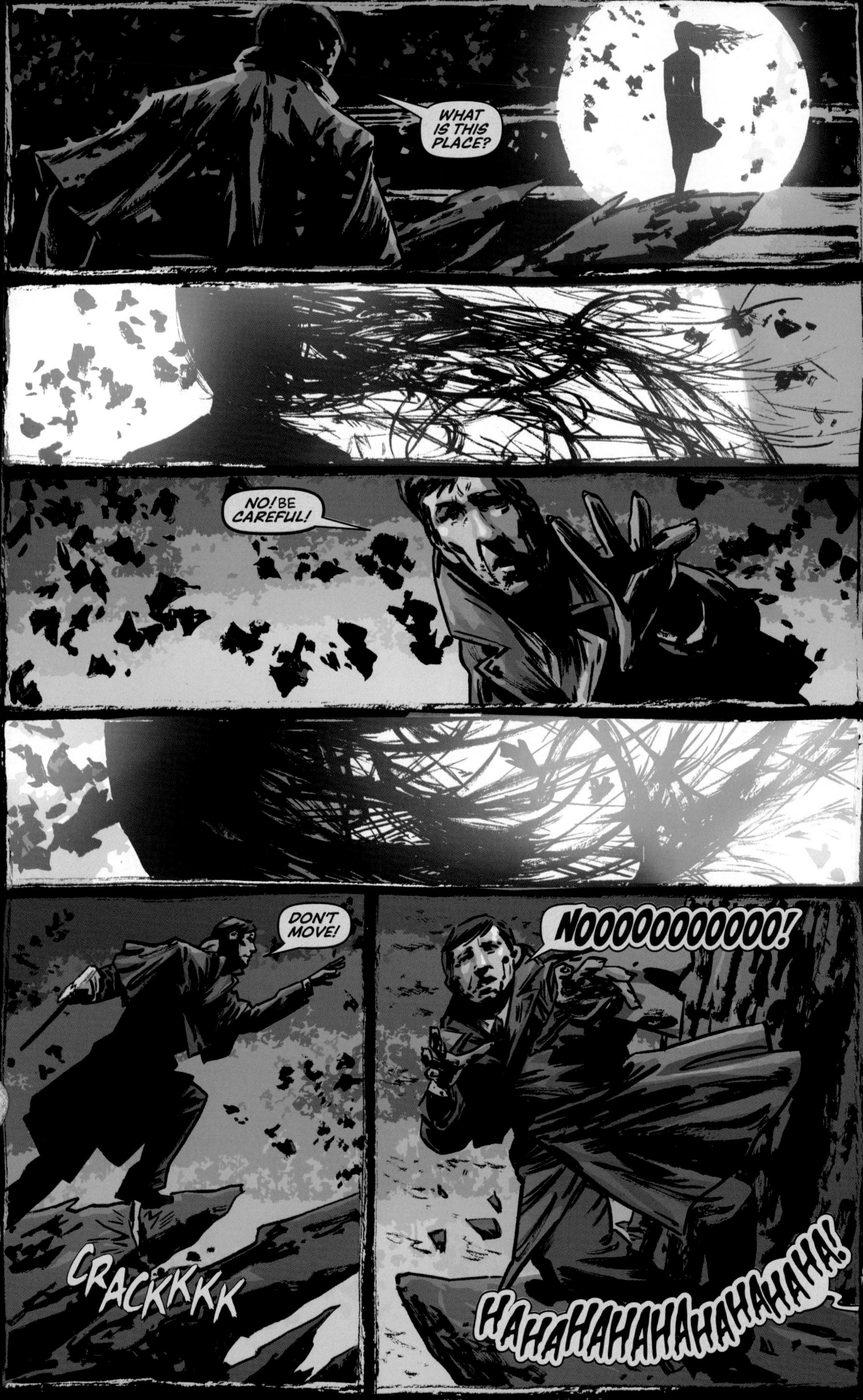
WHAT IS THIS PLACE?
NO! BE CAREFUL!
DON'T MOVE!
CRACKKKK
NOOOOOOOOOOO!
HAHAHAHAHAHAHAHAHAHA!

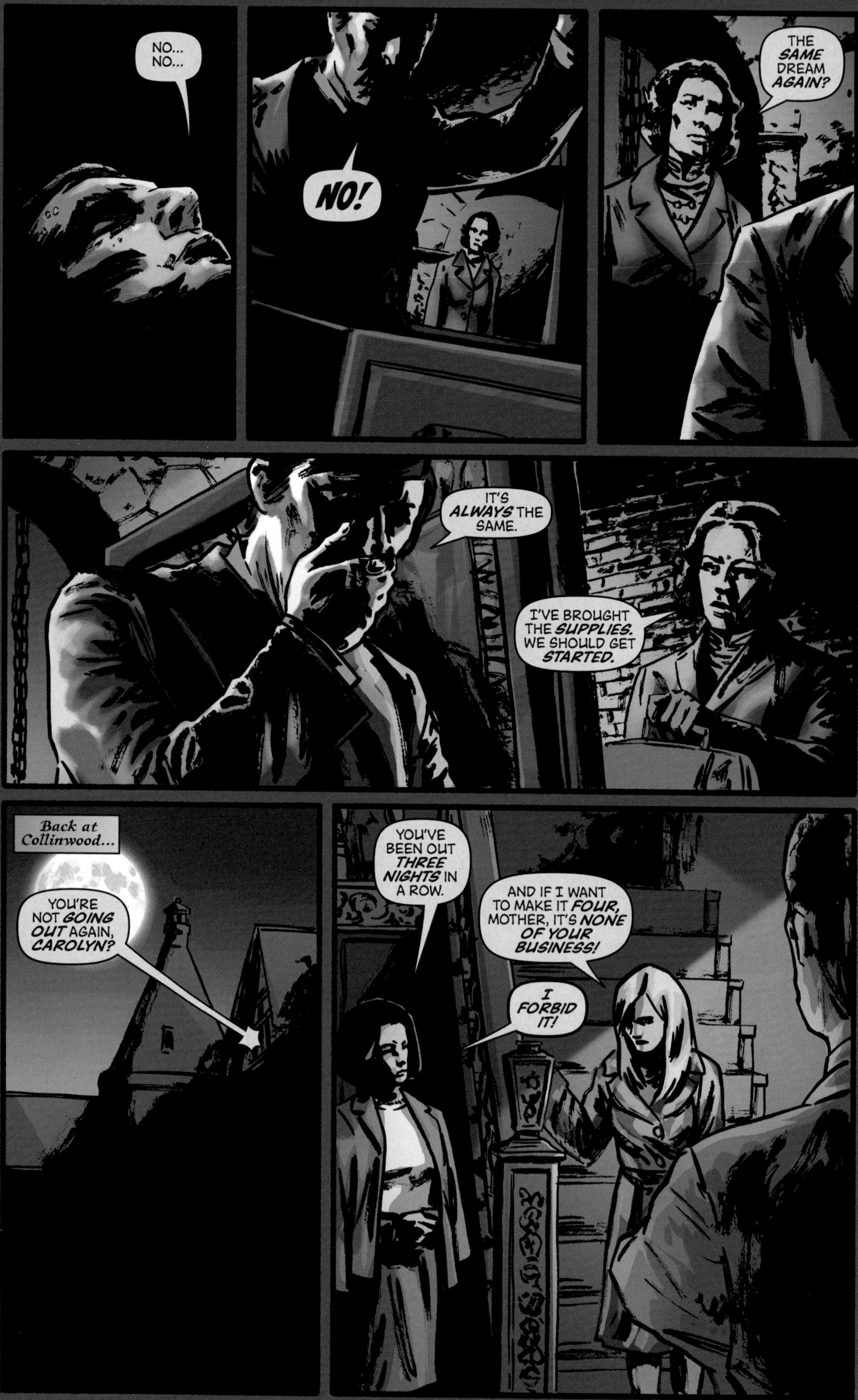
NO... NO...
NO!
THE SAME DREAM AGAIN?
IT'S ALWAYS THE SAME.
I'VE BROUGHT THE SUPPLIES. WE SHOULD GET STARTED.
Back at Collinwood...
YOU'RE NOT GOING OUT AGAIN, CAROLYN?
YOU'VE BEEN OUT THREE NIGHTS IN A ROW.
AND IF I WANT TO MAKE IT FOUR, MOTHER, IT'S NONE OF YOUR BUSINESS!
I FORBID IT!

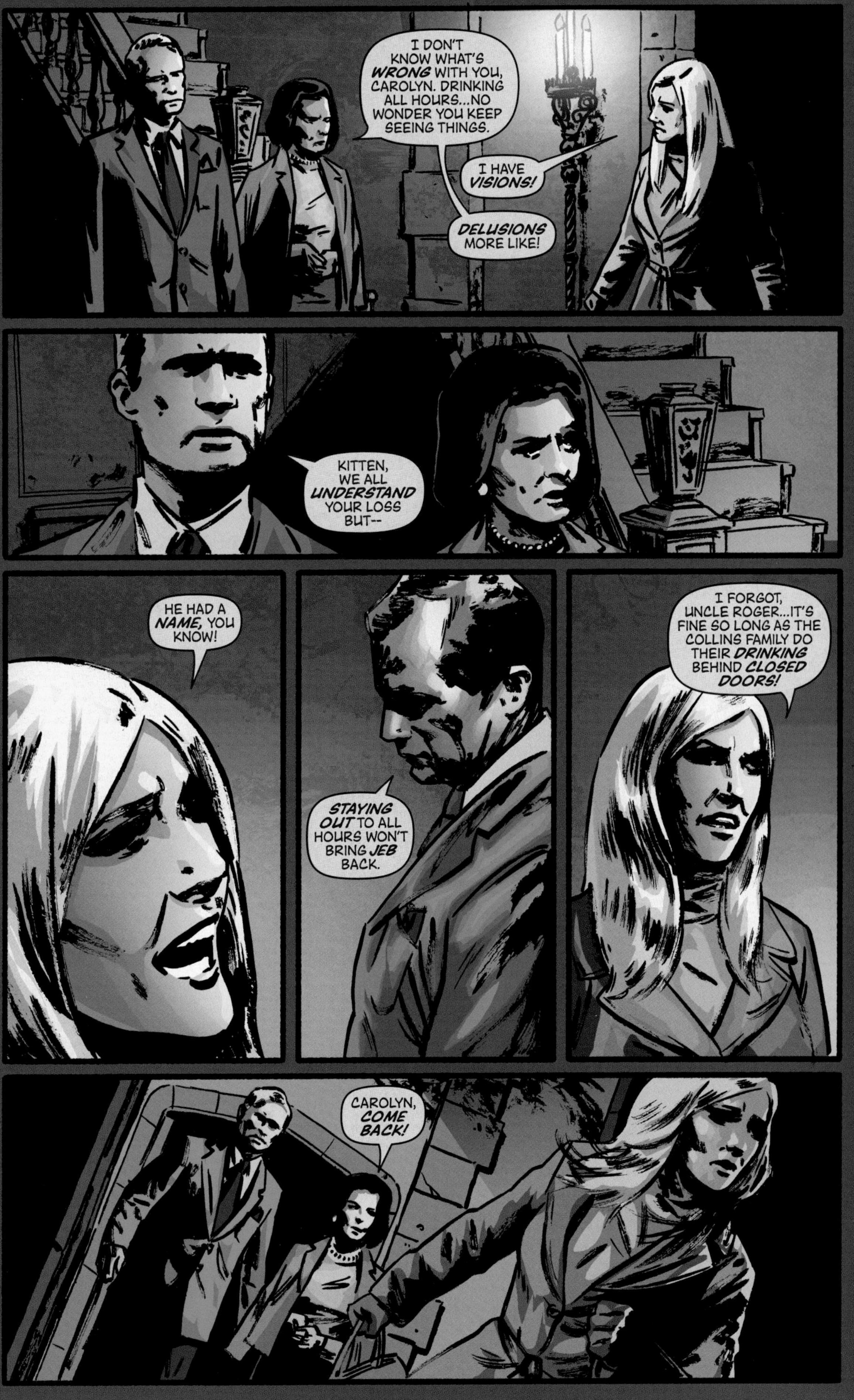
I DON'T KNOW WHAT'S WRONG WITH YOU, CAROLYN. DRINKING ALL HOURS...NO WONDER YOU KEEP SEEING THINGS.
I HAVE VISIONS!
DELUSIONS MORE LIKE!
KITTEN, WE ALL UNDERSTAND YOUR LOSS BUT--
HE HAD A NAME, YOU KNOW!
STAYING OUT TO ALL HOURS WON'T BRING JEB BACK.
I FORGOT, UNCLE ROGER...IT'S FINE SO LONG AS THE COLLINS FAMILY DO THEIR DRINKING BEHIND CLOSED DOORS!
CAROLYN, COME BACK!

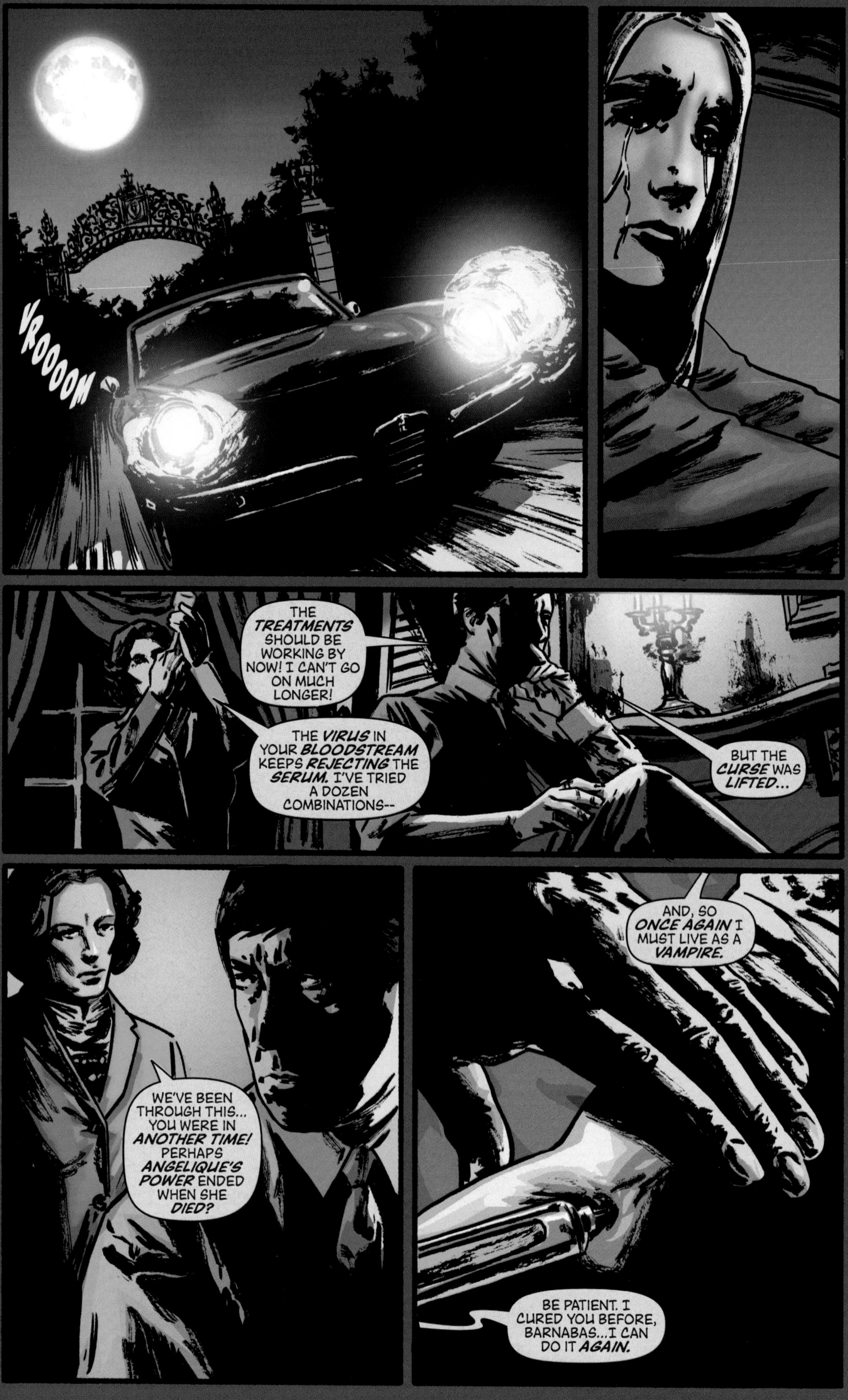
VROOOOM
THE TREATMENTS SHOULD BE WORKING BY NOW! I CAN'T GO ON MUCH LONGER!
THE VIRUS IN YOUR BLOODSTREAM KEEPS REJECTING THE SERUM. I'VE TRIED A DOZEN COMBINATIONS--
BUT THE CURSE WAS LIFTED...
WE'VE BEEN THROUGH THIS... YOU WERE IN ANOTHER TIME! PERHAPS ANGELIQUE'S POWER ENDED WHEN SHE DIED?
AND, SO ONCE AGAIN I MUST LIVE AS A VAMPIRE.
BE PATIENT. I CURED YOU BEFORE, BARNABAS... I CAN DO IT AGAIN.

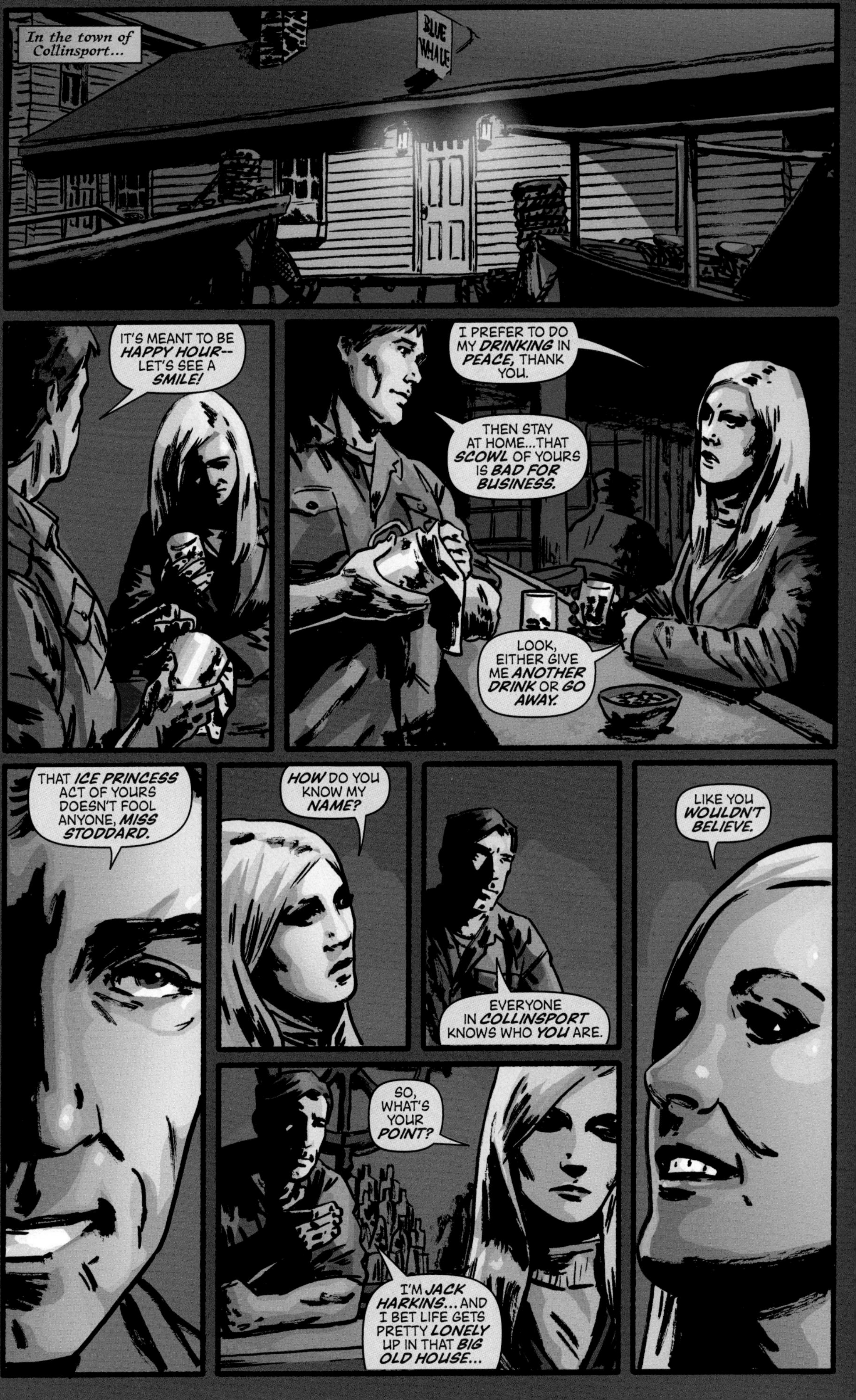
In the town of Collinsport...
BLUE WHALE
IT'S MEANT TO BE HAPPY HOUR-- LET'S SEE A SMILE!
I PREFER TO DO MY DRINKING IN PEACE, THANK YOU.
THEN STAY AT HOME...THAT SCOWL OF YOURS IS BAD FOR BUSINESS.
LOOK, EITHER GIVE ME ANOTHER DRINK OR GO AWAY.
THAT ICE PRINCESS ACT OF YOURS DOESN'T FOOL ANYONE, MISS STODDARD.
HOW DO YOU KNOW MY NAME?
EVERYONE IN COLLINSPORT KNOWS WHO YOU ARE.
SO, WHAT'S YOUR POINT?
I'M JACK HARKINS... AND I BET LIFE GETS PRETTY LONELY UP IN THAT BIG OLD HOUSE...
LIKE YOU WOULDN'T BELIEVE.

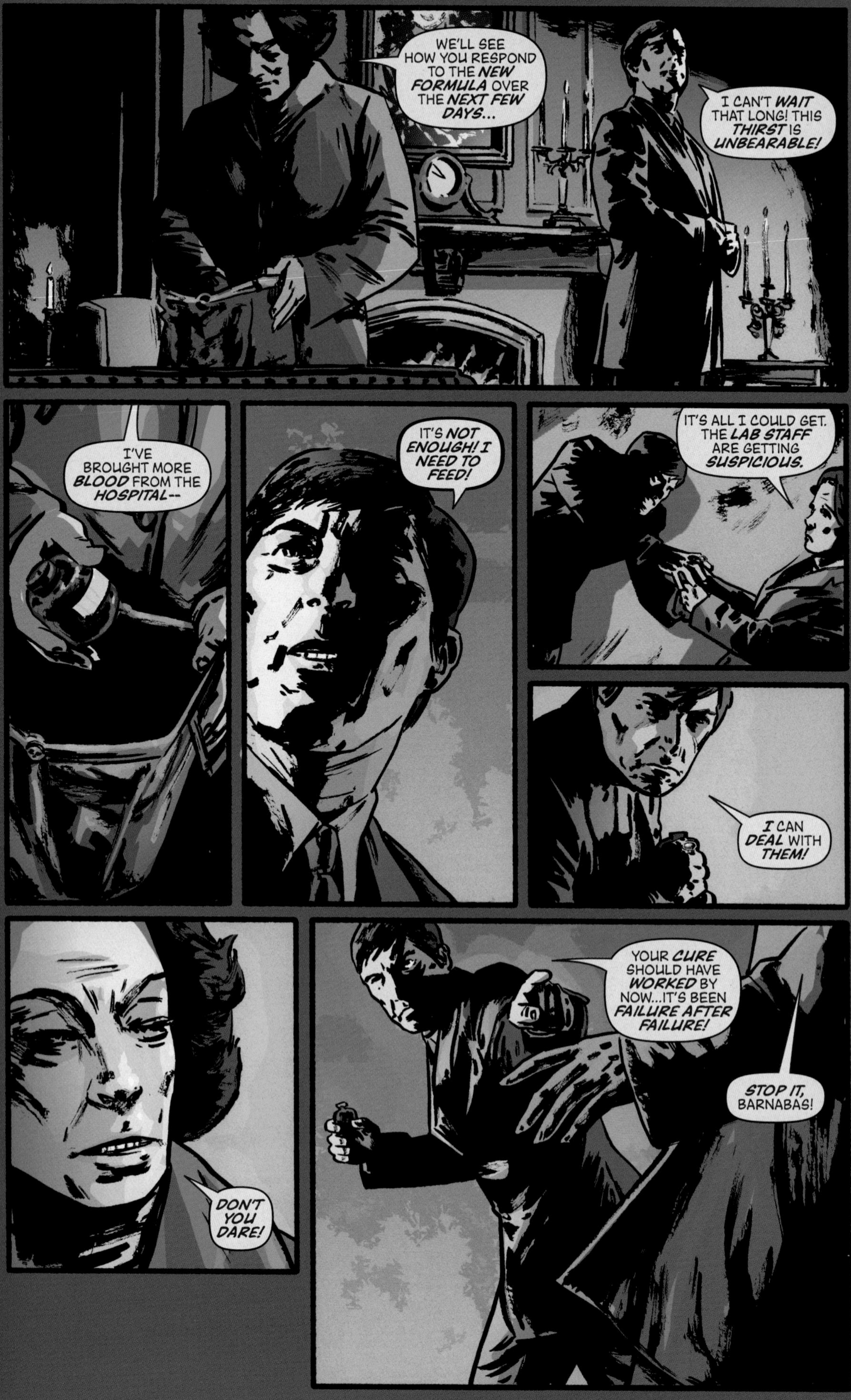
WE'LL SEE HOW YOU RESPOND TO THE NEW FORMULA OVER THE NEXT FEW DAYS...
I CAN'T WAIT THAT LONG! THIS THIRST IS UNBEARABLE!
I'VE BROUGHT MORE BLOOD FROM THE HOSPITAL--
IT'S NOT ENOUGH! I NEED TO FEED!
IT'S ALL I COULD GET. THE LAB STAFF ARE GETTING SUSPICIOUS.
I CAN DEAL WITH THEM!
DON'T YOU DARE!
YOUR CURE SHOULD HAVE WORKED BY NOW...IT'S BEEN FAILURE AFTER FAILURE!
STOP IT, BARNABAS!

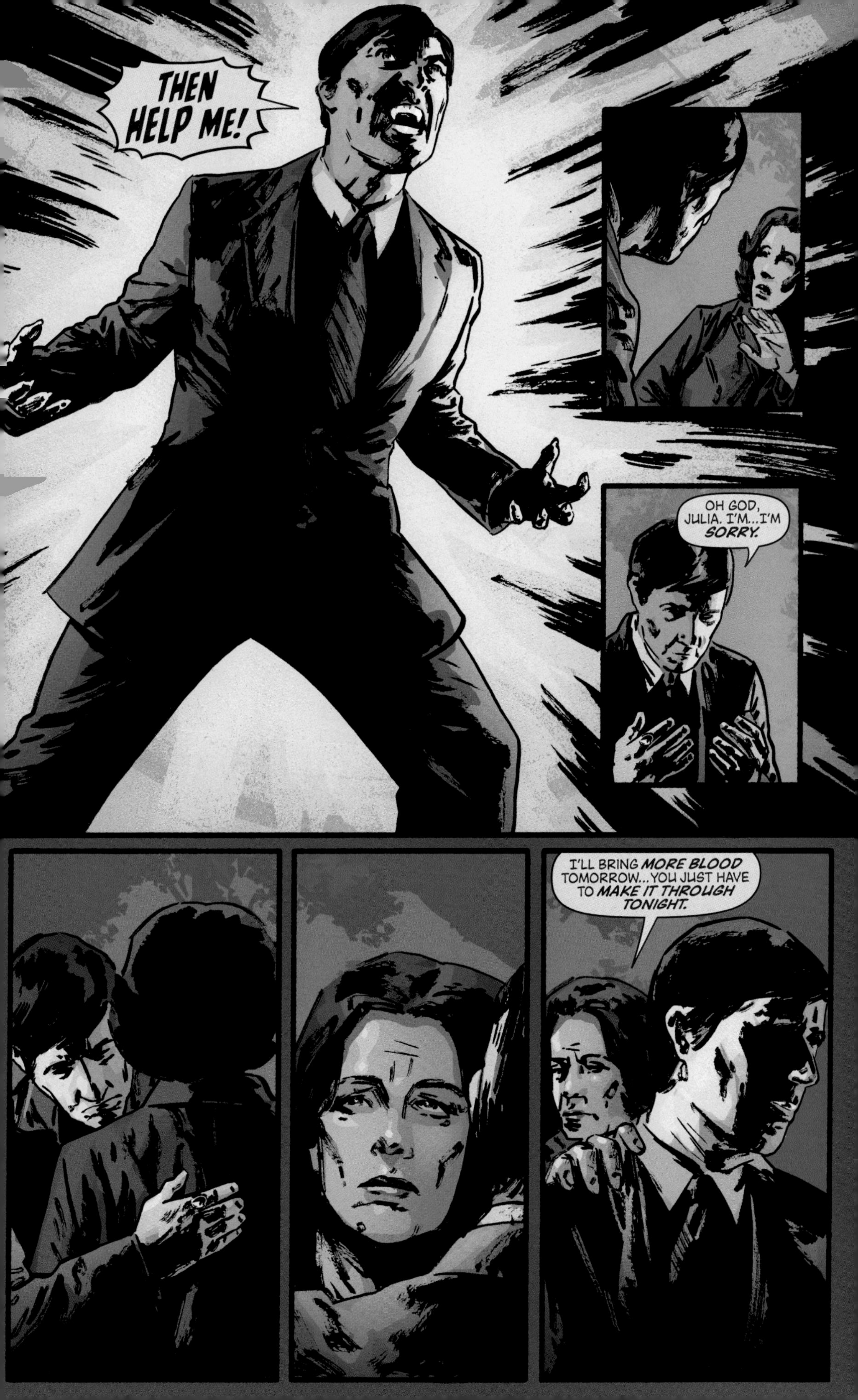
THEN HELP ME!
OH GOD, JULIA. I'M...I'M SORRY.
I'LL BRING MORE BLOOD TOMORROW...YOU JUST HAVE TO MAKE IT THROUGH TONIGHT.

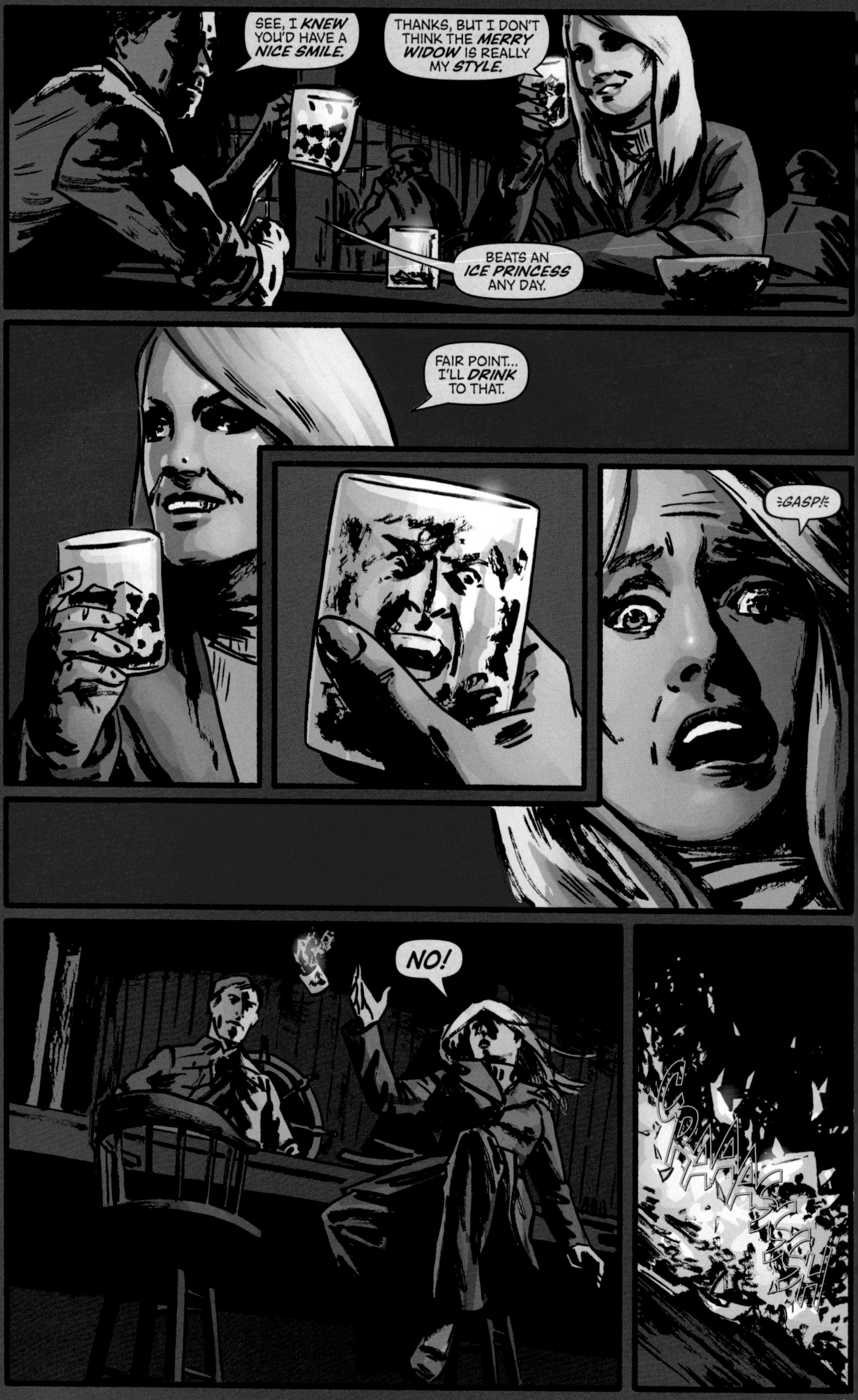
SEE, I KNEW YOU'D HAVE A NICE SMILE.
THANKS, BUT I DON'T THINK THE MERRY WIDOW IS REALLY MY STYLE.
BEATS AN ICE PRINCESS ANY DAY.
FAIR POINT... I'LL DRINK TO THAT.
GASP!
NO!

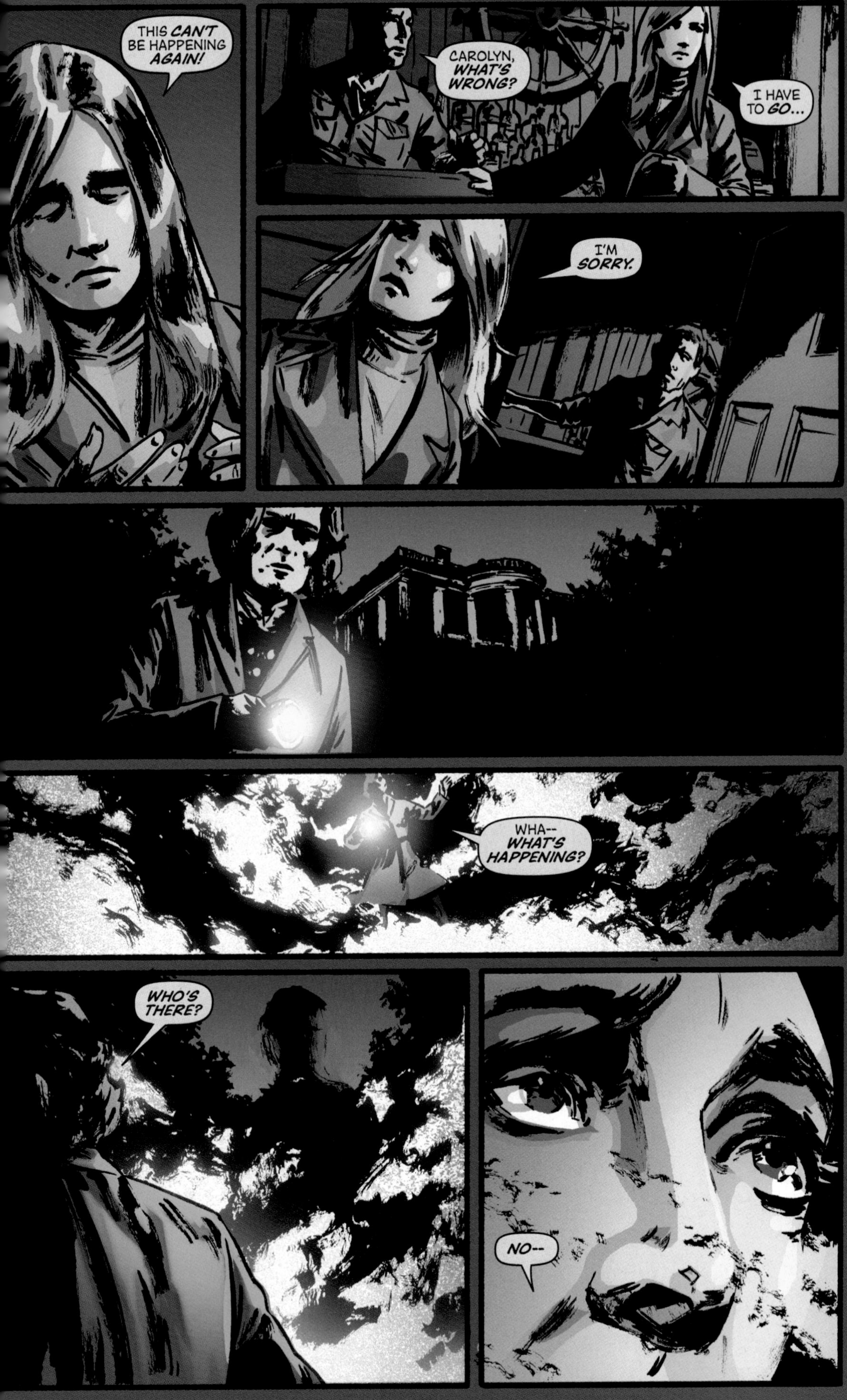
THIS CAN'T BE HAPPENING AGAIN!
CAROLYN, WHAT'S WRONG?
I HAVE TO GO...
I'M SORRY.
WHA-- WHAT'S HAPPENING?
WHO'S THERE?
NO--

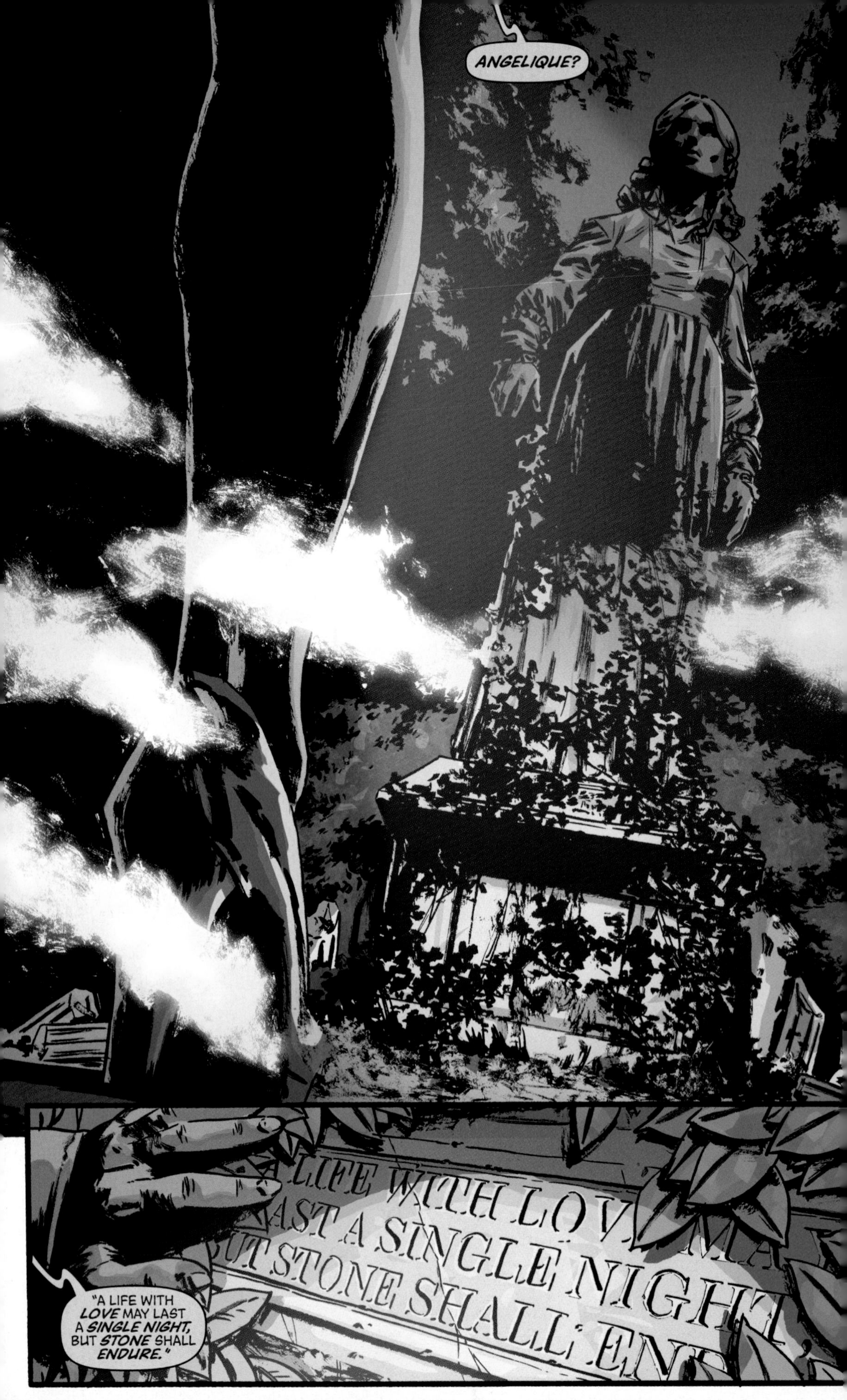
ANGELIQUE?
"A LIFE WITH LOVE MAY LAST A SINGLE NIGHT, BUT STONE SHALL ENDURE."

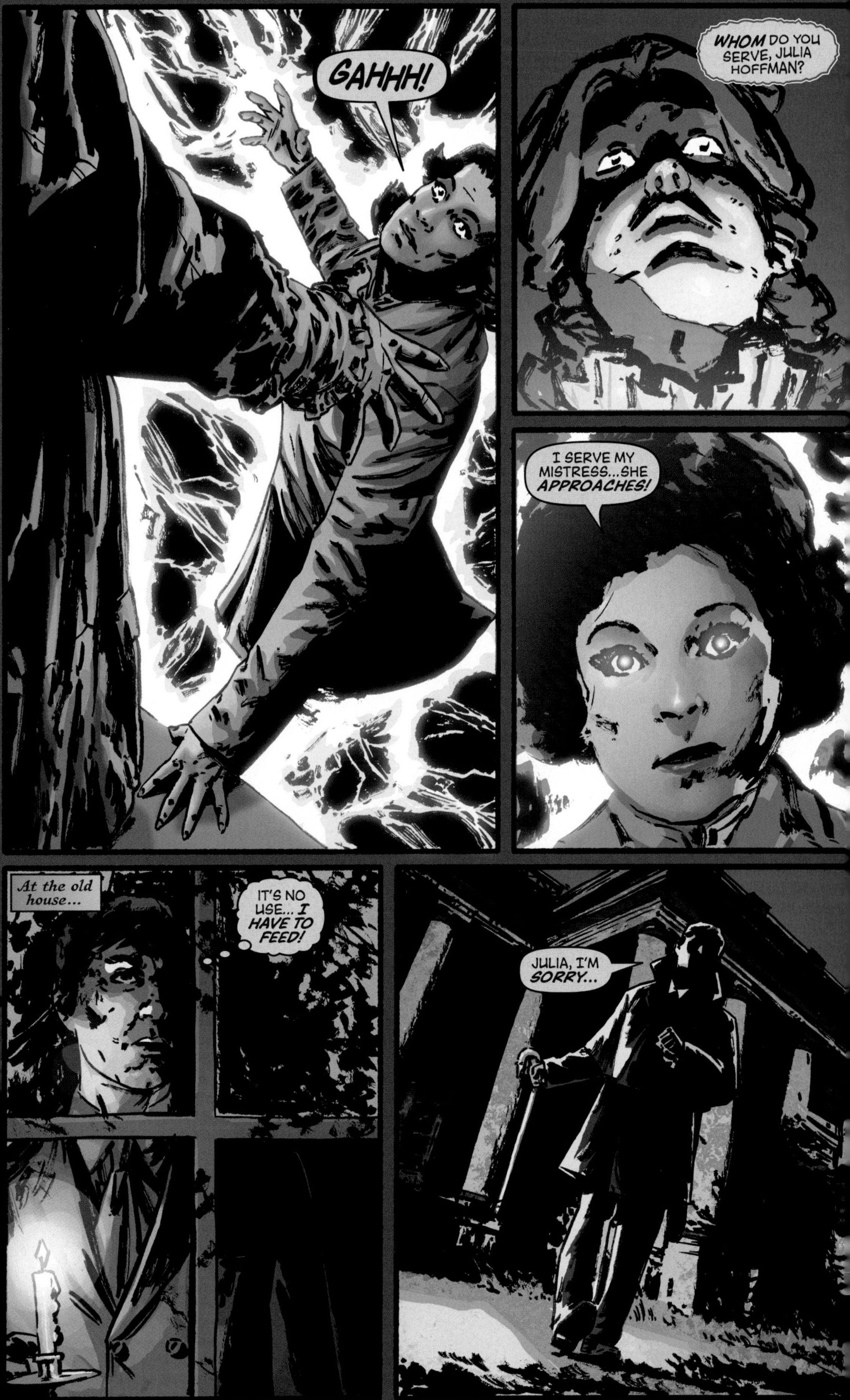
GAHHH!
WHOM DO YOU SERVE, JULIA HOFFMAN?
I SERVE MY MISTRESS...SHE APPROACHES!
At the old house...
IT'S NO USE... I HAVE TO FEED!
JULIA, I'M SORRY...

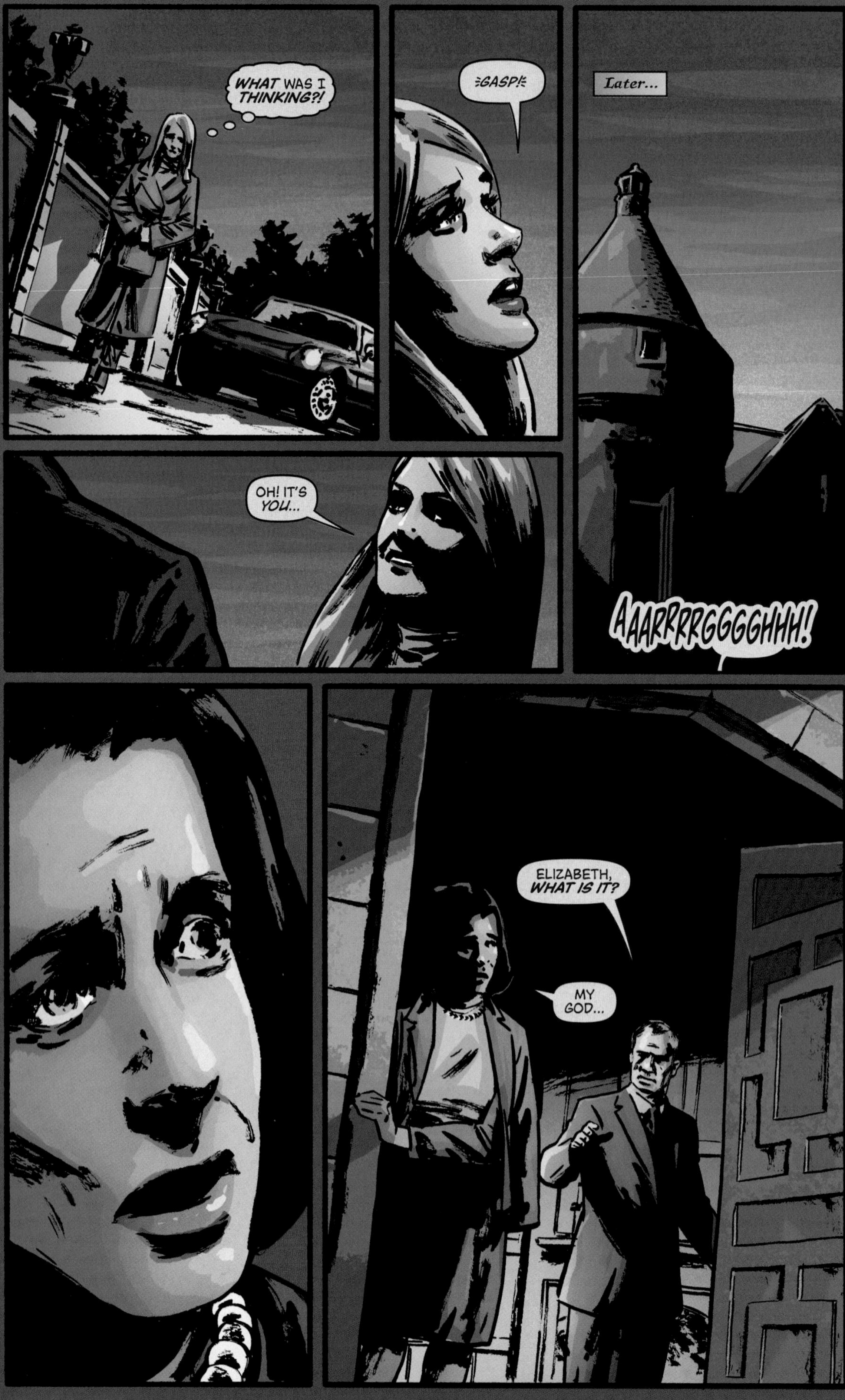
WHAT WAS I THINKING?!
GASP!
Later...
OH! IT'S YOU...
AAARRRRGGGGHHH!
ELIZABETH, WHAT IS IT?
MY GOD...

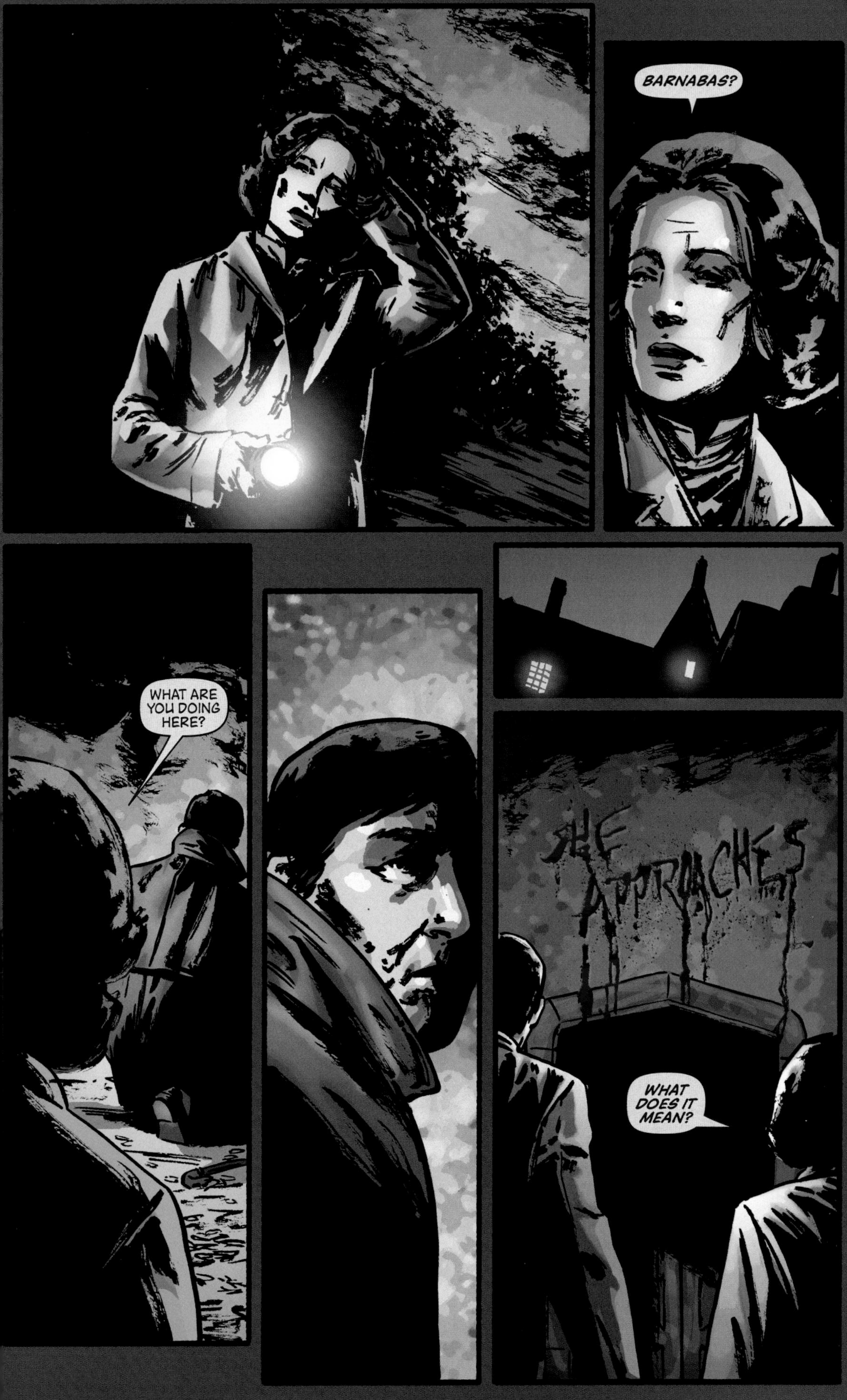
BARNABAS?
WHAT ARE YOU DOING HERE?
SHE APPROACHES
WHAT DOES IT MEAN?

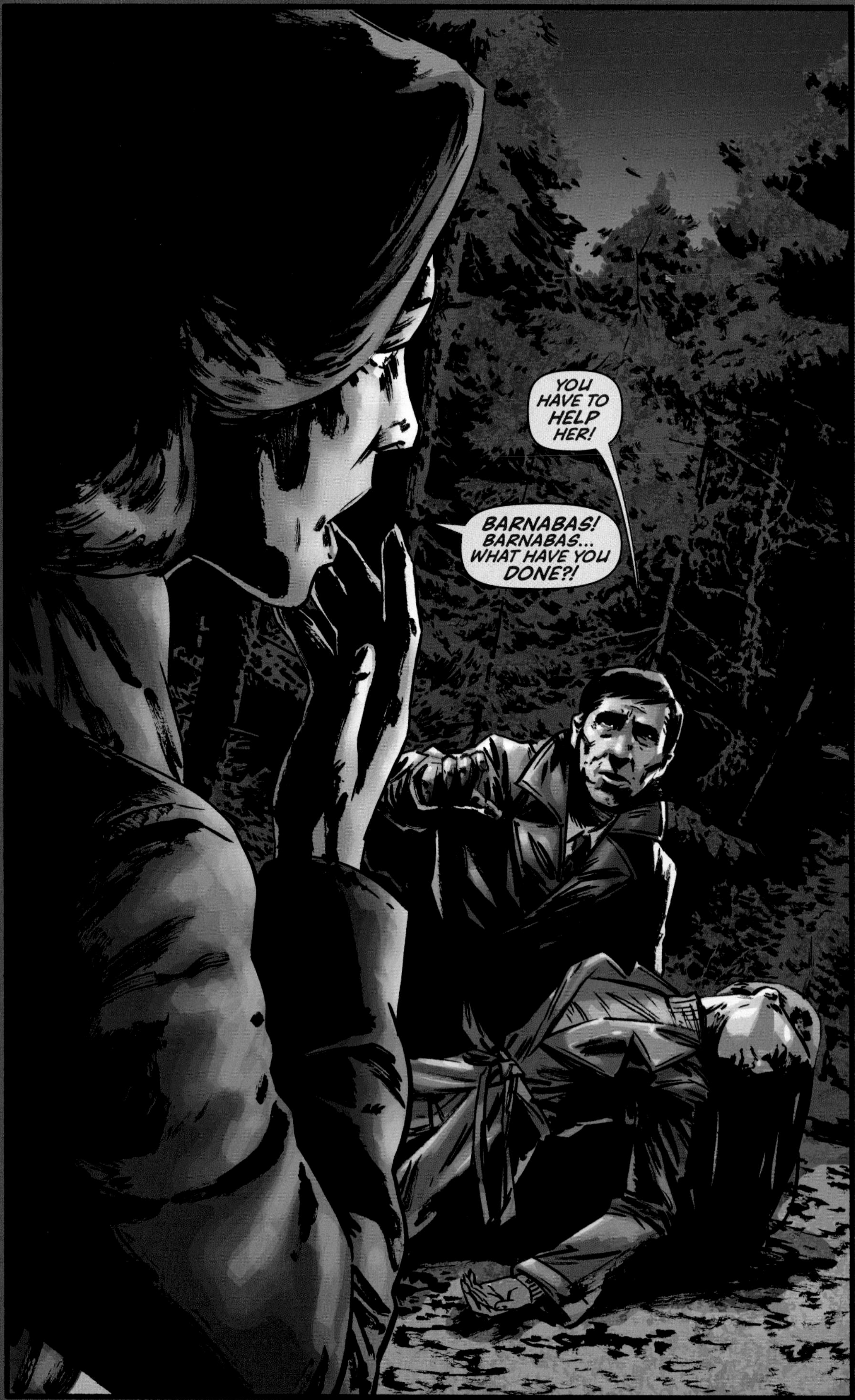
YOU HAVE TO HELP HER!
BARNABAS! BARNABAS... WHAT HAVE YOU DONE?!

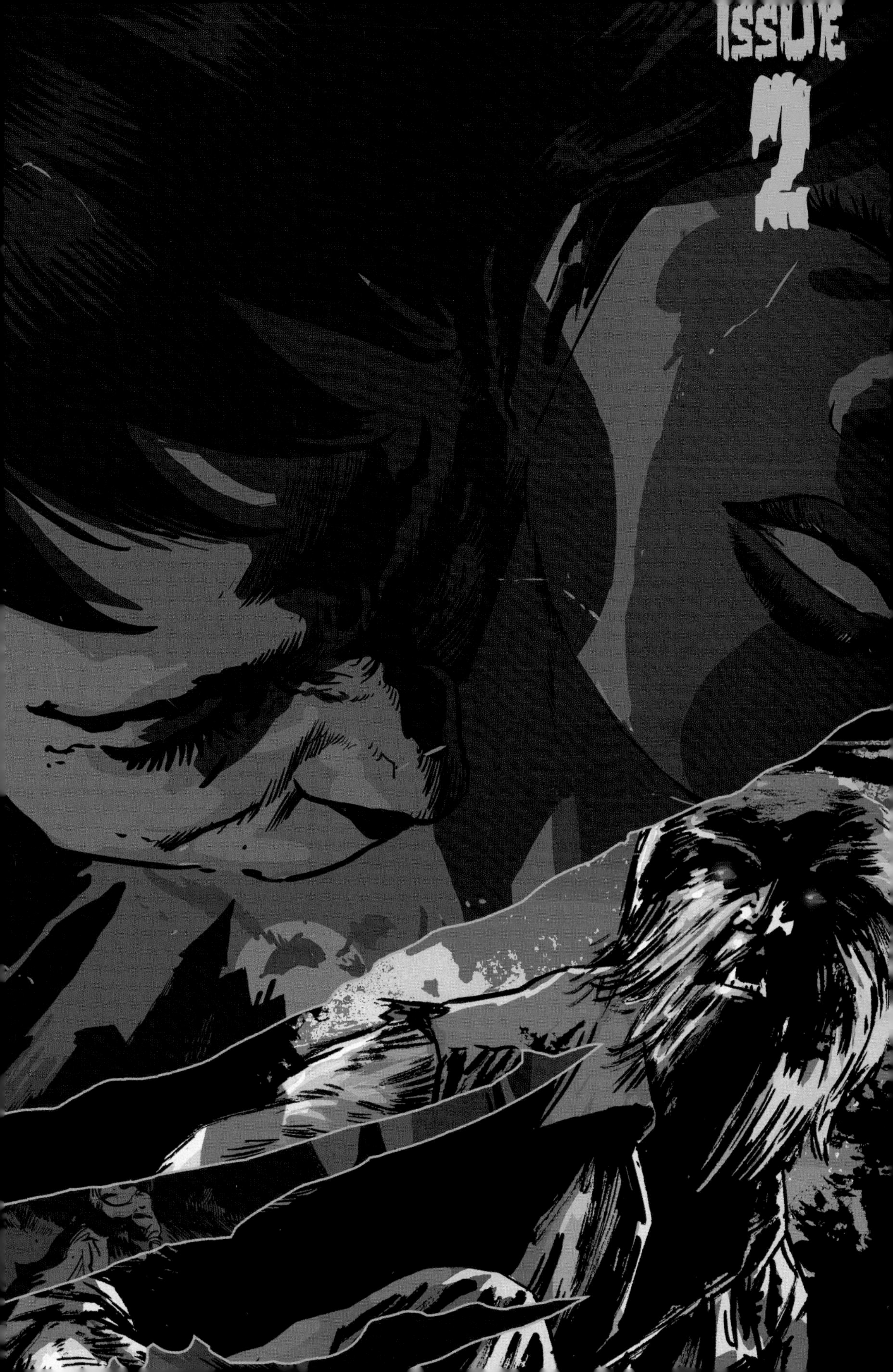
ISSUE
2

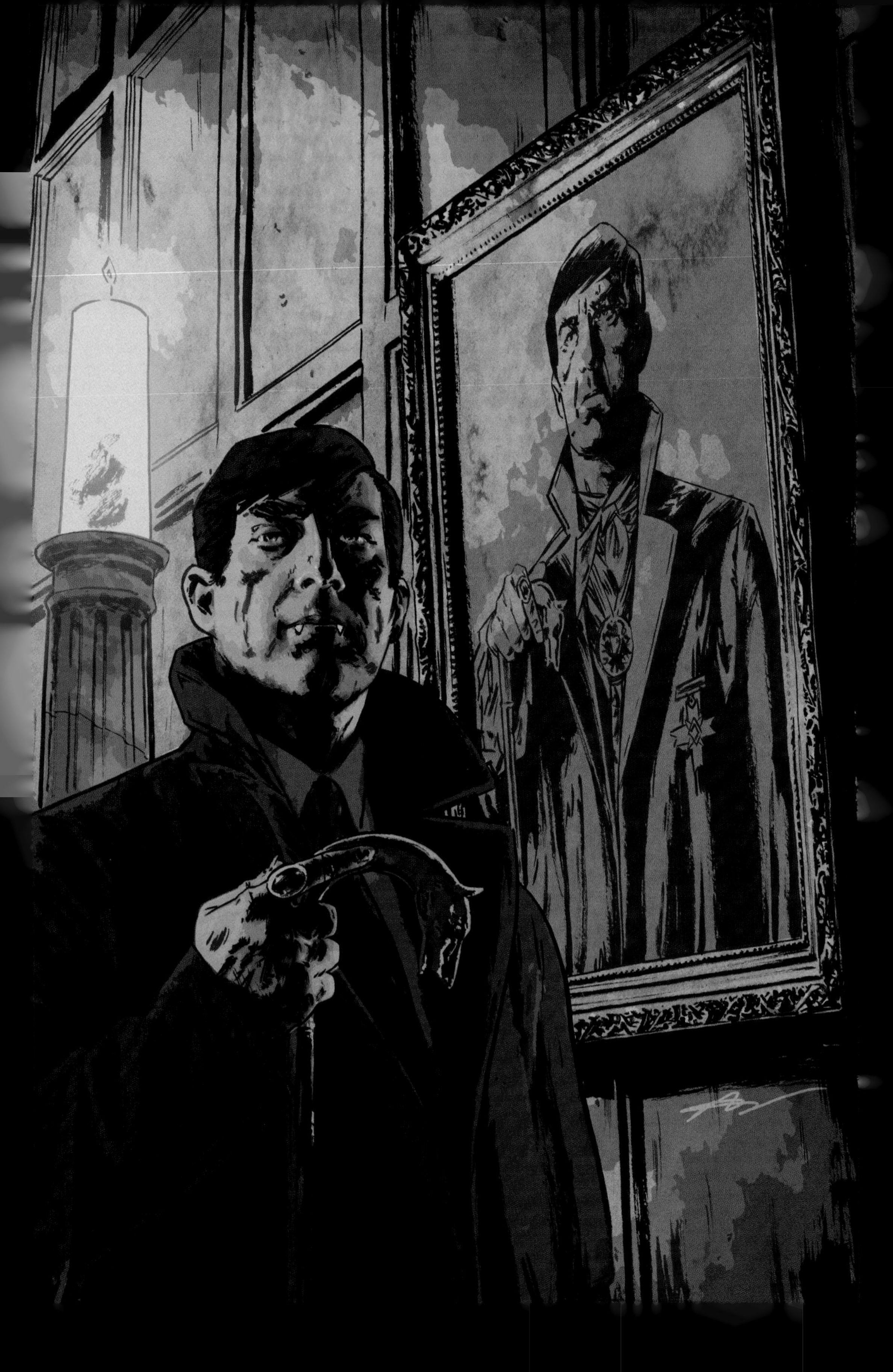

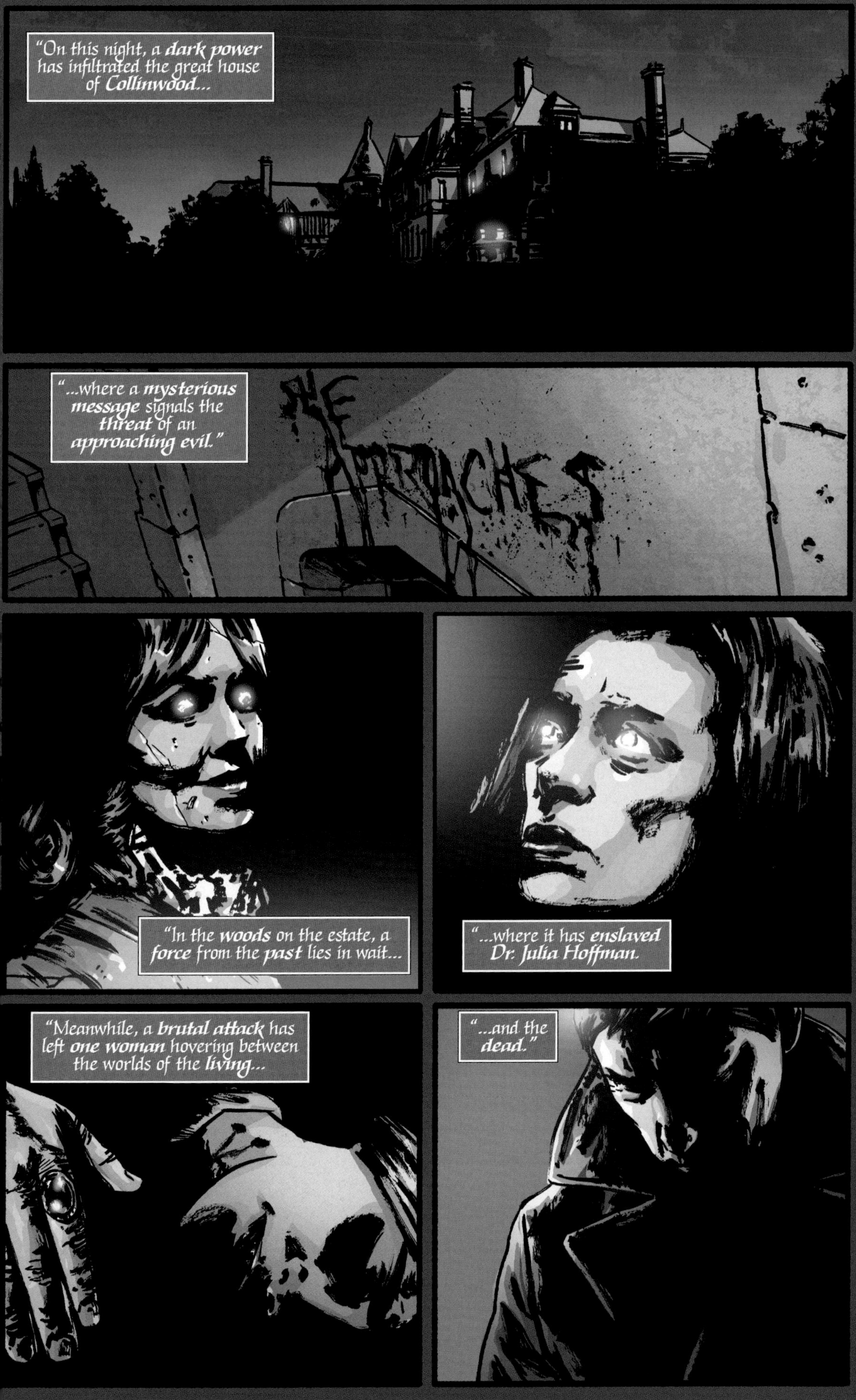
"On this night, a **dark power** has infiltrated the great house of **Collinwood**...
"...where a **mysterious message** signals the **threat** of an **approaching evil**."
"In the **woods** on the estate, a **force** from the **past** lies in wait...
"...where it has **enslaved** **Dr. Julia Hoffman**.
"Meanwhile, a **brutal attack** has left **one woman** hovering between the worlds of the **living**...
"...and the **dead**."

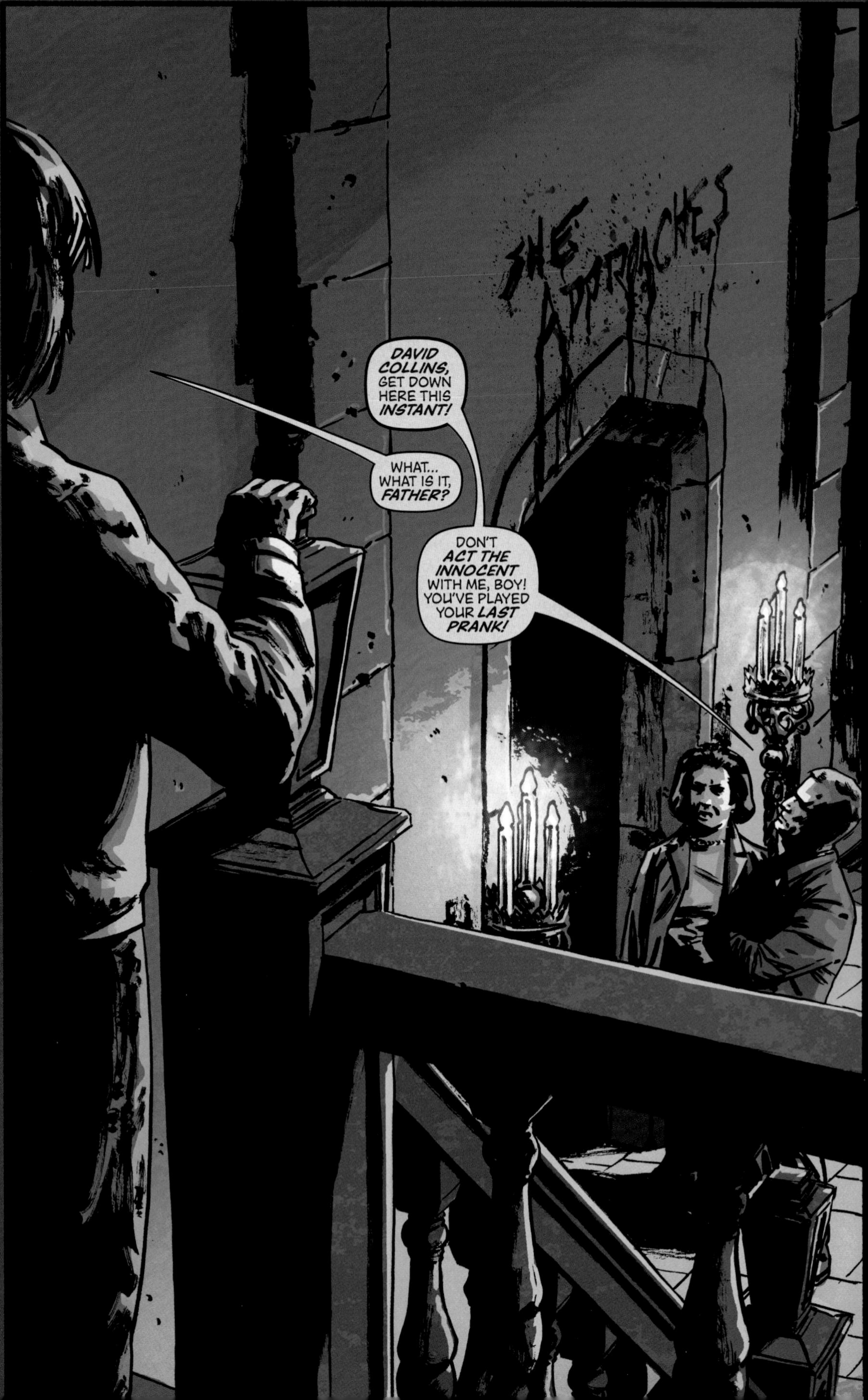
SHE APPROACHES
DAVID COLLINS, GET DOWN HERE THIS INSTANT!
WHAT... WHAT IS IT, FATHER?
DON'T ACT THE INNOCENT WITH ME, BOY! YOU'VE PLAYED YOUR LAST PRANK!

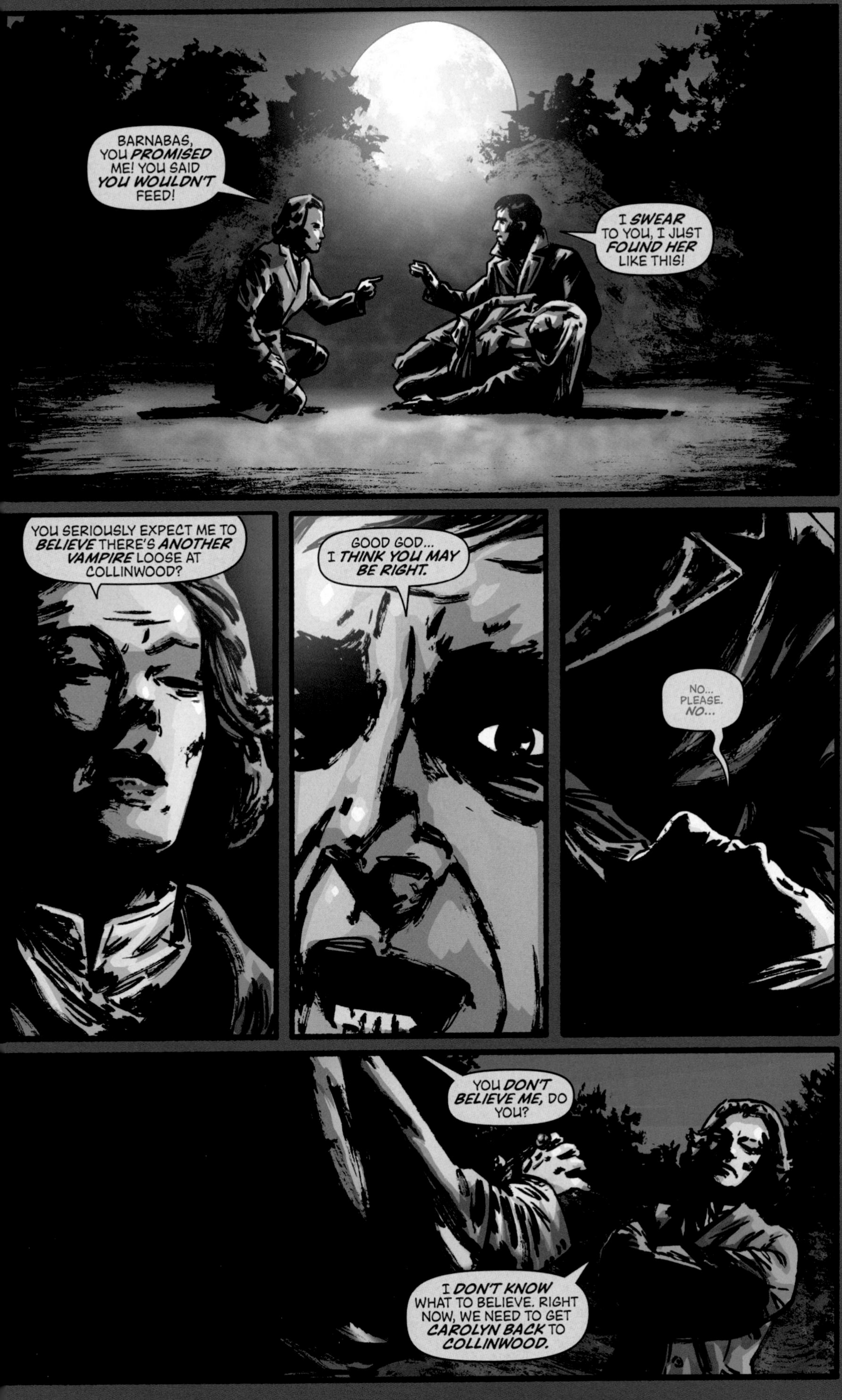
BARNABAS, YOU PROMISED ME! YOU SAID YOU WOULDN'T FEED!
I SWEAR TO YOU, I JUST FOUND HER LIKE THIS!
YOU SERIOUSLY EXPECT ME TO BELIEVE THERE'S ANOTHER VAMPIRE LOOSE AT COLLINWOOD?
GOOD GOD... I THINK YOU MAY BE RIGHT.
NO... PLEASE. NO...
YOU DON'T BELIEVE ME, DO YOU?
I DON'T KNOW WHAT TO BELIEVE. RIGHT NOW, WE NEED TO GET CAROLYN BACK TO COLLINWOOD.

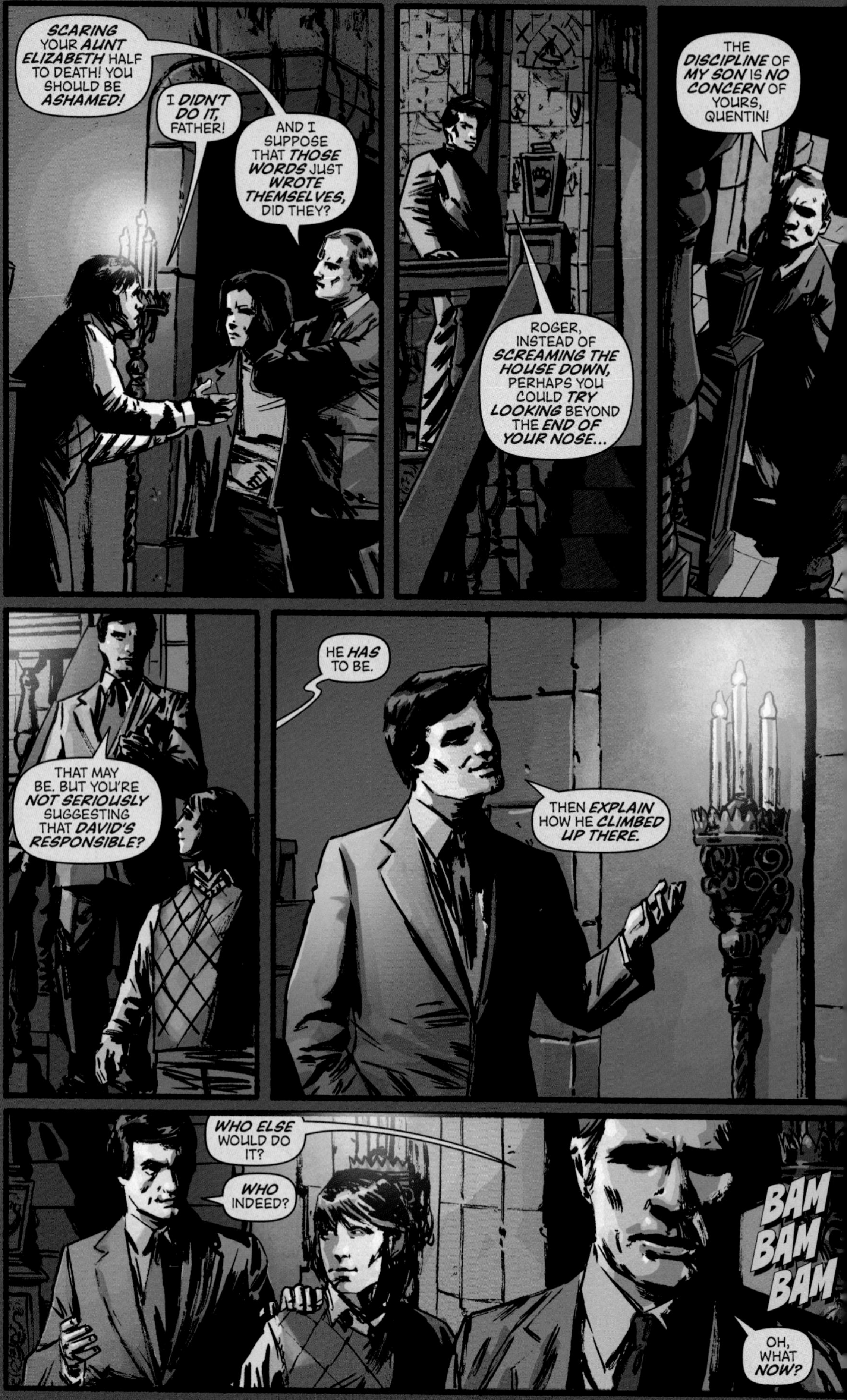
SCARING YOUR AUNT ELIZABETH HALF TO DEATH! YOU SHOULD BE ASHAMED!
I DIDN'T DO IT, FATHER!
AND I SUPPOSE THAT THOSE WORDS JUST WROTE THEMSELVES, DID THEY?
ROGER, INSTEAD OF SCREAMING THE HOUSE DOWN, PERHAPS YOU COULD TRY LOOKING BEYOND THE END OF YOUR NOSE...
THE DISCIPLINE OF MY SON IS NO CONCERN OF YOURS, QUENTIN!
THAT MAY BE. BUT YOU'RE NOT SERIOUSLY SUGGESTING THAT DAVID'S RESPONSIBLE?
HE HAS TO BE.
THEN EXPLAIN HOW HE CLIMBED UP THERE.
WHO ELSE WOULD DO IT?
WHO INDEED?
BAM BAM BAM
OH, WHAT NOW?

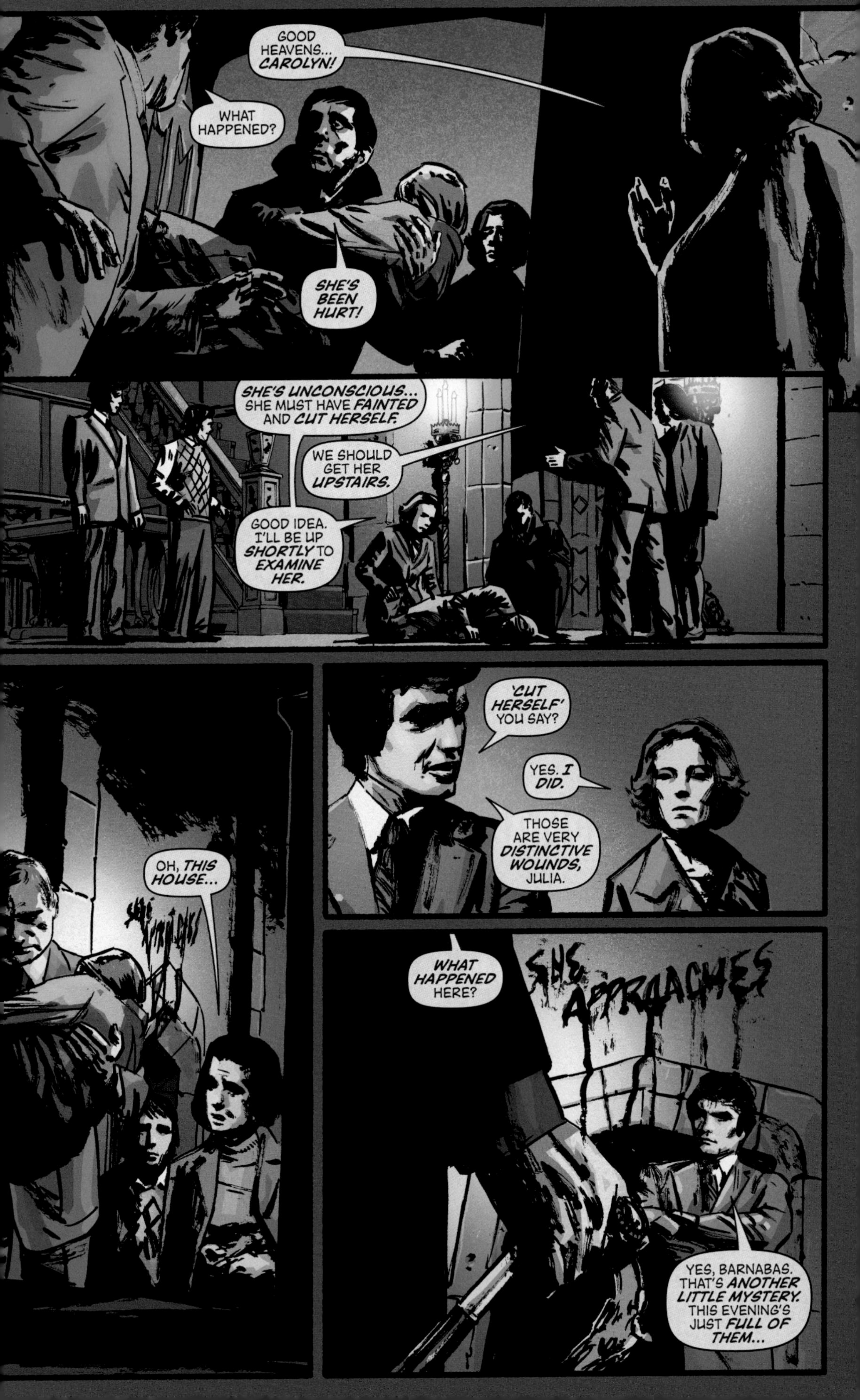
GOOD HEAVENS... CAROLYN!
WHAT HAPPENED?
SHE'S BEEN HURT!
SHE'S UNCONSCIOUS... SHE MUST HAVE FAINTED AND CUT HERSELF.
WE SHOULD GET HER UPSTAIRS.
GOOD IDEA. I'LL BE UP SHORTLY TO EXAMINE HER.
OH, THIS HOUSE...
'CUT HERSELF' YOU SAY?
YES. I DID.
THOSE ARE VERY DISTINCTIVE WOUNDS, JULIA.
WHAT HAPPENED HERE?
SHE APPROACHES
YES, BARNABAS. THAT'S ANOTHER LITTLE MYSTERY. THIS EVENING'S JUST FULL OF THEM...

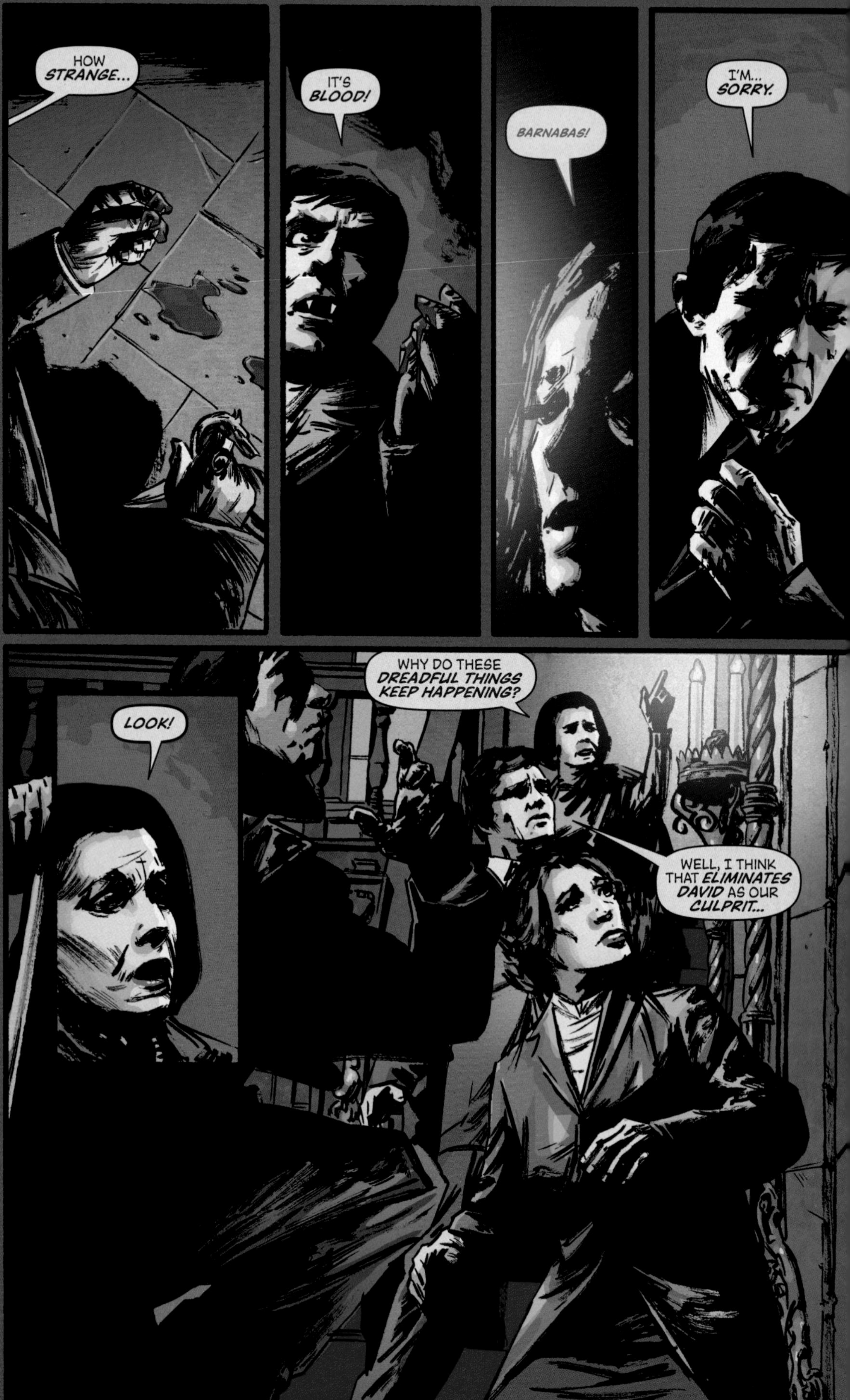
HOW STRANGE...
IT'S BLOOD!
BARNABAS!
I'M... SORRY.
LOOK!
WHY DO THESE DREADFUL THINGS KEEP HAPPENING?
WELL, I THINK THAT ELIMINATES DAVID AS OUR CULPRIT...

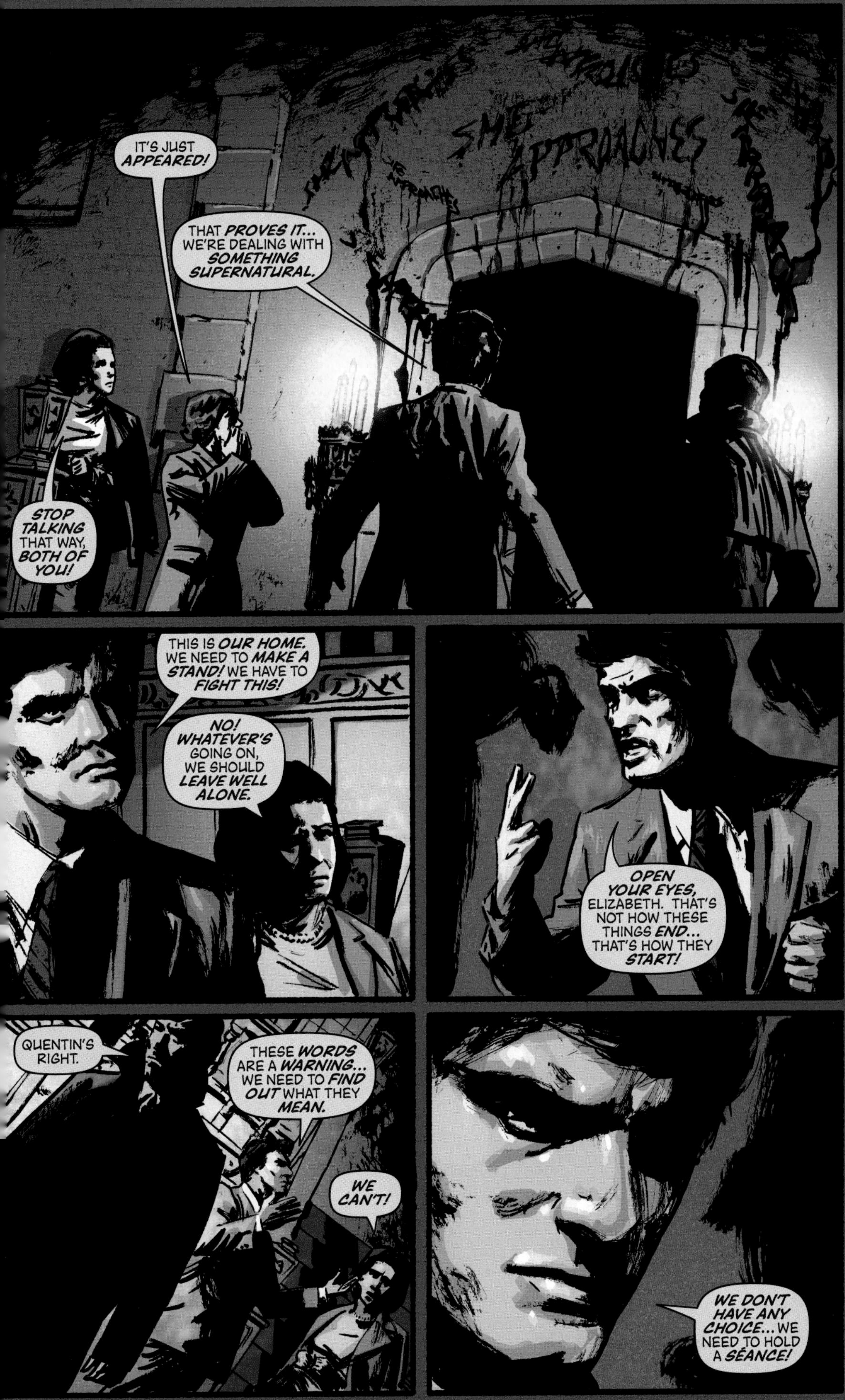
SHE APPROACHES
IT'S JUST APPEARED!
THAT PROVES IT... WE'RE DEALING WITH SOMETHING SUPERNATURAL.
STOP TALKING THAT WAY, BOTH OF YOU!
THIS IS OUR HOME. WE NEED TO MAKE A STAND! WE HAVE TO FIGHT THIS!
NO! WHATEVER'S GOING ON, WE SHOULD LEAVE WELL ALONE.
OPEN YOUR EYES, ELIZABETH. THAT'S NOT HOW THESE THINGS END... THAT'S HOW THEY START!
QUENTIN'S RIGHT.
THESE WORDS ARE A WARNING... WE NEED TO FIND OUT WHAT THEY MEAN.
WE CAN'T!
WE DON'T HAVE ANY CHOICE... WE NEED TO HOLD A SÉANCE!

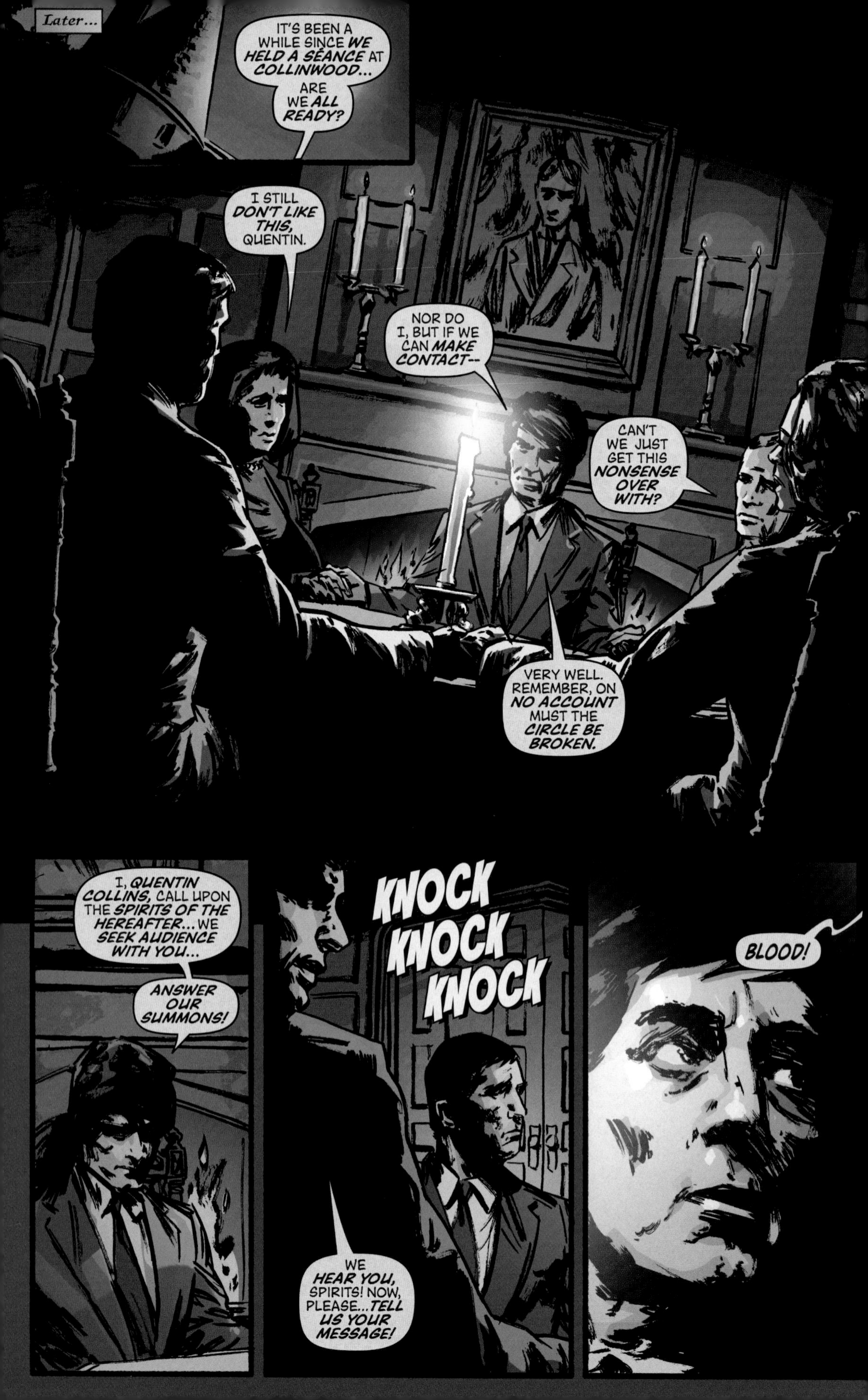
Later...
IT'S BEEN A WHILE SINCE WE HELD A SÉANCE AT COLLINWOOD... ARE WE ALL READY?
I STILL DON'T LIKE THIS, QUENTIN.
NOR DO I, BUT IF WE CAN MAKE CONTACT--
CAN'T WE JUST GET THIS NONSENSE OVER WITH?
VERY WELL. REMEMBER, ON NO ACCOUNT MUST THE CIRCLE BE BROKEN.
I, QUENTIN COLLINS, CALL UPON THE SPIRITS OF THE HEREAFTER... WE SEEK AUDIENCE WITH YOU...
ANSWER OUR SUMMONS!
KNOCK KNOCK KNOCK
WE HEAR YOU, SPIRITS! NOW, PLEASE... TELL US YOUR MESSAGE!
BLOOD!

IT NEEDS BLOOD!

CAROLYN!

SHE'S DELIRIOUS.

NO, SHE'S IN A TRANCE! IT'S USING HER TO SPEAK TO US.

QUENTIN, WE HAVE TO STOP THIS!

NO! WE CAN'T BREAK THE CIRCLE!

CAROLYN, TELL US... WHY DOES IT NEED BLOOD?

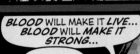

BLOOD WILL MAKE IT LIVE... BLOOD WILL MAKE IT STRONG...

AND CAN YOU TELL US ITS NAME?

ITS NAME?

YES, CAROLYN, PLEASE... TELL US!

IT IS AN ANCIENT EVIL, KNOWN TO YOU... NOURISHED, SPILLED BY BLOOD... HIDING IN PLAIN SIGHT. AND THE NAME OF THE EVIL IS--

STOP IT! CAN'T YOU SEE SHE'S SUFFERED ENOUGH!

BARNABAS, NO!

GGGAAAAAGGHH!

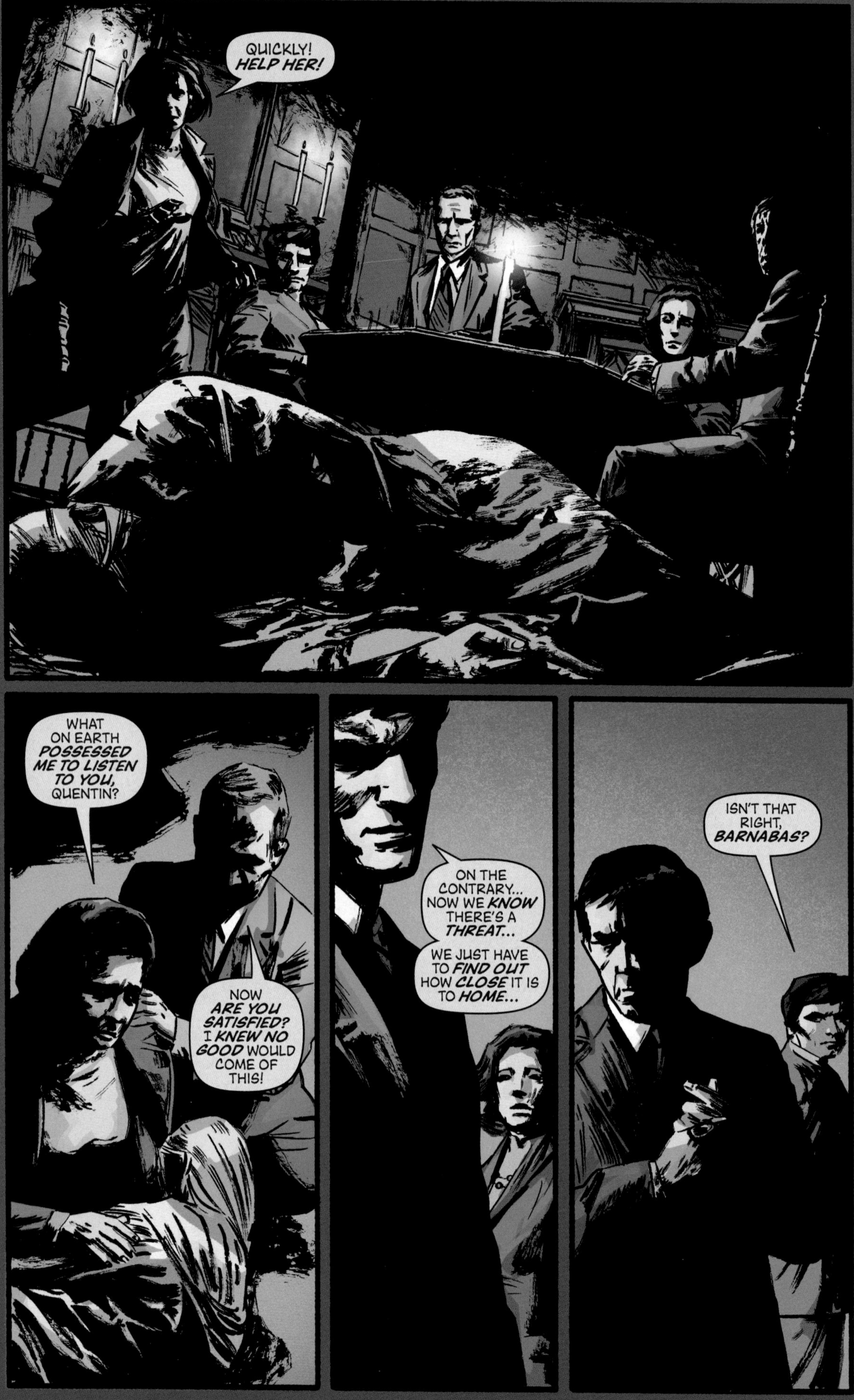
QUICKLY! HELP HER!
WHAT ON EARTH POSSESSED ME TO LISTEN TO YOU, QUENTIN?
NOW ARE YOU SATISFIED? I KNEW NO GOOD WOULD COME OF THIS!
ON THE CONTRARY... NOW WE KNOW THERE'S A THREAT...
WE JUST HAVE TO FIND OUT HOW CLOSE IT IS TO HOME...
ISN'T THAT RIGHT, BARNABAS?

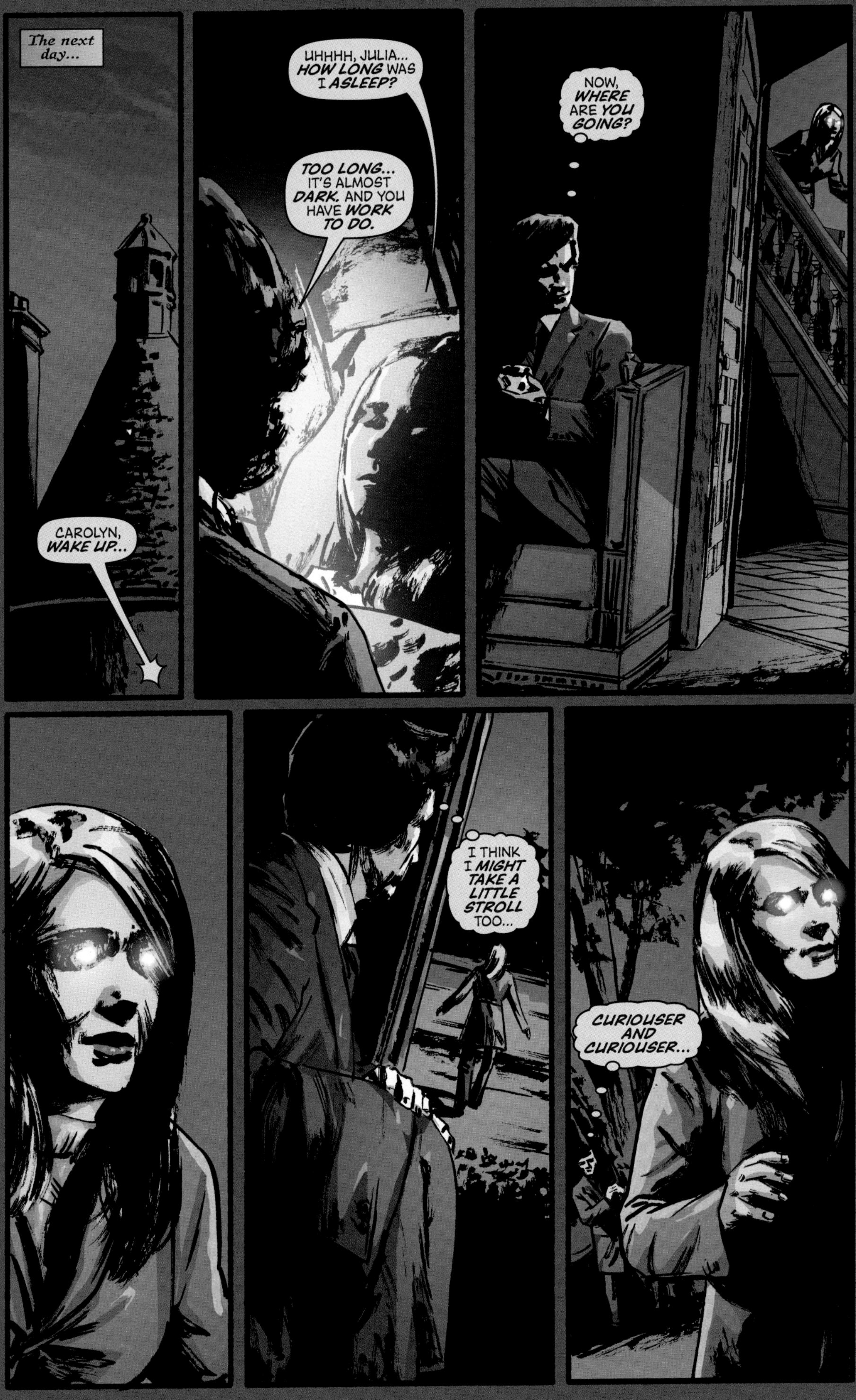
The next day...
CAROLYN, WAKE UP...
UHHHH, JULIA... HOW LONG WAS I ASLEEP?
TOO LONG... IT'S ALMOST DARK. AND YOU HAVE WORK TO DO.
NOW, WHERE ARE YOU GOING?
I THINK I MIGHT TAKE A LITTLE STROLL TOO...
CURIOUSER AND CURIOUSER...

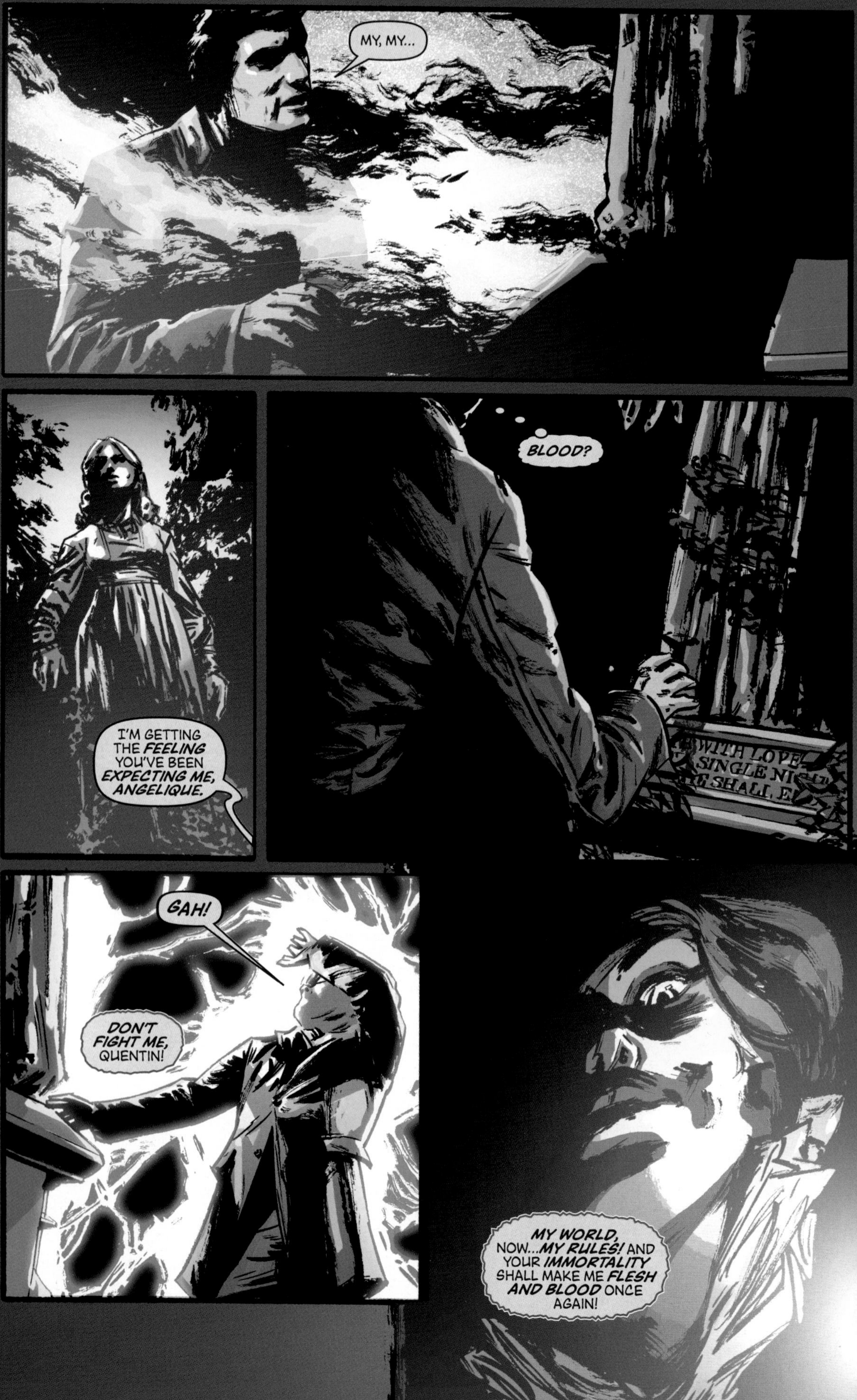
MY, MY...
I'M GETTING THE FEELING YOU'VE BEEN EXPECTING ME, ANGELIQUE.
BLOOD?
WITH LOVE
SINGLE NI
SHALL E
GAH!
DON'T FIGHT ME, QUENTIN!
MY WORLD, NOW...MY RULES! AND YOUR IMMORTALITY SHALL MAKE ME FLESH AND BLOOD ONCE AGAIN!

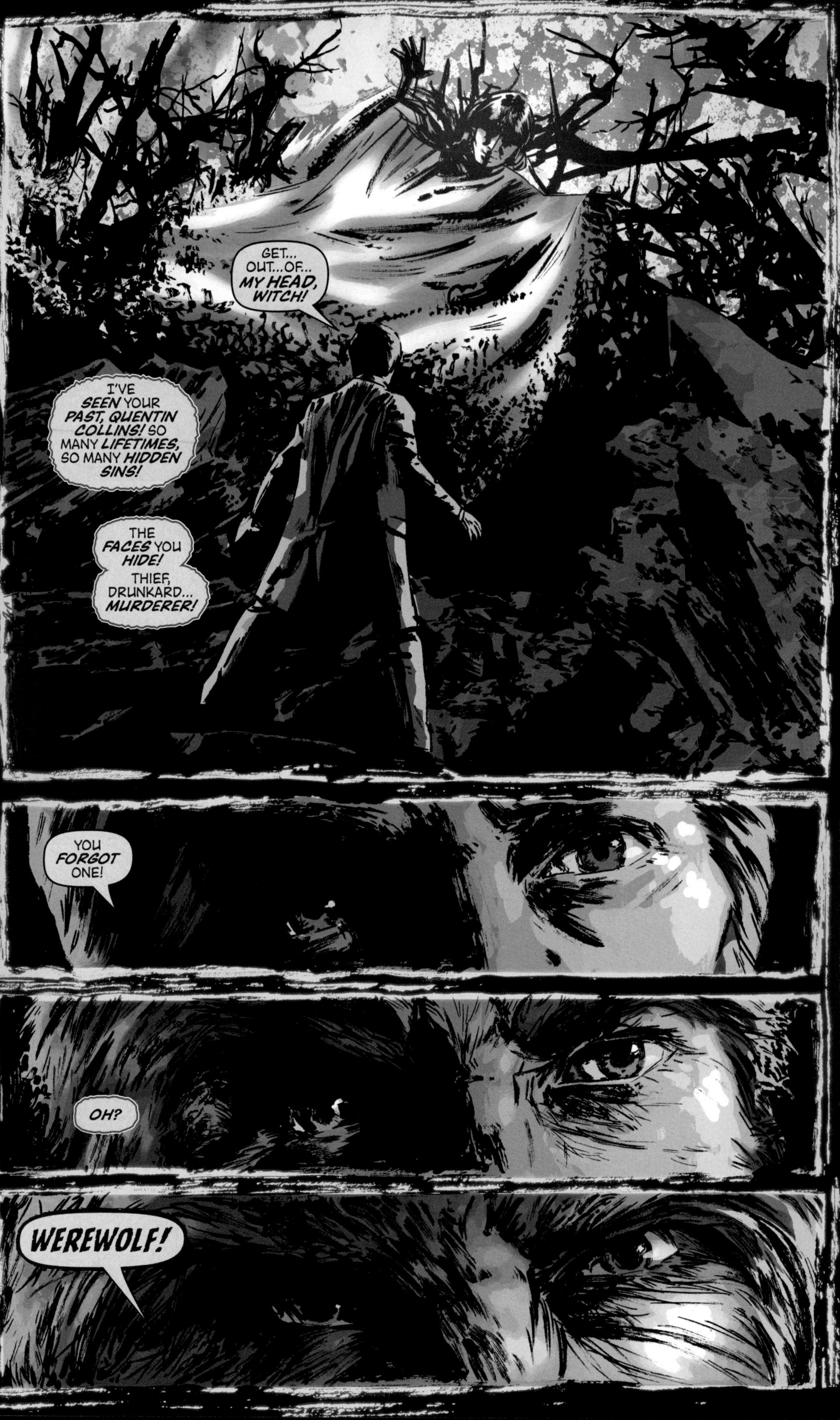
GET... OUT...OF... MY HEAD, WITCH!
I'VE SEEN YOUR PAST, QUENTIN COLLINS! SO MANY LIFETIMES, SO MANY HIDDEN SINS!
THE FACES YOU HIDE!
THIEF, DRUNKARD... MURDERER!
YOU FORGOT ONE!
OH?
WEREWOLF!

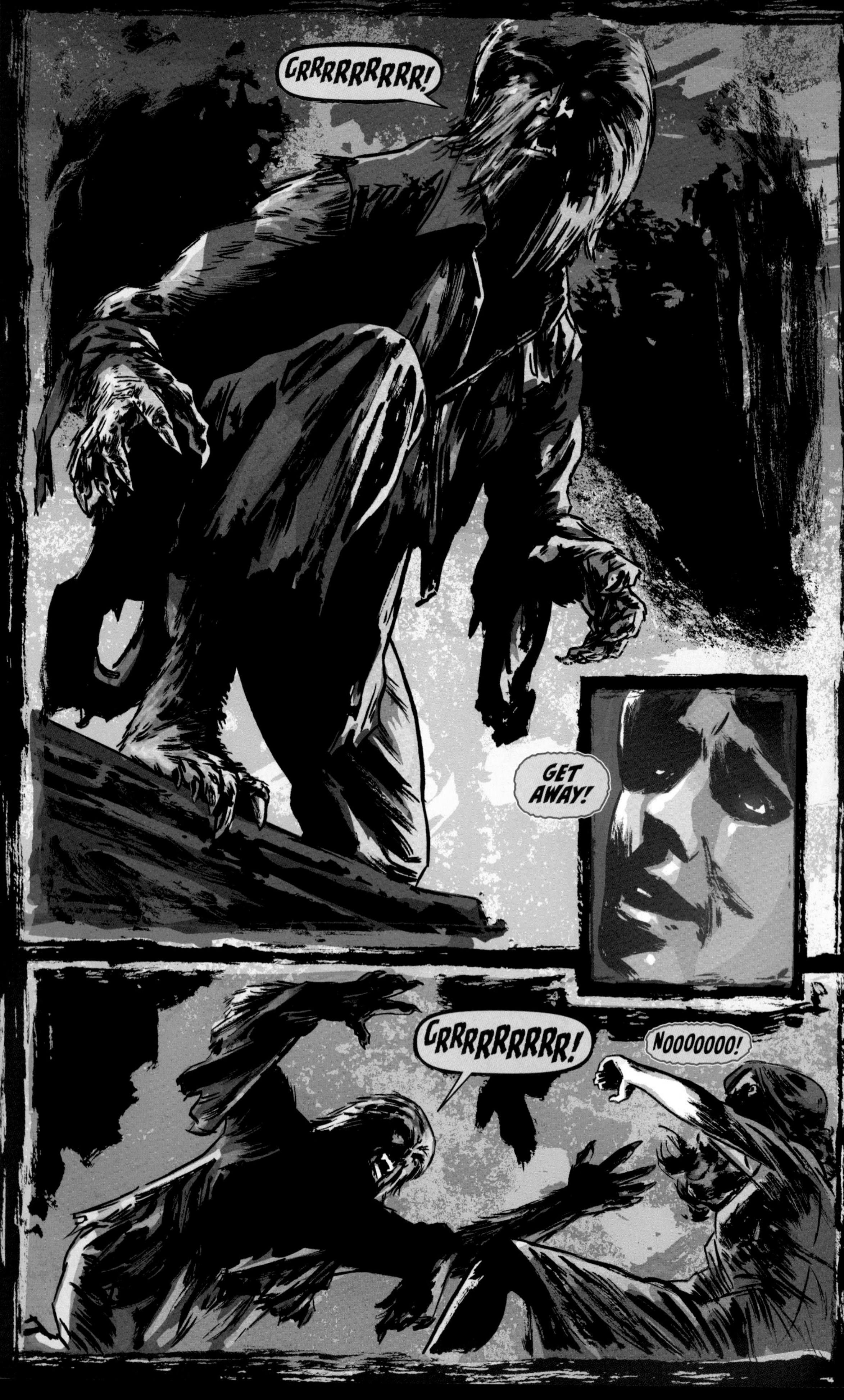
GRRRRRRRRR!
GET AWAY!
GRRRRRRRRR!
NOOOOOOO!

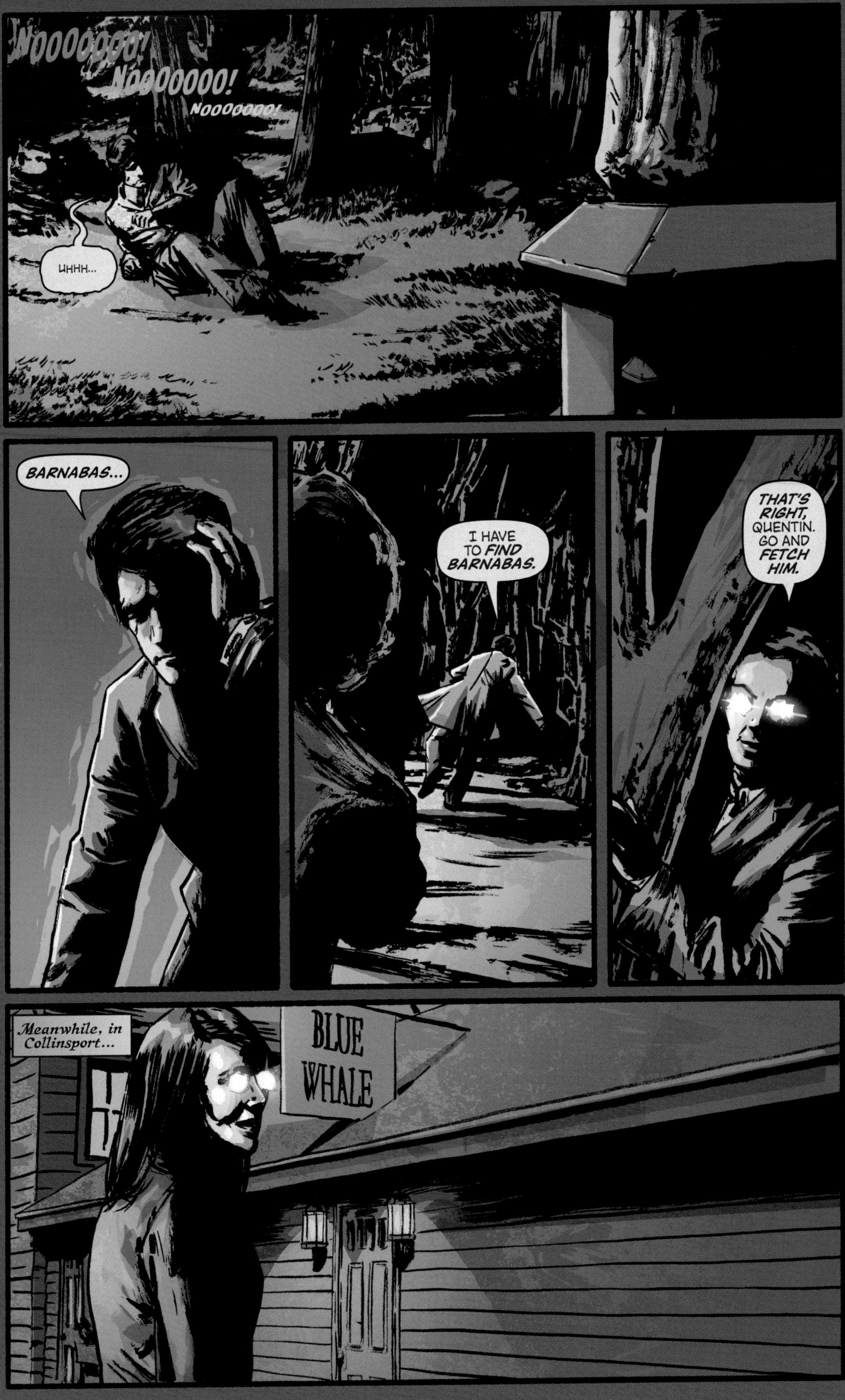
NOOOOOOO!
NOOOOOOO!
NOOOOOOO!
UHHH...
BARNABAS...
I HAVE TO FIND BARNABAS.
THAT'S RIGHT, QUENTIN. GO AND FETCH HIM.
Meanwhile, in Collinsport...
BLUE WHALE

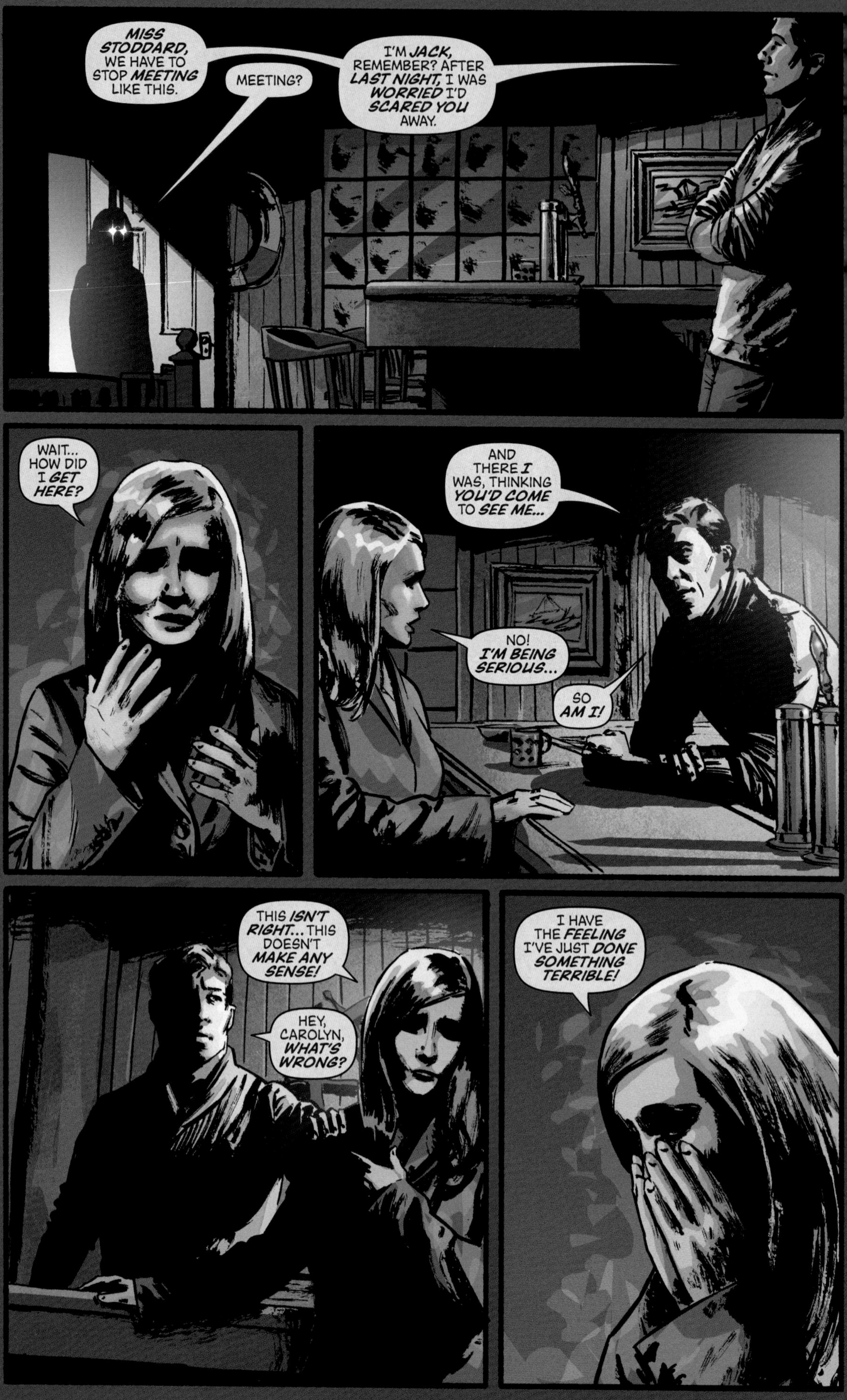
MISS STODDARD, WE HAVE TO STOP MEETING LIKE THIS.
MEETING?
I'M JACK, REMEMBER? AFTER LAST NIGHT, I WAS WORRIED I'D SCARED YOU AWAY.
WAIT... HOW DID I GET HERE?
AND THERE I WAS, THINKING YOU'D COME TO SEE ME...
NO! I'M BEING SERIOUS...
SO AM I!
THIS ISN'T RIGHT... THIS DOESN'T MAKE ANY SENSE!
HEY, CAROLYN, WHAT'S WRONG?
I HAVE THE FEELING I'VE JUST DONE SOMETHING TERRIBLE!

At the old house...

RATTATTATT

BARNABAS, OPEN UP!

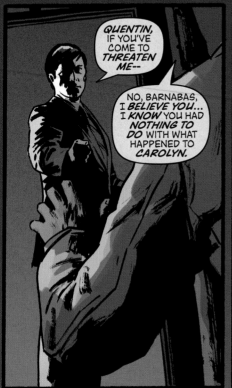

QUENTIN, IF YOU'VE COME TO THREATEN ME--

NO, BARNABAS, I BELIEVE YOU... I KNOW YOU HAD NOTHING TO DO WITH WHAT HAPPENED TO CAROLYN.

I FEAR WE'RE DEALING WITH ANOTHER VAMPIRE.

NO, YOU'RE WRONG...IT'S SOMETHING MUCH WORSE!

YOU WANNA TALK ABOUT IT?

DO YOU EVER WORRY THAT YOU'RE MISSING THINGS? LIKE THERE'S A WHOLE SCARY WORLD GOING ON AROUND YOU AND SOMEHOW YOU JUST CAN'T SEE IT?

YOU THINK TOO MUCH, PRINCESS. YOU NEED TO GET A JOB!

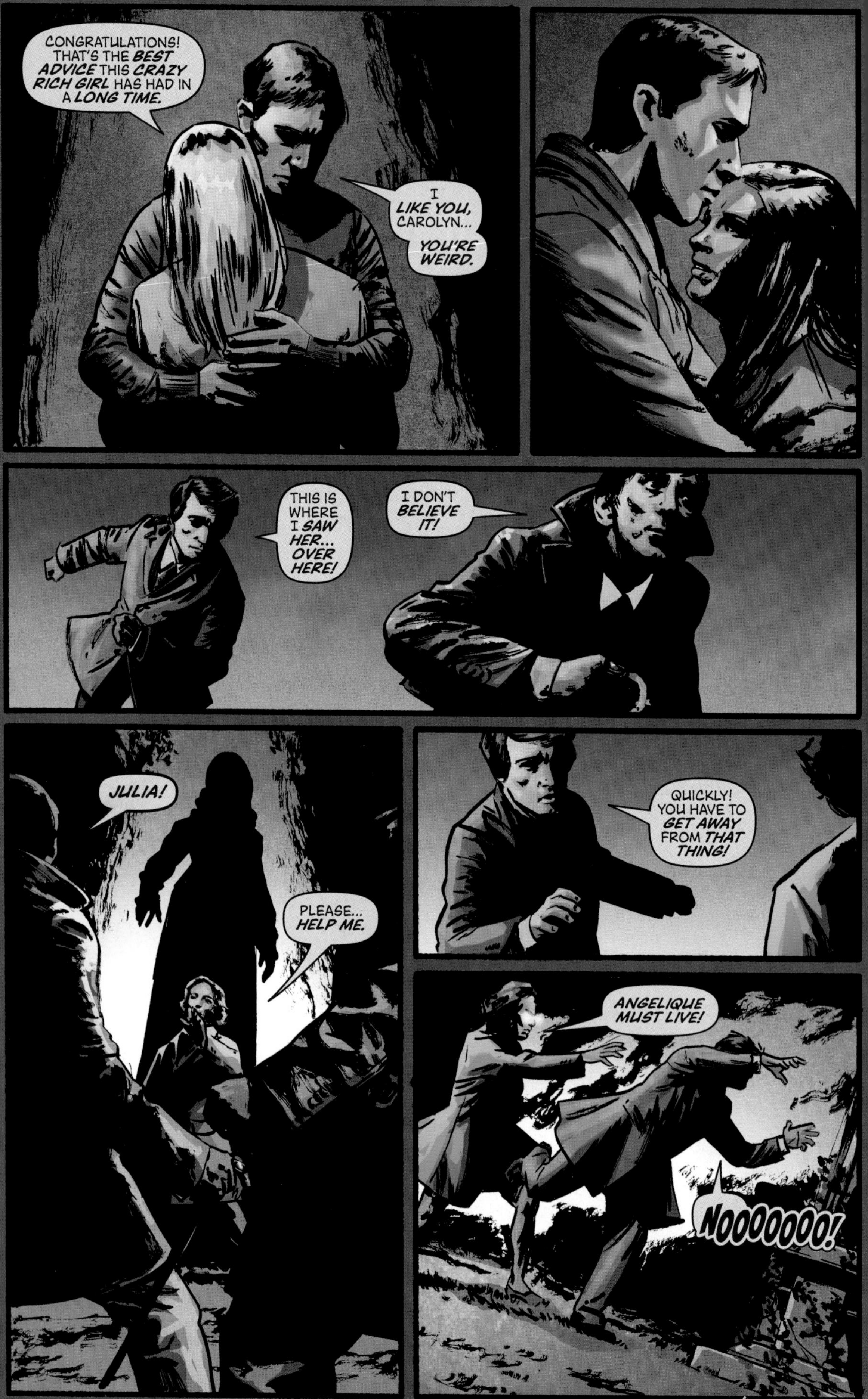
CONGRATULATIONS! THAT'S THE BEST ADVICE THIS CRAZY RICH GIRL HAS HAD IN A LONG TIME.
I LIKE YOU, CAROLYN... YOU'RE WEIRD.
THIS IS WHERE I SAW HER... OVER HERE!
I DON'T BELIEVE IT!
JULIA!
PLEASE... HELP ME.
QUICKLY! YOU HAVE TO GET AWAY FROM THAT THING!
ANGELIQUE MUST LIVE!
NOOOOOOO!

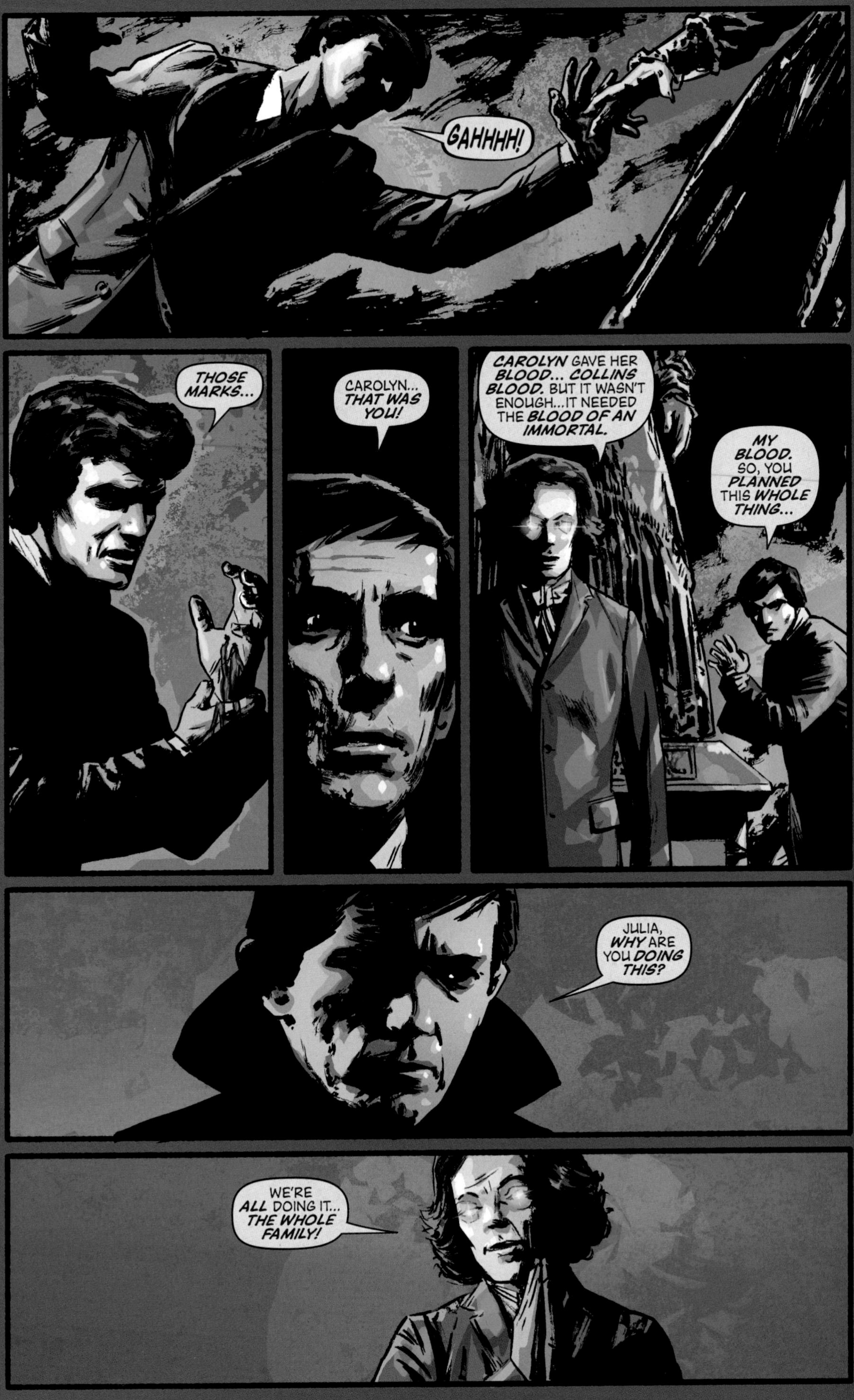
GAHHHH!
THOSE MARKS...
CAROLYN... THAT WAS YOU!
CAROLYN GAVE HER BLOOD... COLLINS BLOOD. BUT IT WASN'T ENOUGH...IT NEEDED THE BLOOD OF AN IMMORTAL.
MY BLOOD. SO, YOU PLANNED THIS WHOLE THING...
JULIA, WHY ARE YOU DOING THIS?
WE'RE ALL DOING IT... THE WHOLE FAMILY!

SHE APPROACHES!

SHE APPROACHES
SHE APPROACHES
SHE APPROACHES
SHE APPROACHES
SHE APPROACHES
SHE APPROACHES
SHE APPROACHES

NOT LONG NOW...

SHE'S ALMOST HERE.

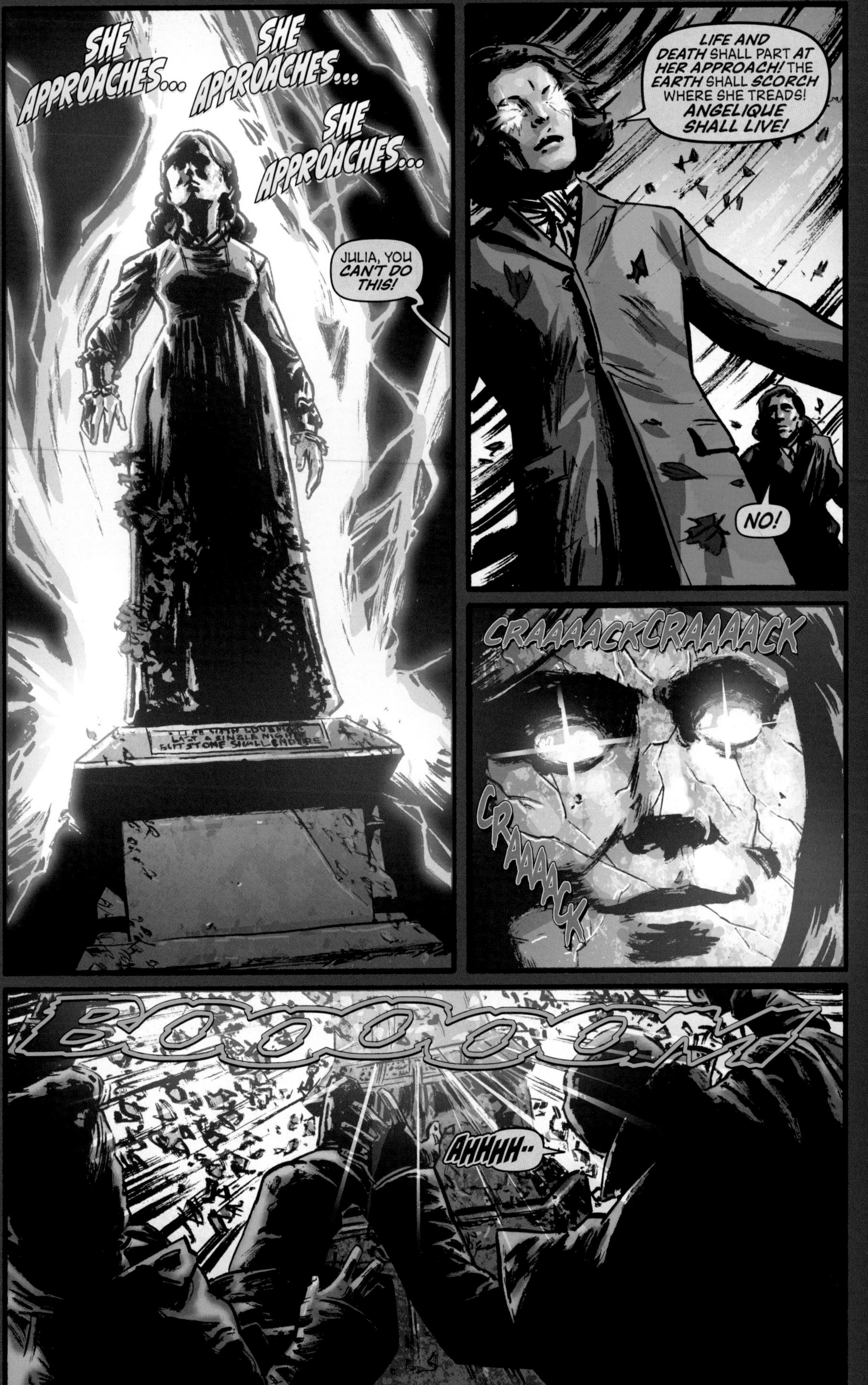
SHE APPROACHES... SHE APPROACHES... SHE APPROACHES...
JULIA, YOU CAN'T DO THIS!
LIFE AND DEATH SHALL PART AT HER APPROACH! THE EARTH SHALL SCORCH WHERE SHE TREADS! ANGELIQUE SHALL LIVE!
NO!
CRAAAACKCRAAAACK
CRAAAAACK
BOOOOOM!
AHHHH..

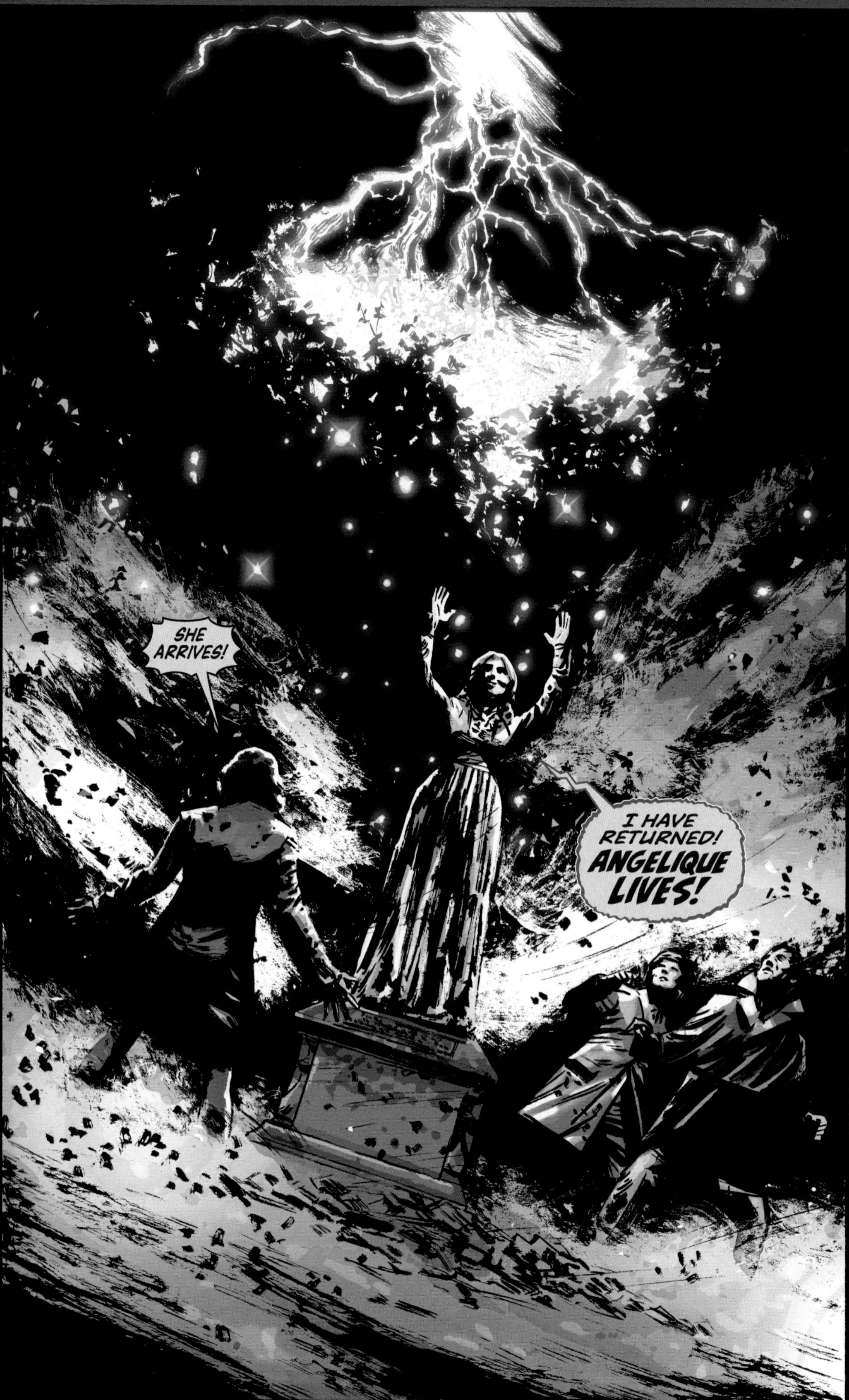
SHE ARRIVES!
I HAVE RETURNED! ANGELIQUE LIVES!

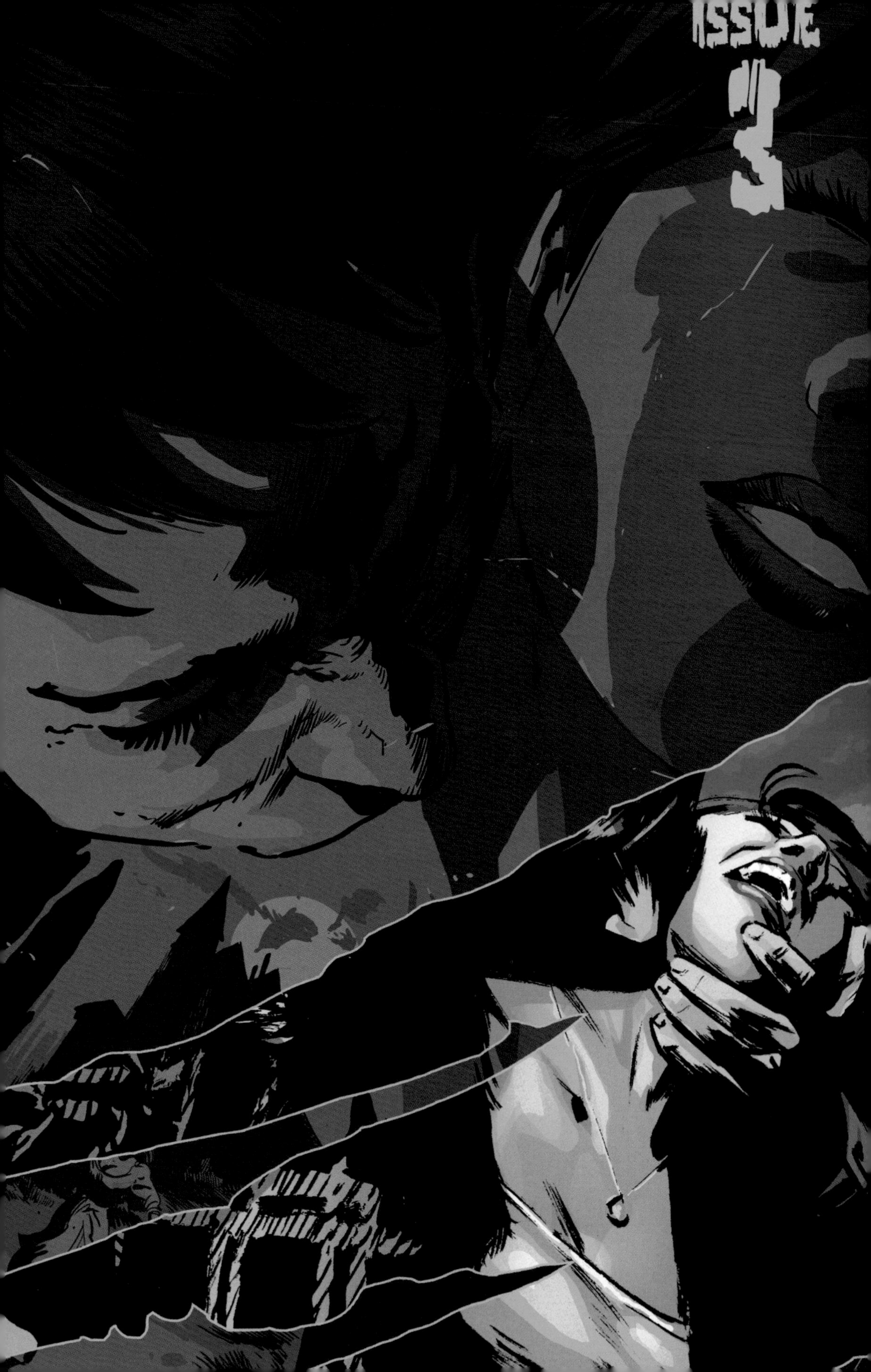
ISSUE
3

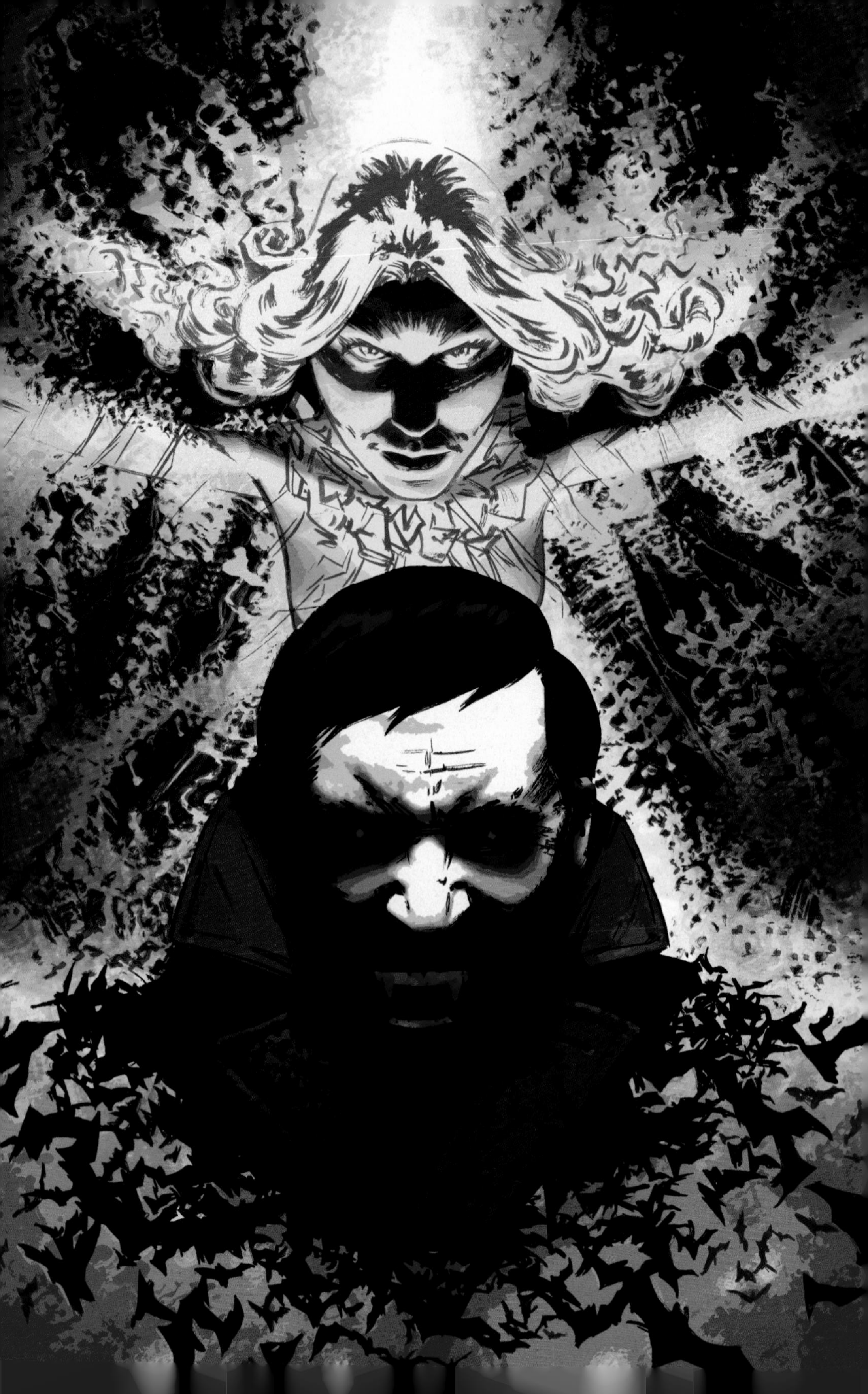

"*Darkness* draws in on the great estate of *Collinwood*..."

A LIFE WITH LOVE MAY LAST A SINGLE NIGHT, BUT STONE SHALL ENDURE

"On a night that has brought the *fulfilment* of an *age-old prophecy*."

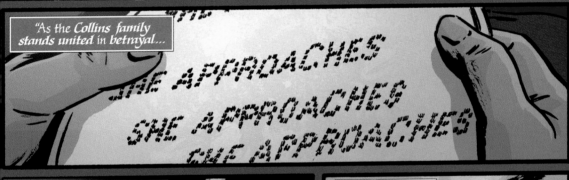

"As the *Collins* family stands united in betrayal..."

THE APPROACHES

SHE APPROACHES

SHE APPROACHES

"*Their actions* begin a sequence of events to *contact* a *powerful spirit*..."

"...and *grant the gift* of life."

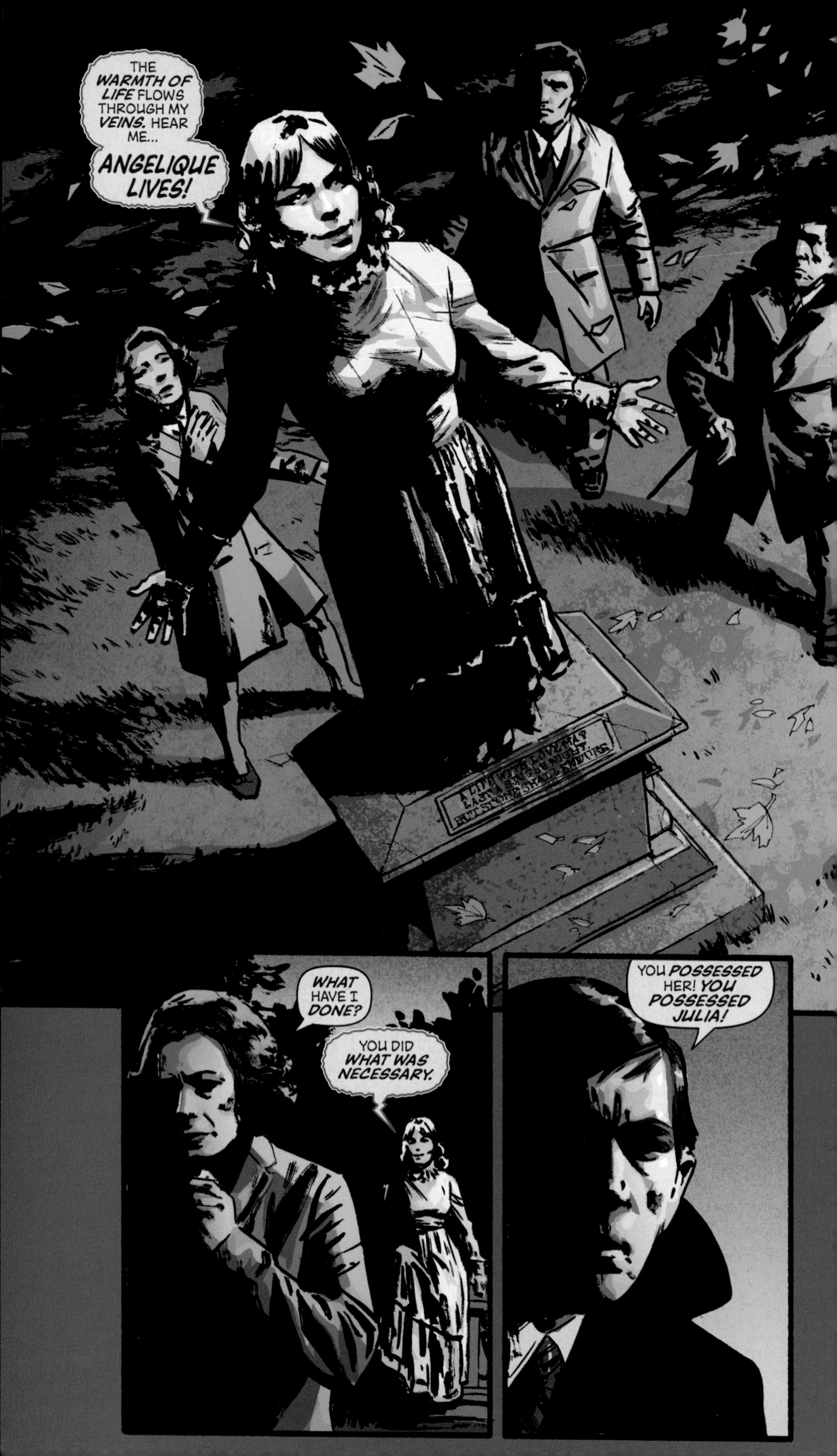
THE WARMTH OF LIFE FLOWS THROUGH MY VEINS. HEAR ME... ANGELIQUE LIVES!
WHAT HAVE I DONE?
YOU DID WHAT WAS NECESSARY.
YOU POSSESSED HER! YOU POSSESSED JULIA!

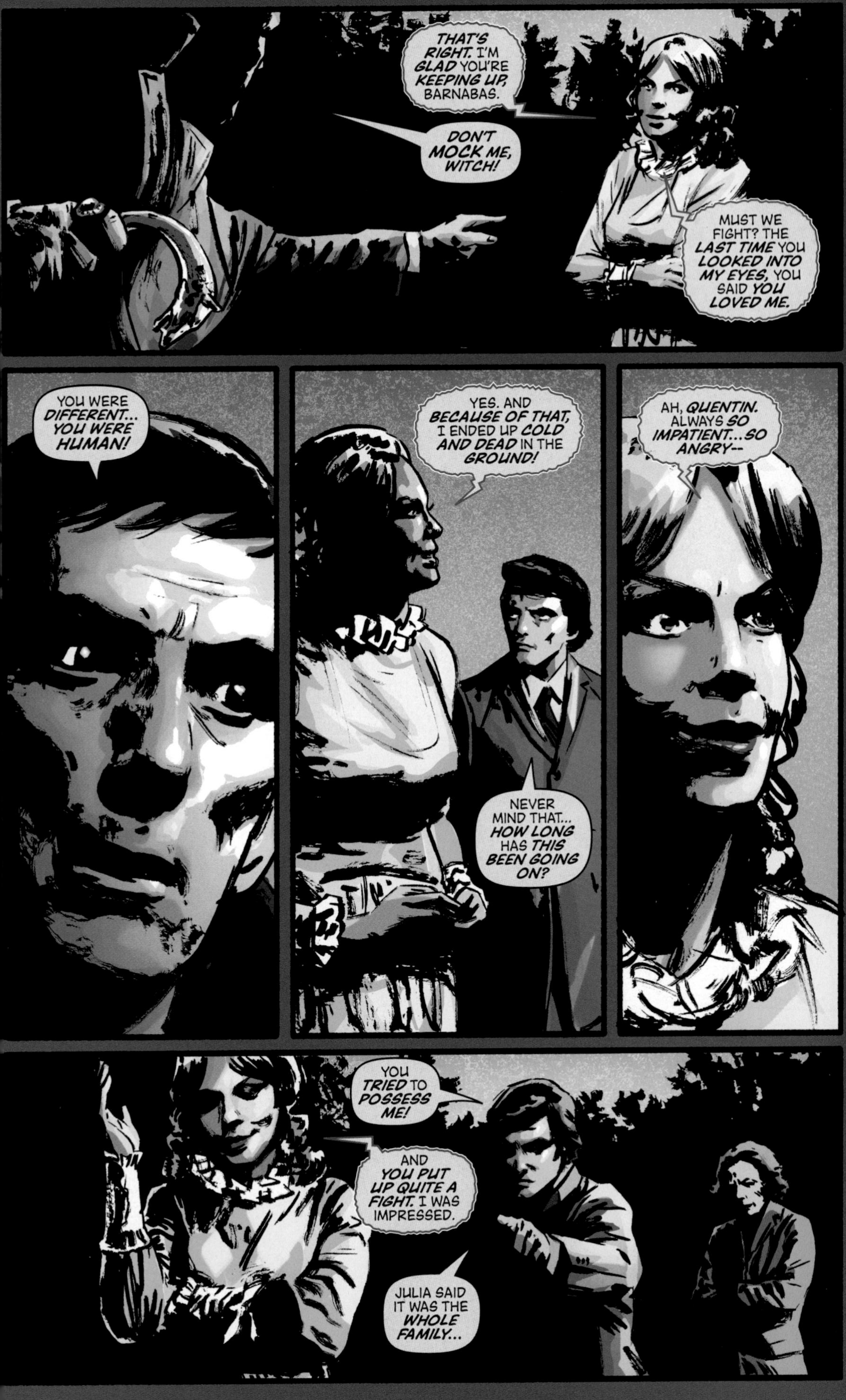
THAT'S RIGHT. I'M GLAD YOU'RE KEEPING UP, BARNABAS.
DON'T MOCK ME, WITCH!
MUST WE FIGHT? THE LAST TIME YOU LOOKED INTO MY EYES, YOU SAID YOU LOVED ME.
YOU WERE DIFFERENT... YOU WERE HUMAN!
YES. AND BECAUSE OF THAT, I ENDED UP COLD AND DEAD IN THE GROUND!
NEVER MIND THAT... HOW LONG HAS THIS BEEN GOING ON?
AH, QUENTIN. ALWAYS SO IMPATIENT... SO ANGRY--
YOU TRIED TO POSSESS ME!
AND YOU PUT UP QUITE A FIGHT. I WAS IMPRESSED.
JULIA SAID IT WAS THE WHOLE FAMILY...

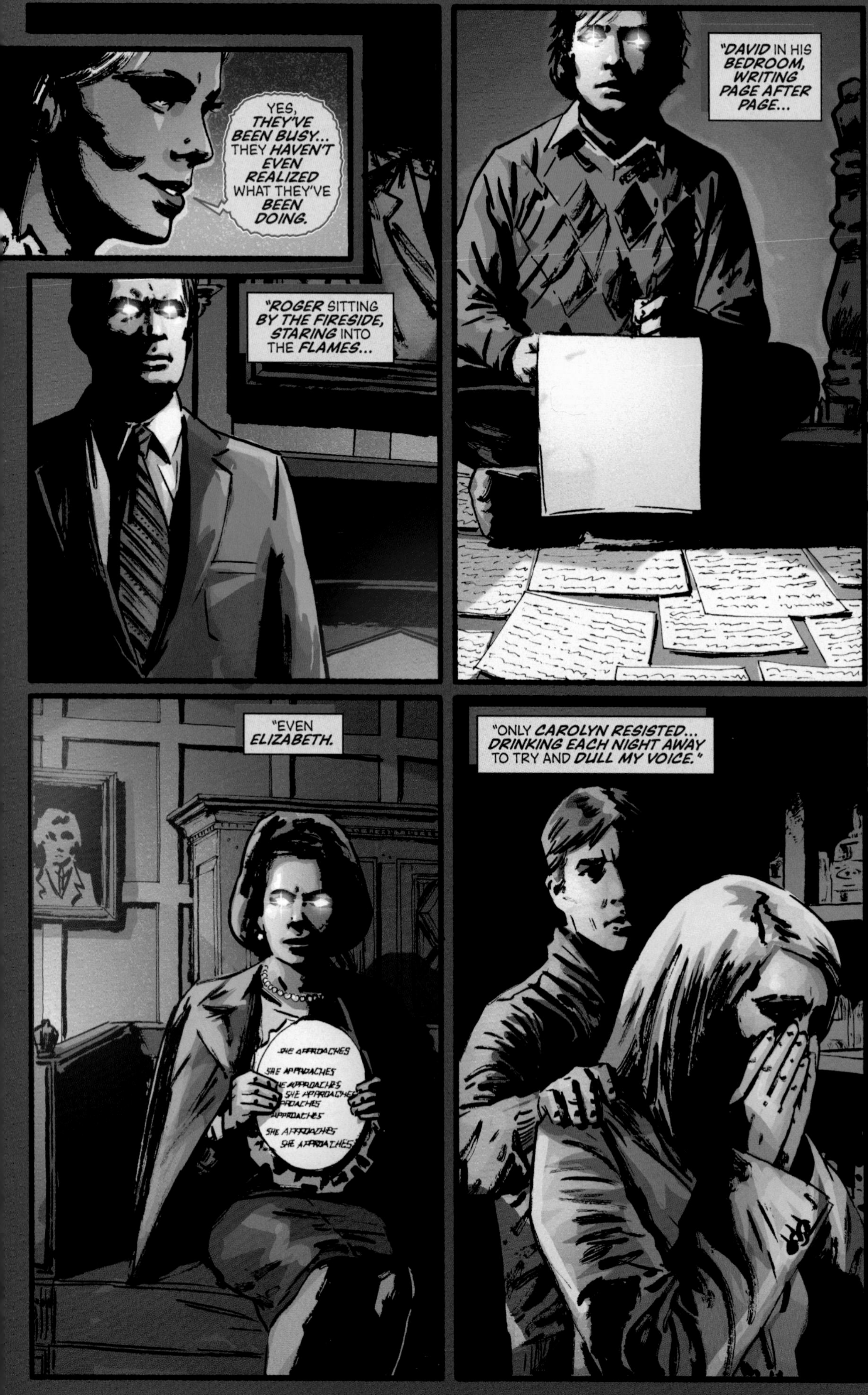
YES, THEY'VE BEEN BUSY... THEY HAVEN'T EVEN REALIZED WHAT THEY'VE BEEN DOING.
"DAVID IN HIS BEDROOM, WRITING PAGE AFTER PAGE...
"ROGER SITTING BY THE FIRESIDE, STARING INTO THE FLAMES...
"EVEN ELIZABETH.
SHE APPROACHES
SHE APPROACHES
SHE APPROACHES
SHE APPROACHES
SHE APPROACHES
"ONLY CAROLYN RESISTED... DRINKING EACH NIGHT AWAY TO TRY AND DULL MY VOICE."

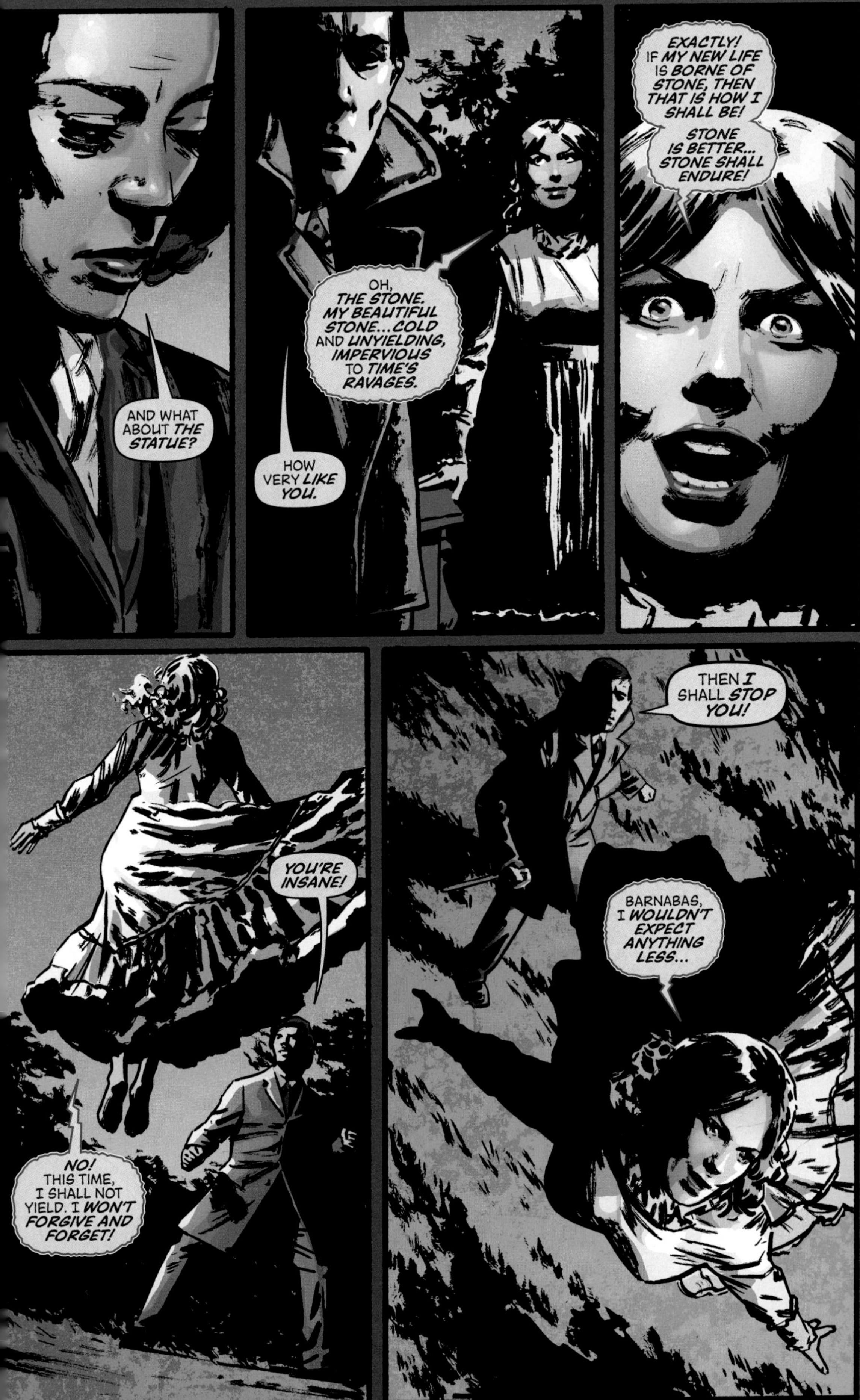
AND WHAT ABOUT THE STATUE?
OH, THE STONE. MY BEAUTIFUL STONE...COLD AND UNYIELDING, IMPERVIOUS TO TIME'S RAVAGES.
HOW VERY LIKE YOU.
EXACTLY! IF MY NEW LIFE IS BORNE OF STONE, THEN THAT IS HOW I SHALL BE!
STONE IS BETTER... STONE SHALL ENDURE!
YOU'RE INSANE!
NO! THIS TIME, I SHALL NOT YIELD. I WON'T FORGIVE AND FORGET!
THEN I SHALL STOP YOU!
BARNABAS, I WOULDN'T EXPECT ANYTHING LESS...

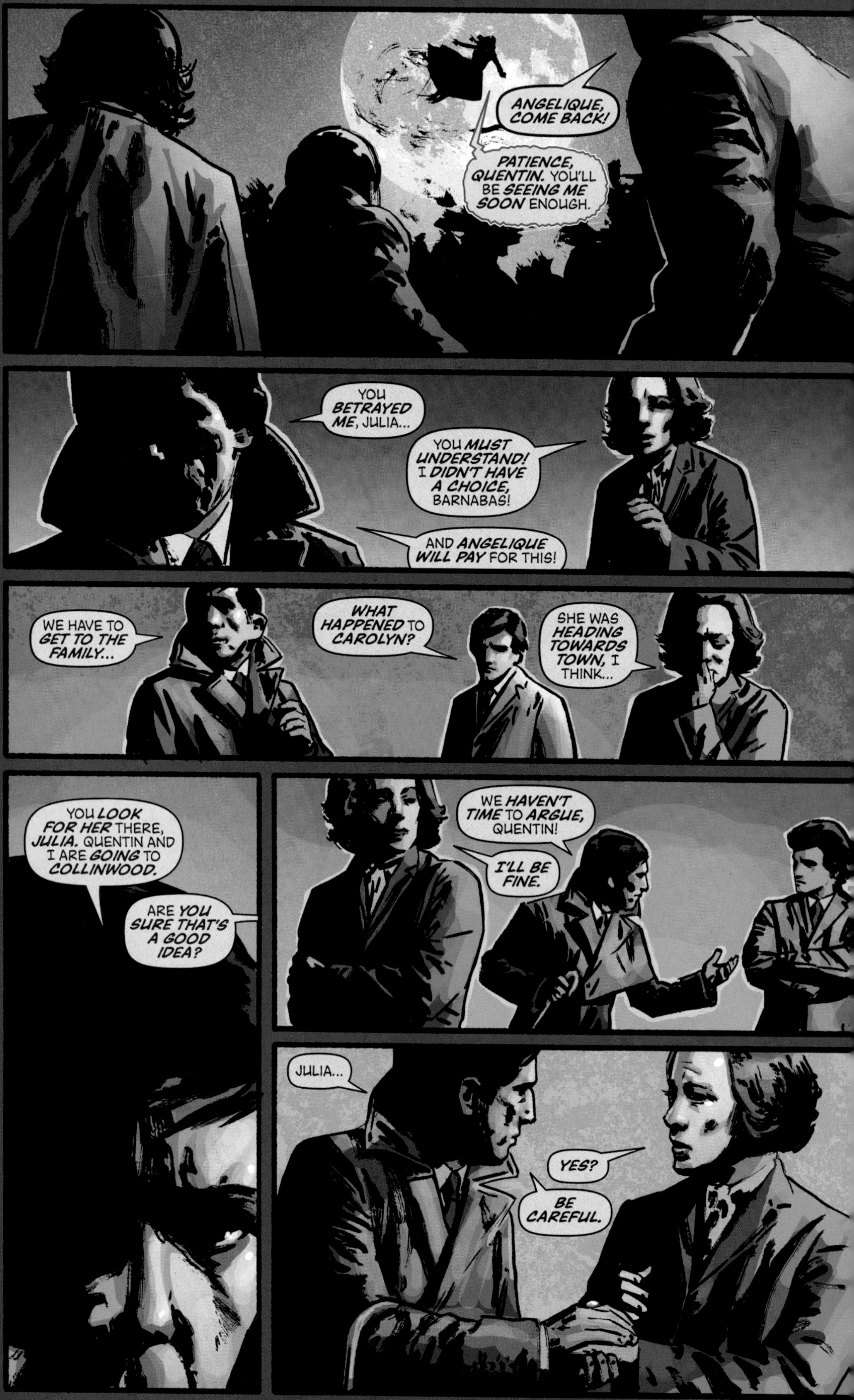
ANGELIQUE, COME BACK!
PATIENCE, QUENTIN. YOU'LL BE SEEING ME SOON ENOUGH.
YOU BETRAYED ME, JULIA...
YOU MUST UNDERSTAND! I DIDN'T HAVE A CHOICE, BARNABAS!
AND ANGELIQUE WILL PAY FOR THIS!
WE HAVE TO GET TO THE FAMILY...
WHAT HAPPENED TO CAROLYN?
SHE WAS HEADING TOWARDS TOWN, I THINK...
YOU LOOK FOR HER THERE, JULIA. QUENTIN AND I ARE GOING TO COLLINWOOD.
ARE YOU SURE THAT'S A GOOD IDEA?
WE HAVEN'T TIME TO ARGUE, QUENTIN!
I'LL BE FINE.
JULIA...
YES?
BE CAREFUL.

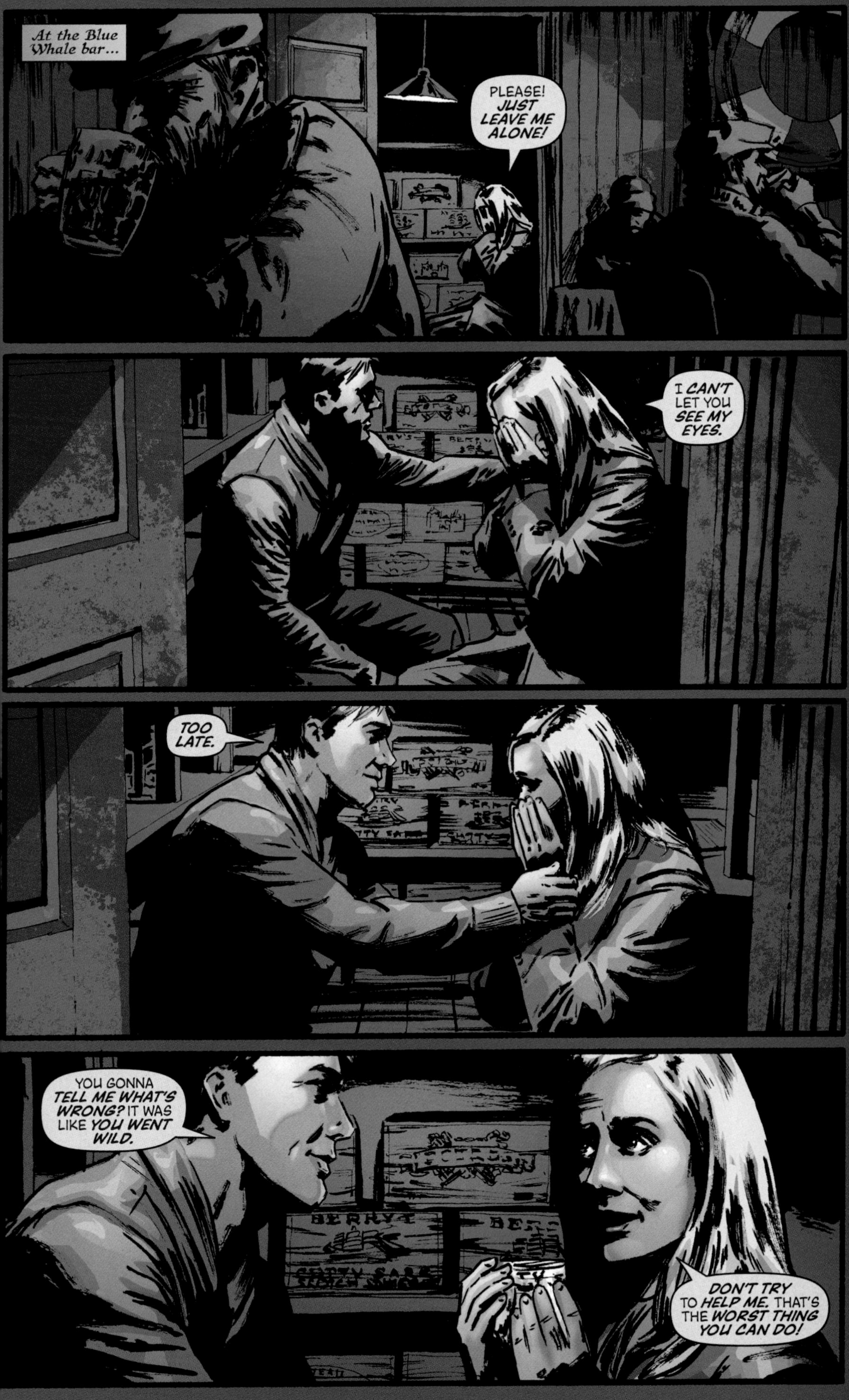
At the Blue Whale bar...
PLEASE! JUST LEAVE ME ALONE!
I CAN'T LET YOU SEE MY EYES.
TOO LATE.
YOU GONNA TELL ME WHAT'S WRONG? IT WAS LIKE YOU WENT WILD.
DON'T TRY TO HELP ME. THAT'S THE WORST THING YOU CAN DO!

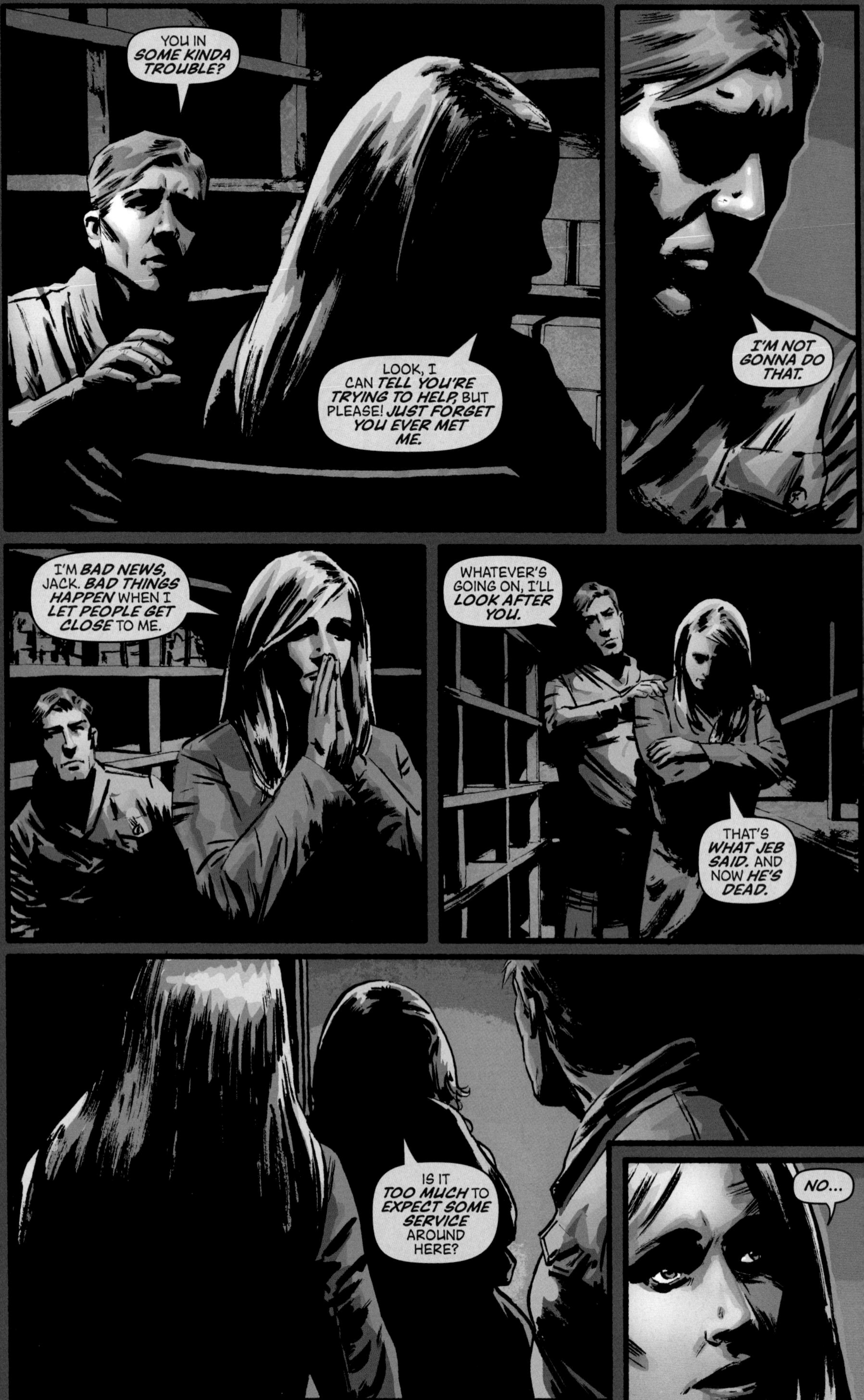
YOU IN SOME KINDA TROUBLE?
LOOK, I CAN TELL YOU'RE TRYING TO HELP, BUT PLEASE! JUST FORGET YOU EVER MET ME.
I'M NOT GONNA DO THAT.
I'M BAD NEWS, JACK. BAD THINGS HAPPEN WHEN I LET PEOPLE GET CLOSE TO ME.
WHATEVER'S GOING ON, I'LL LOOK AFTER YOU.
THAT'S WHAT JEB SAID. AND NOW HE'S DEAD.
IS IT TOO MUCH TO EXPECT SOME SERVICE AROUND HERE?
NO...

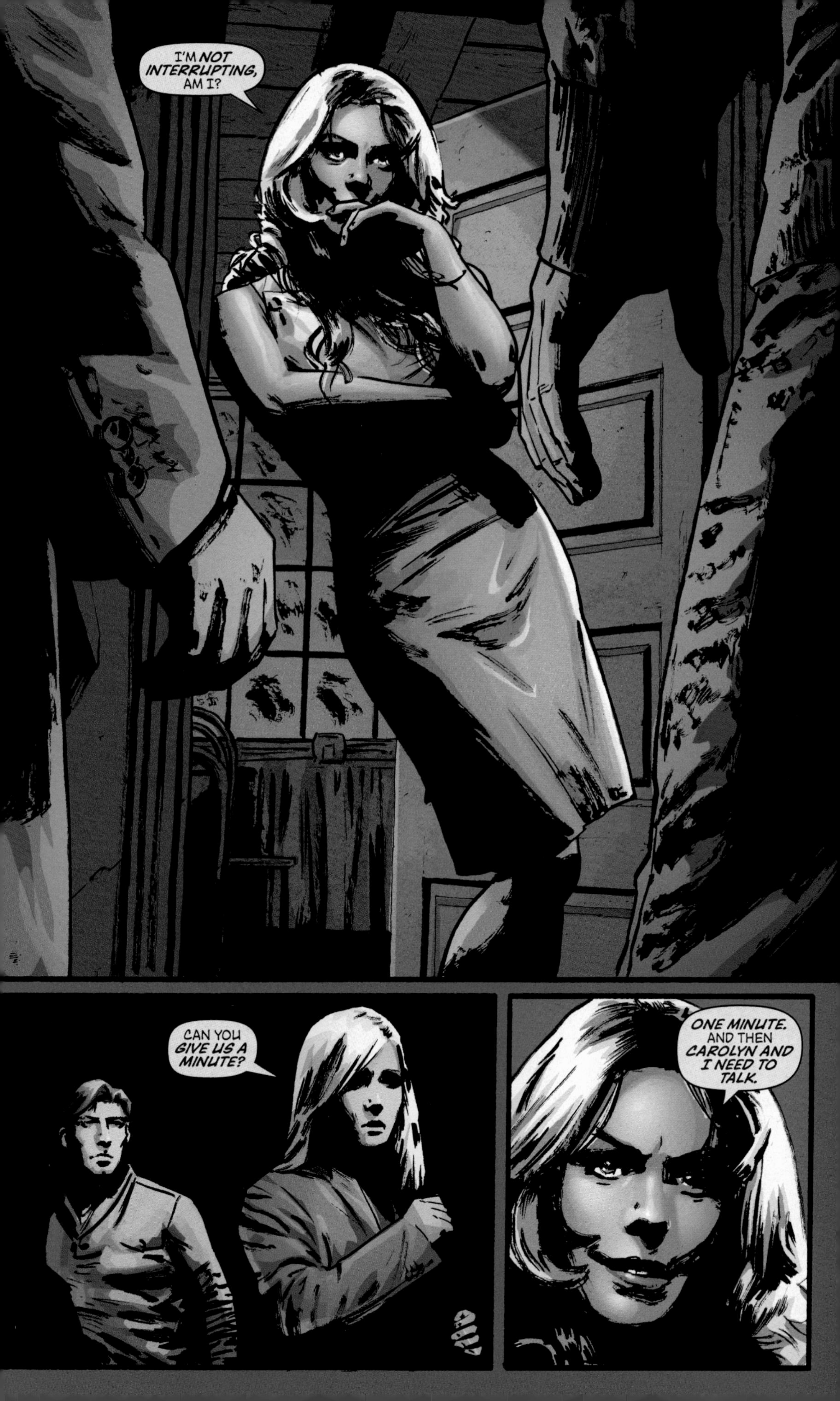
I'M NOT INTERRUPTING, AM I?
CAN YOU GIVE US A MINUTE?
ONE MINUTE. AND THEN CAROLYN AND I NEED TO TALK.

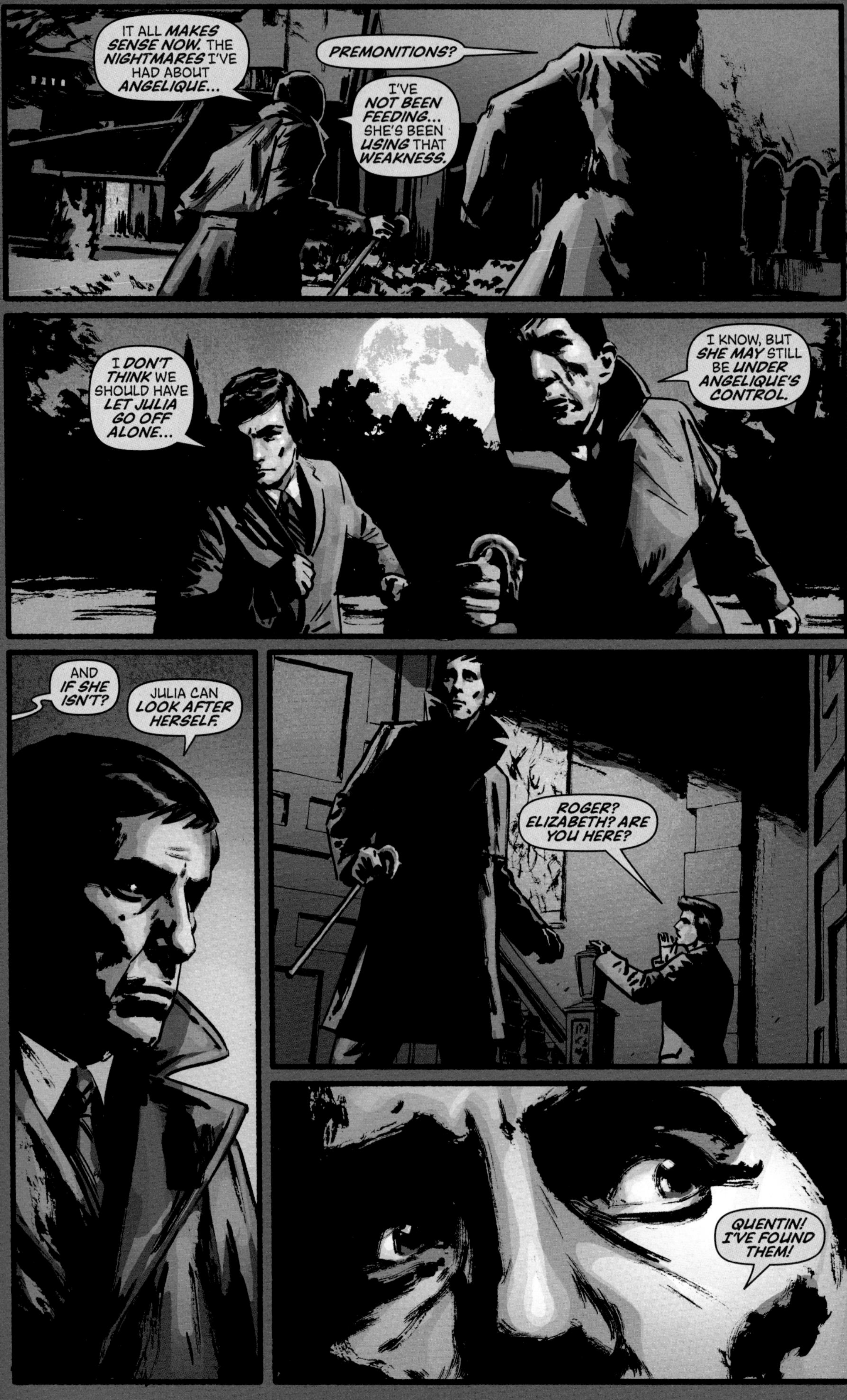
IT ALL MAKES SENSE NOW. THE NIGHTMARES I'VE HAD ABOUT ANGELIQUE...
PREMONITIONS?
I'VE NOT BEEN FEEDING... SHE'S BEEN USING THAT WEAKNESS.
I DON'T THINK WE SHOULD HAVE LET JULIA GO OFF ALONE...
I KNOW, BUT SHE MAY STILL BE UNDER ANGELIQUE'S CONTROL.
AND IF SHE ISN'T?
JULIA CAN LOOK AFTER HERSELF.
ROGER? ELIZABETH? ARE YOU HERE?
QUENTIN! I'VE FOUND THEM!

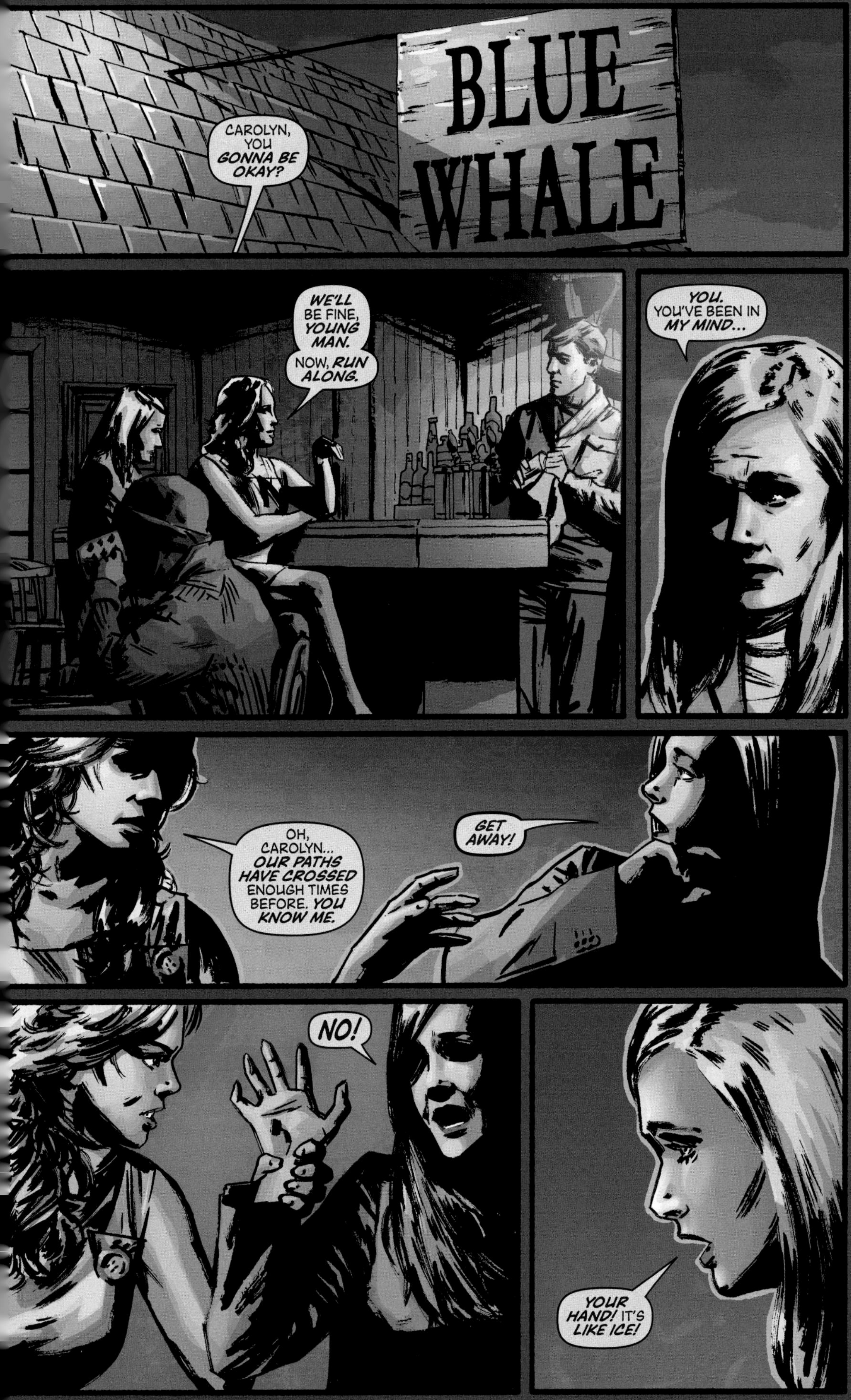
BLUE WHALE
CAROLYN, YOU GONNA BE OKAY?
WE'LL BE FINE, YOUNG MAN.
NOW, RUN ALONG.
YOU. YOU'VE BEEN IN MY MIND...
OH, CAROLYN... OUR PATHS HAVE CROSSED ENOUGH TIMES BEFORE. YOU KNOW ME.
GET AWAY!
NO!
YOUR HAND! IT'S LIKE ICE!

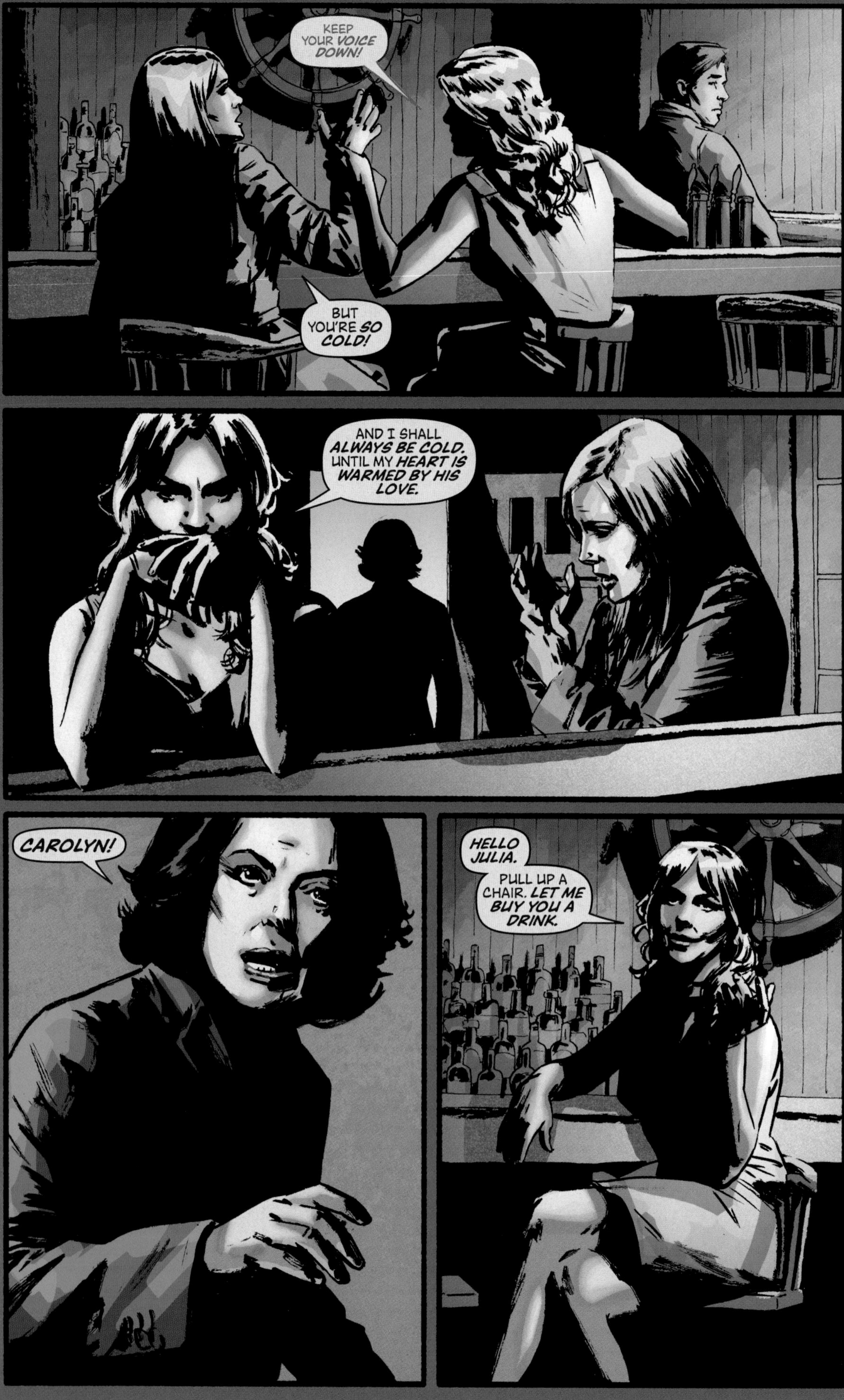
KEEP YOUR VOICE DOWN!
BUT YOU'RE SO COLD!
AND I SHALL ALWAYS BE COLD. UNTIL MY HEART IS WARMED BY HIS LOVE.
CAROLYN!
HELLO JULIA.
PULL UP A CHAIR. LET ME BUY YOU A DRINK.

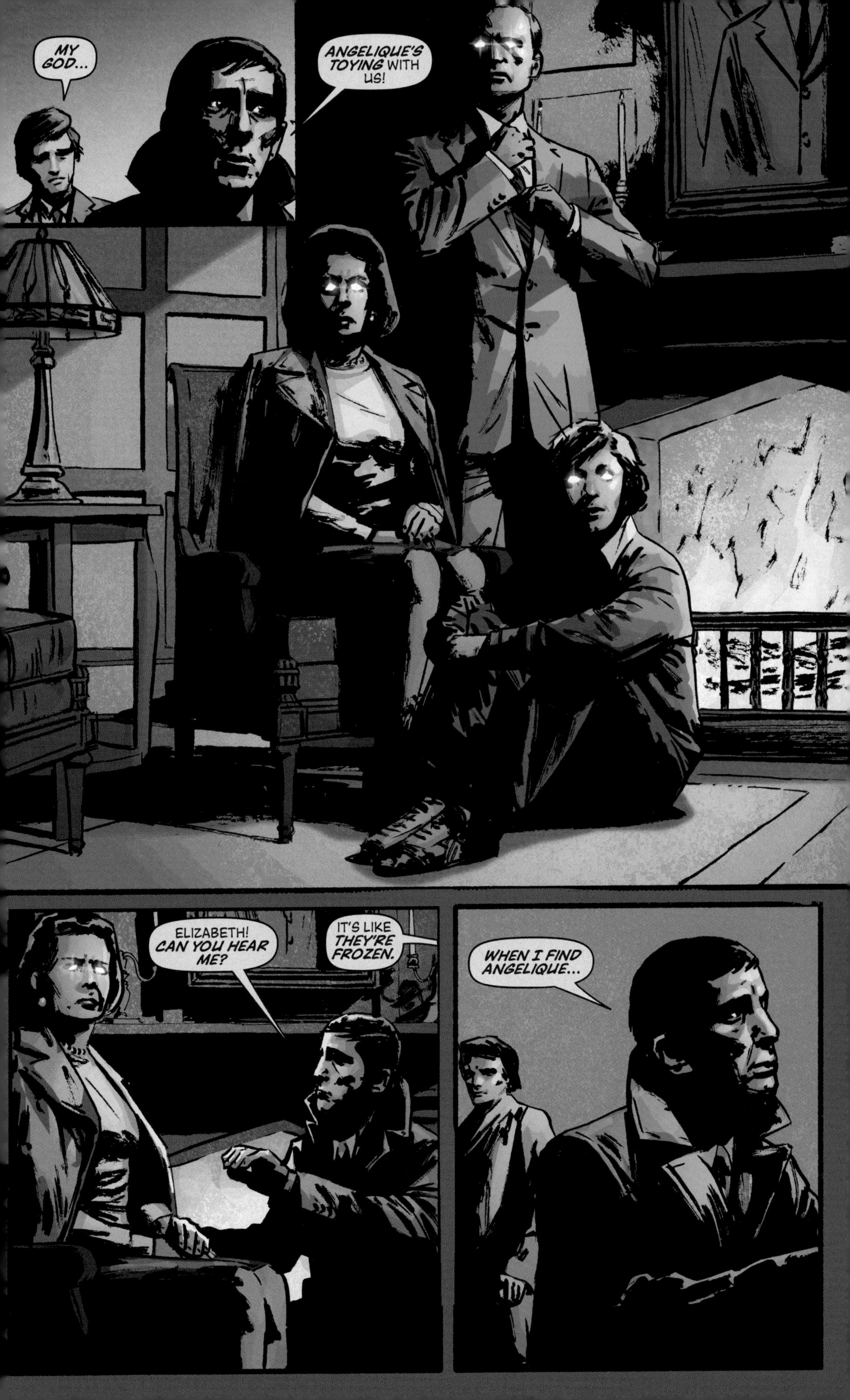
MY GOD...
ANGELIQUE'S TOYING WITH US!
ELIZABETH! CAN YOU HEAR ME?
IT'S LIKE THEY'RE FROZEN.
WHEN I FIND ANGELIQUE...

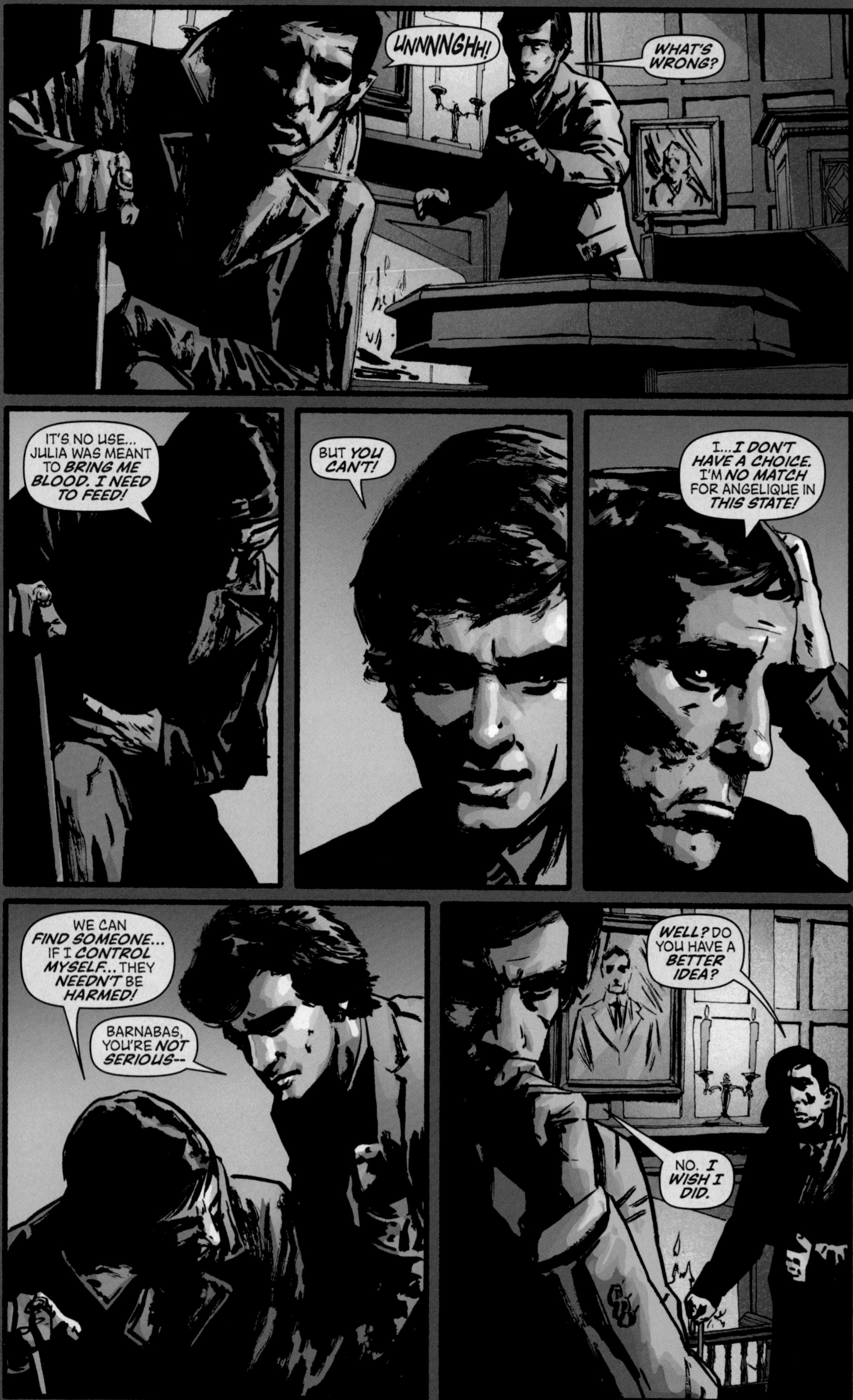
UNNNNGHH!
WHAT'S WRONG?
IT'S NO USE... JULIA WAS MEANT TO BRING ME BLOOD. I NEED TO FEED!
BUT YOU CAN'T!
I...I DON'T HAVE A CHOICE. I'M NO MATCH FOR ANGELIQUE IN THIS STATE!
WE CAN FIND SOMEONE... IF I CONTROL MYSELF...THEY NEEDN'T BE HARMED!
BARNABAS, YOU'RE NOT SERIOUS--
WELL? DO YOU HAVE A BETTER IDEA?
NO. I WISH I DID.

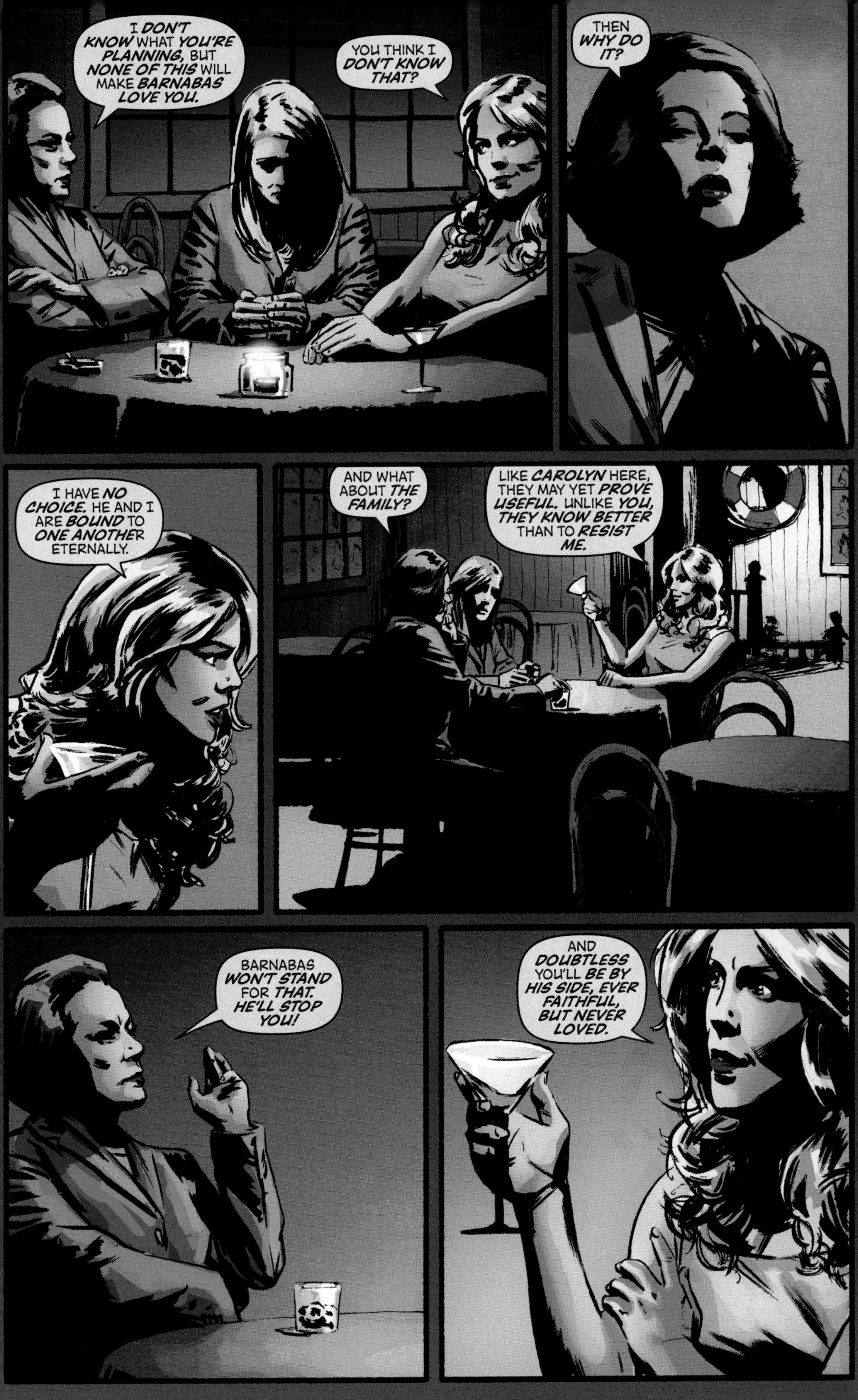
I DON'T KNOW WHAT YOU'RE PLANNING, BUT NONE OF THIS WILL MAKE BARNABAS LOVE YOU.
YOU THINK I DON'T KNOW THAT?
THEN WHY DO IT?
I HAVE NO CHOICE. HE AND I ARE BOUND TO ONE ANOTHER ETERNALLY.
AND WHAT ABOUT THE FAMILY?
LIKE CAROLYN HERE, THEY MAY YET PROVE USEFUL. UNLIKE YOU, THEY KNOW BETTER THAN TO RESIST ME.
BARNABAS WON'T STAND FOR THAT. HE'LL STOP YOU!
AND DOUBTLESS YOU'LL BE BY HIS SIDE, EVER FAITHFUL, BUT NEVER LOVED.

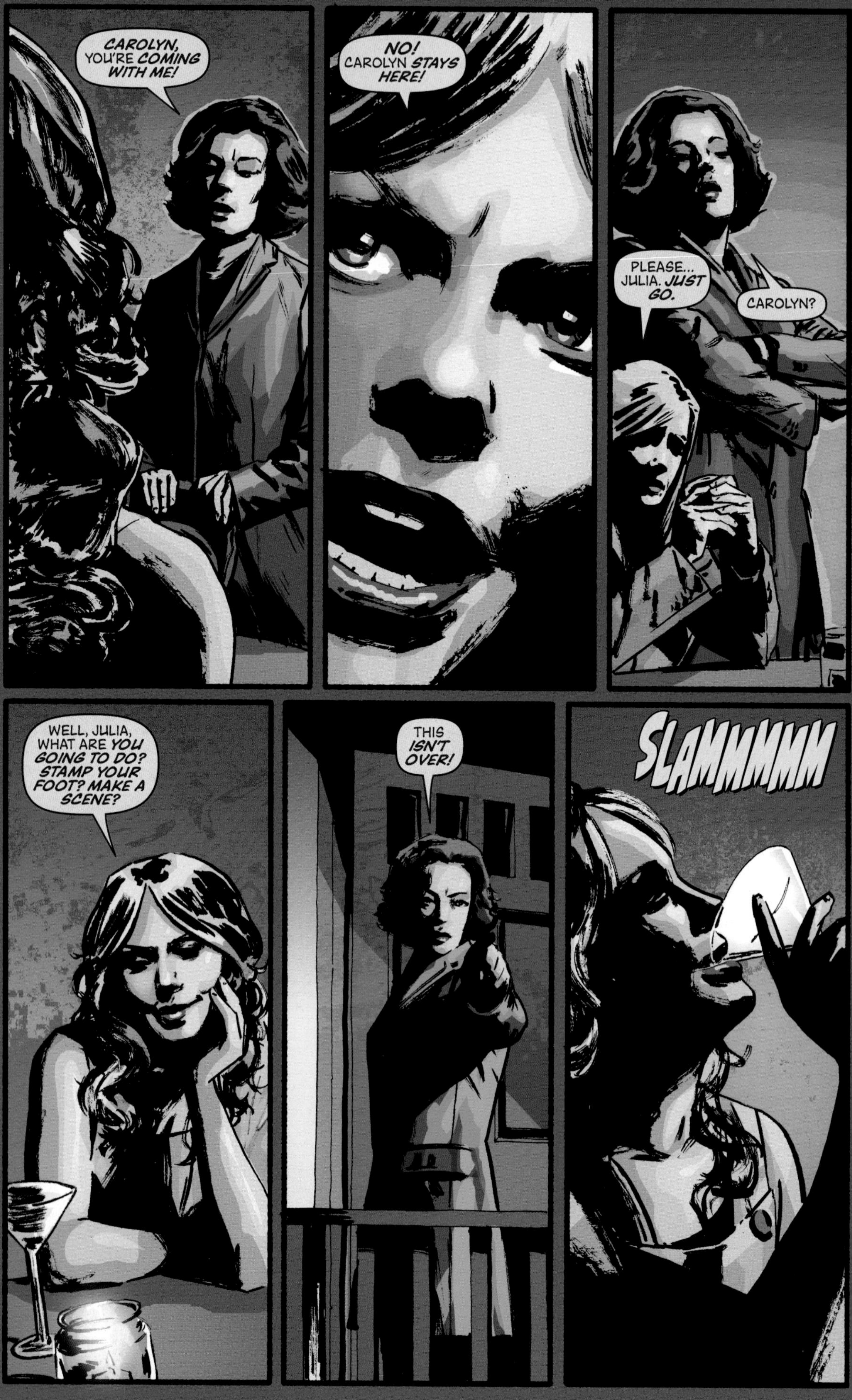
CAROLYN, YOU'RE COMING WITH ME!
NO! CAROLYN STAYS HERE!
PLEASE... JULIA. JUST GO.
CAROLYN?
WELL, JULIA, WHAT ARE YOU GOING TO DO? STAMP YOUR FOOT? MAKE A SCENE?
THIS ISN'T OVER!
SLAMMMMM

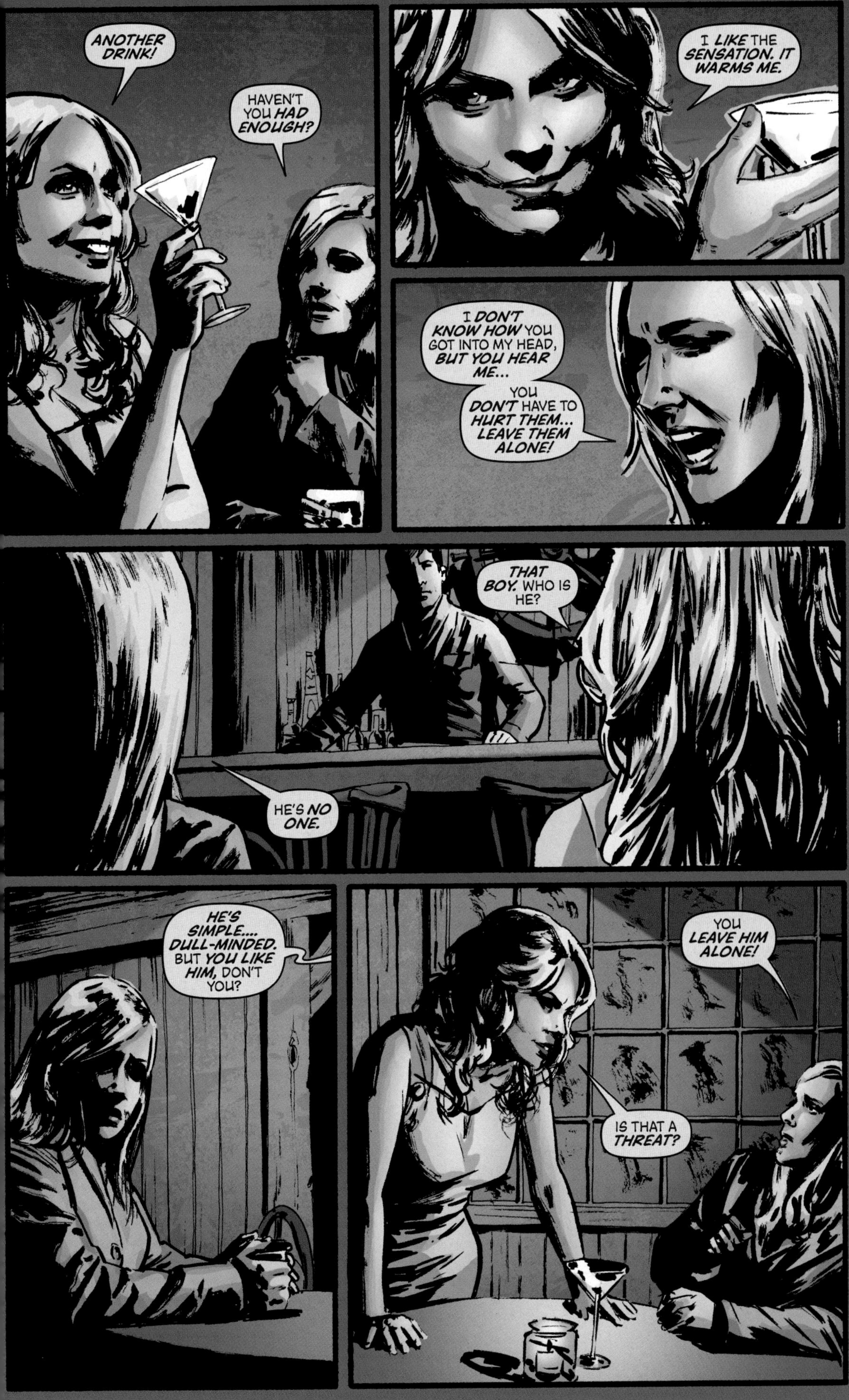
ANOTHER DRINK!
HAVEN'T YOU HAD ENOUGH?
I LIKE THE SENSATION. IT WARMS ME.
I DON'T KNOW HOW YOU GOT INTO MY HEAD, BUT YOU HEAR ME...
YOU DON'T HAVE TO HURT THEM... LEAVE THEM ALONE!
THAT BOY. WHO IS HE?
HE'S NO ONE.
HE'S SIMPLE.... DULL-MINDED. BUT YOU LIKE HIM, DON'T YOU?
YOU LEAVE HIM ALONE!
IS THAT A THREAT?

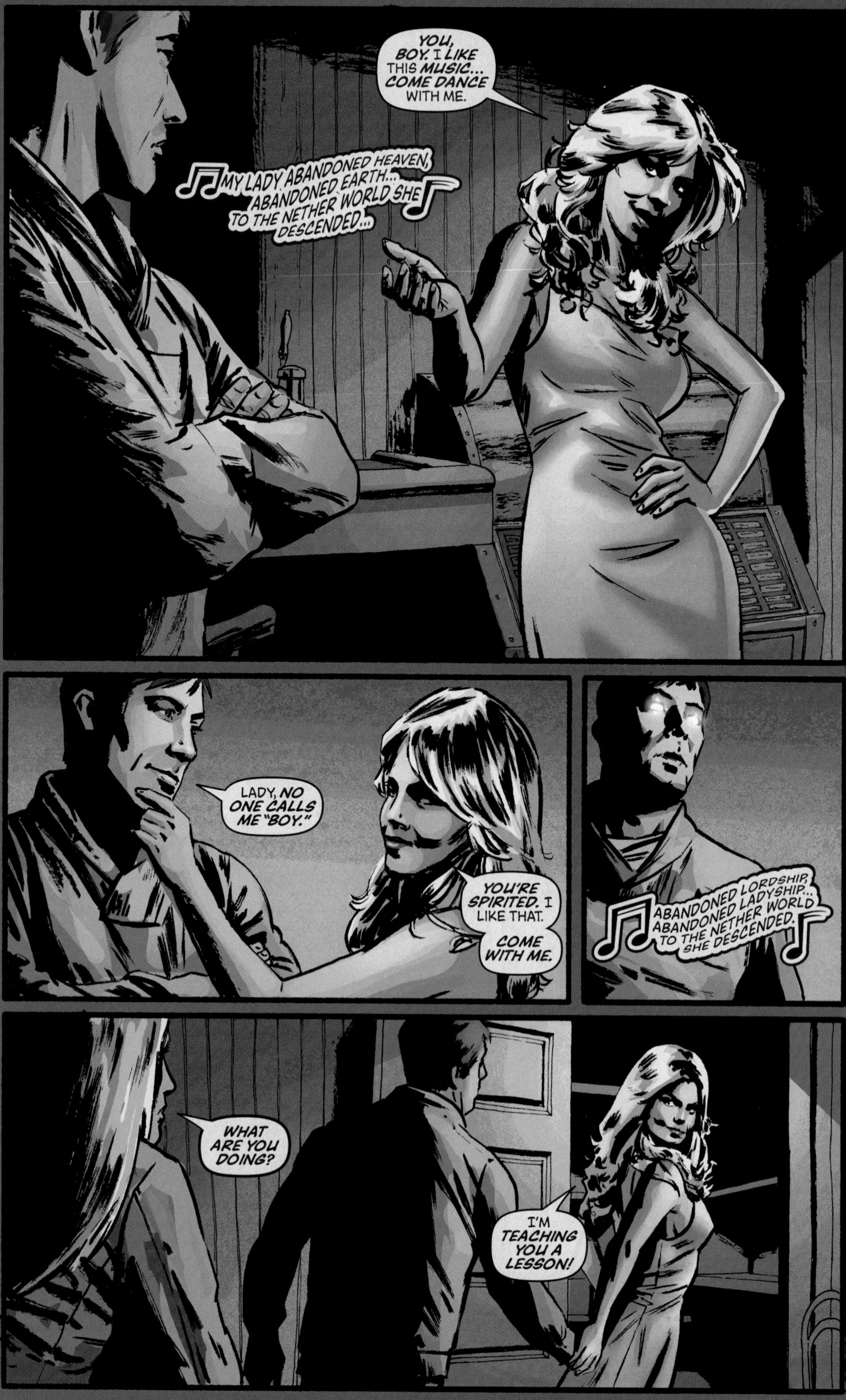
YOU, BOY. I LIKE THIS MUSIC... COME DANCE WITH ME.
MY LADY ABANDONED HEAVEN, ABANDONED EARTH... TO THE NETHER WORLD SHE DESCENDED...
LADY, NO ONE CALLS ME "BOY."
YOU'RE SPIRITED. I LIKE THAT.
COME WITH ME.
ABANDONED LORDSHIP, ABANDONED LADYSHIP... TO THE NETHER WORLD SHE DESCENDED.
WHAT ARE YOU DOING?
I'M TEACHING YOU A LESSON!

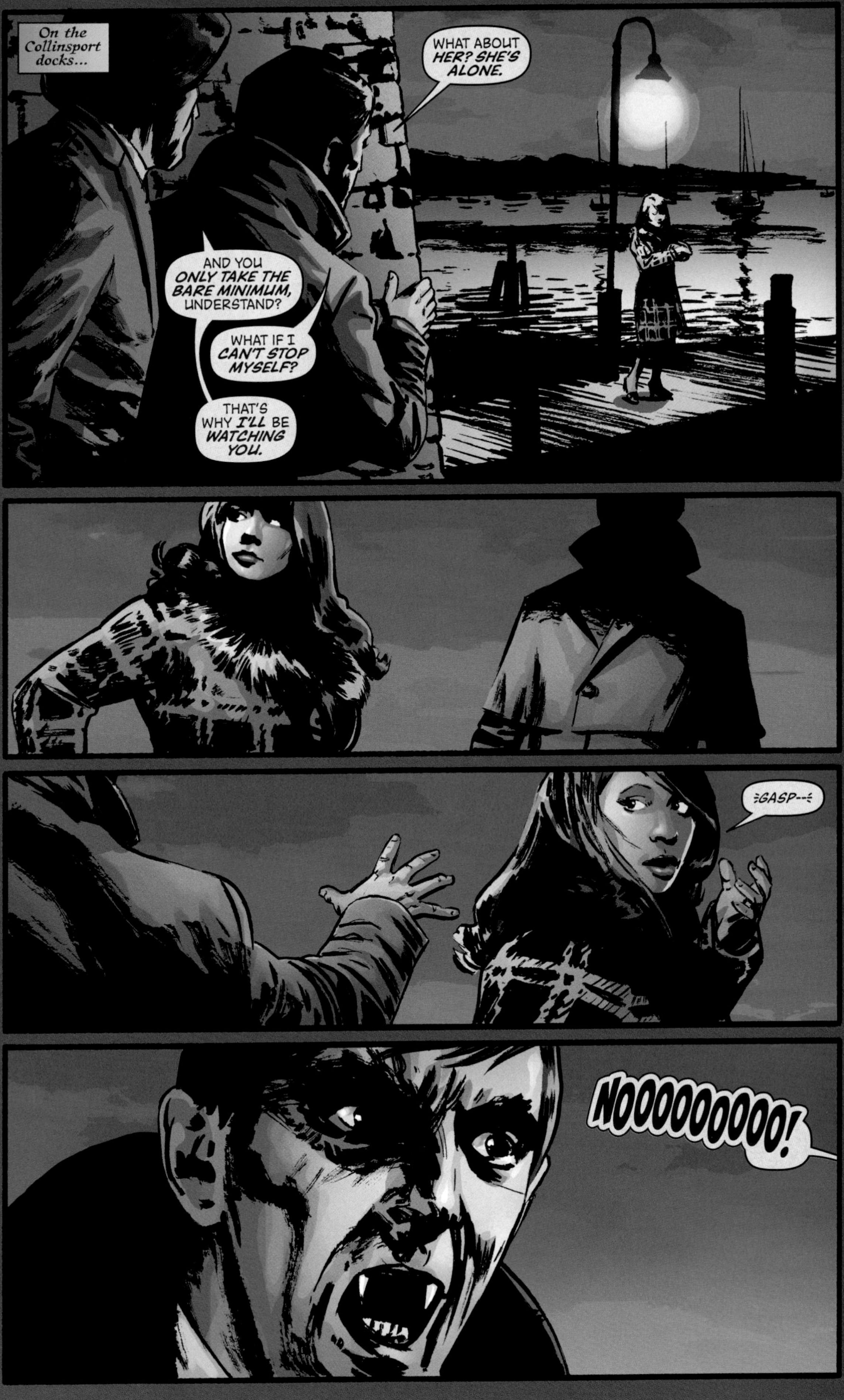
On the Collinsport docks...
WHAT ABOUT HER? SHE'S ALONE.
AND YOU ONLY TAKE THE BARE MINIMUM, UNDERSTAND?
WHAT IF I CAN'T STOP MYSELF?
THAT'S WHY I'LL BE WATCHING YOU.
GASP--
NOOOOOOOOO!

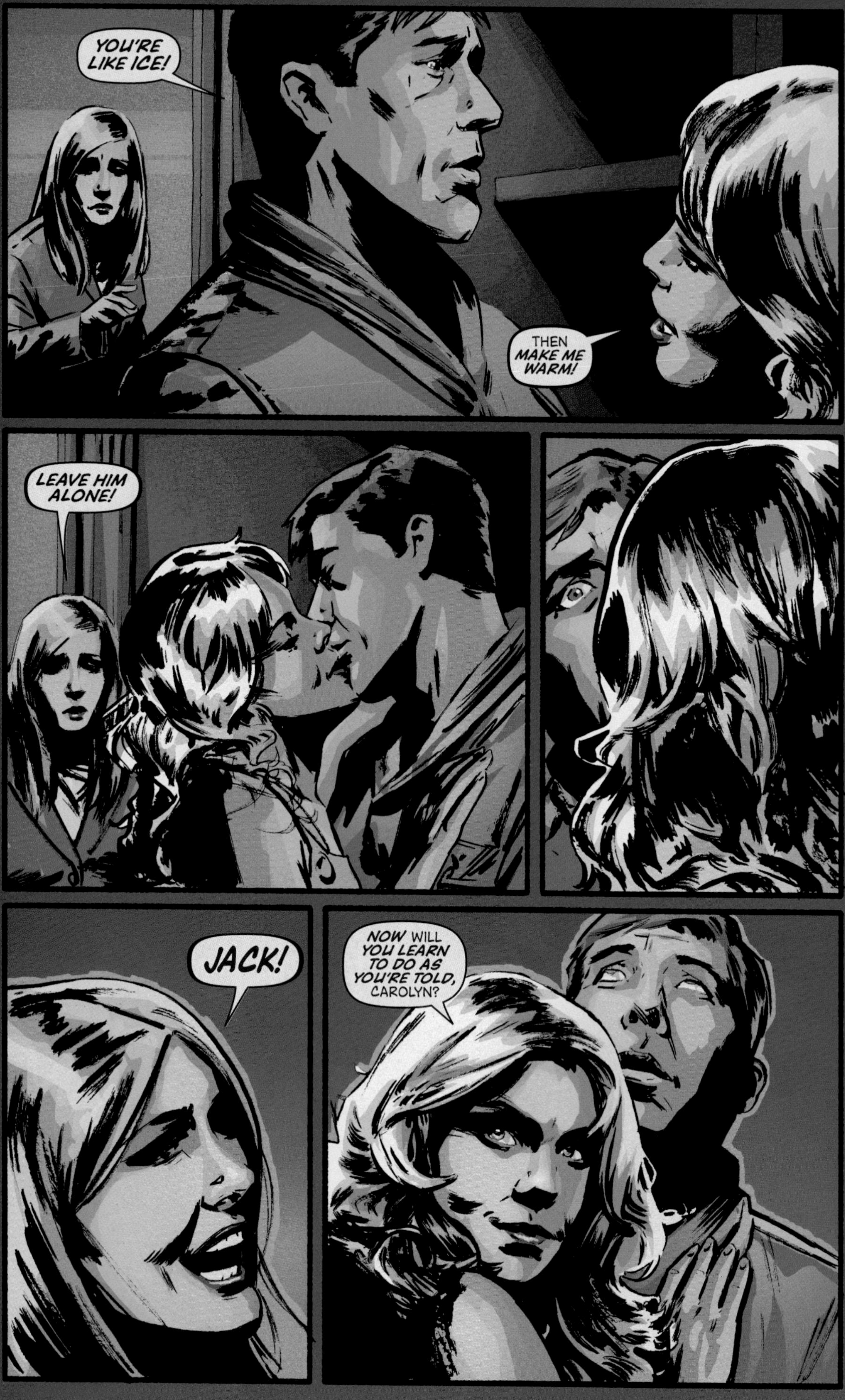
YOU'RE LIKE ICE!
THEN MAKE ME WARM!
LEAVE HIM ALONE!
JACK!
NOW WILL YOU LEARN TO DO AS YOU'RE TOLD, CAROLYN?

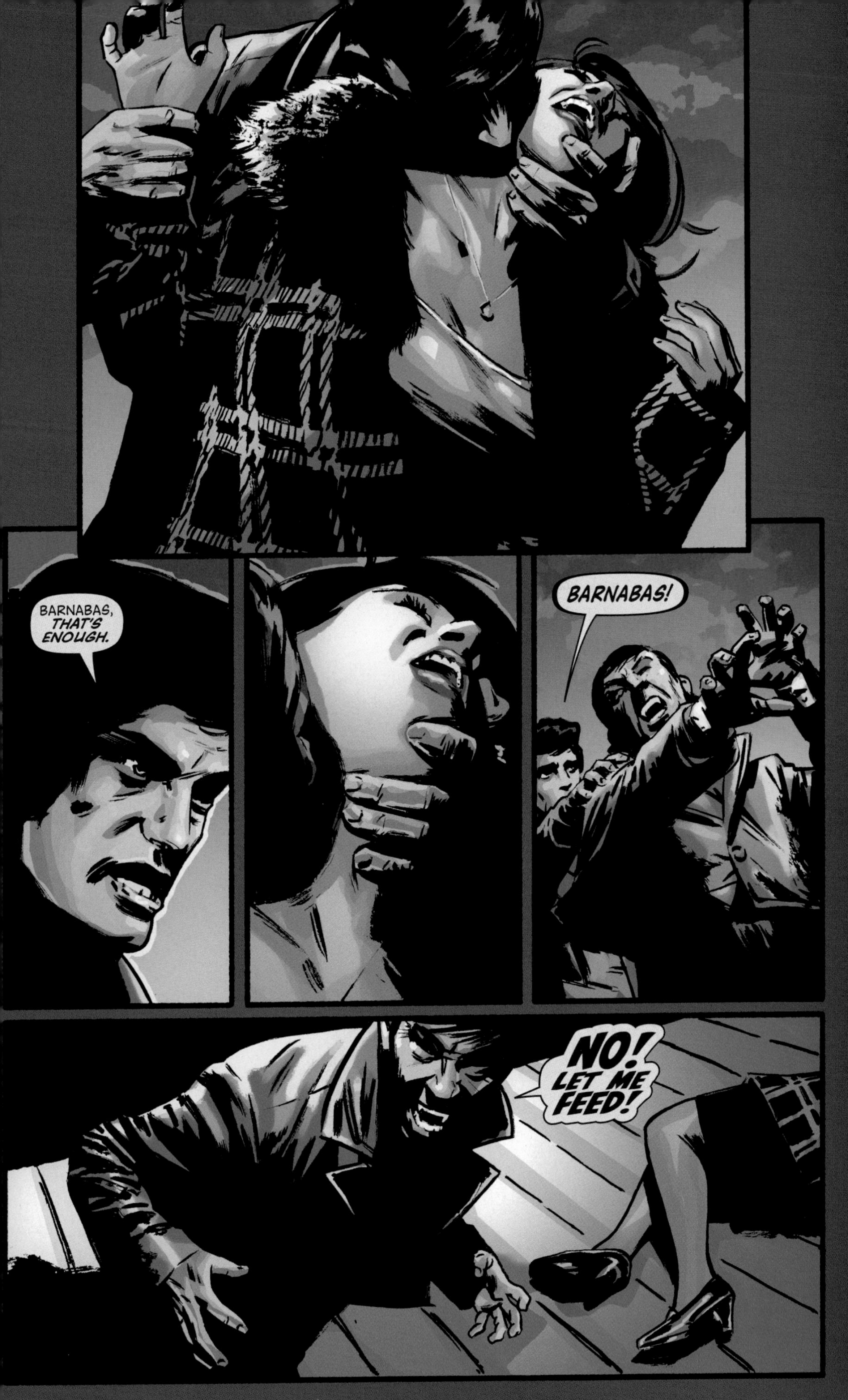
BARNABAS, THAT'S ENOUGH.
BARNABAS!
NO! LET ME FEED!

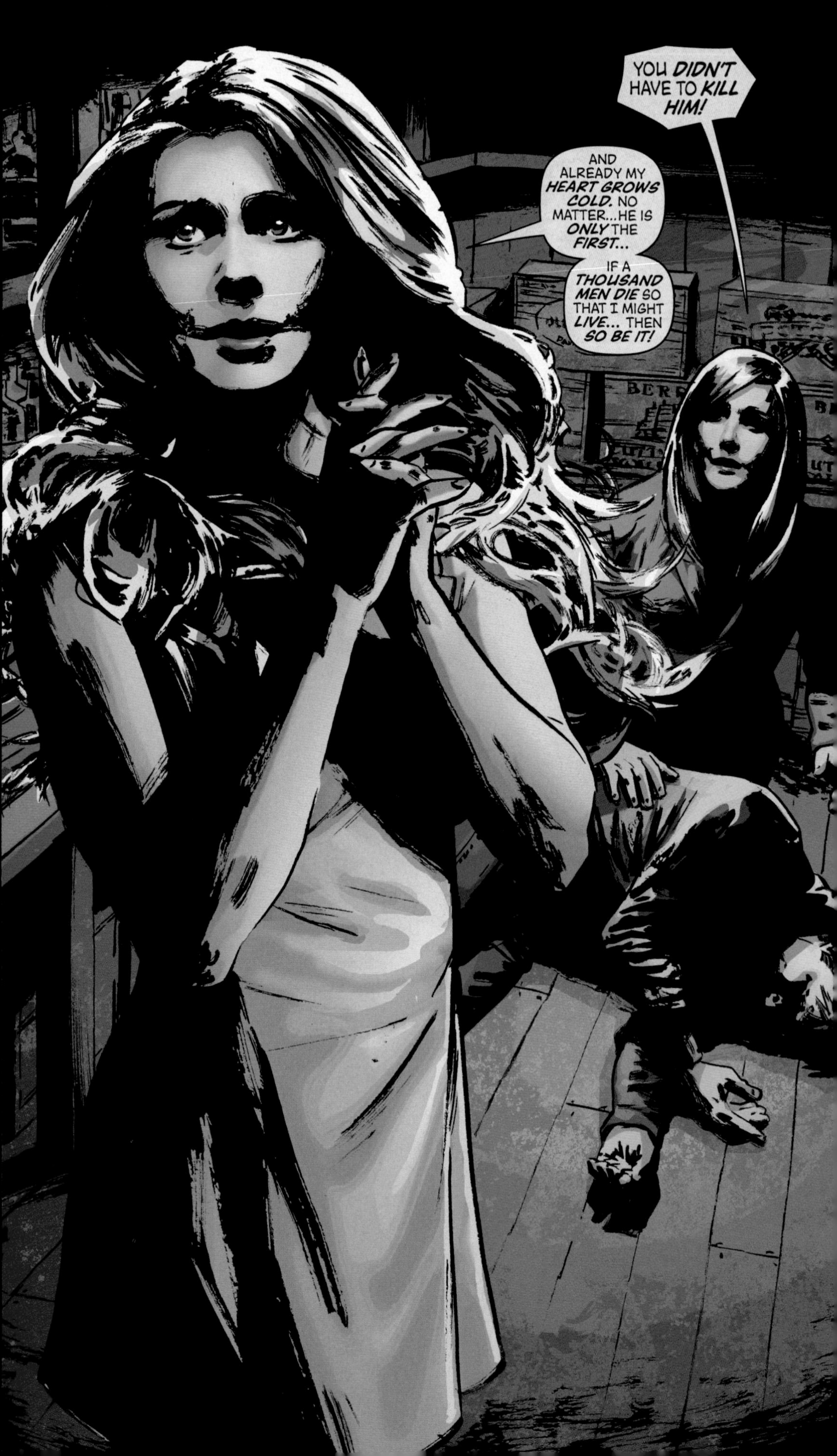
YOU DIDN'T HAVE TO KILL HIM!
AND ALREADY MY HEART GROWS COLD. NO MATTER... HE IS ONLY THE FIRST...
IF A THOUSAND MEN DIE SO THAT I MIGHT LIVE... THEN SO BE IT!

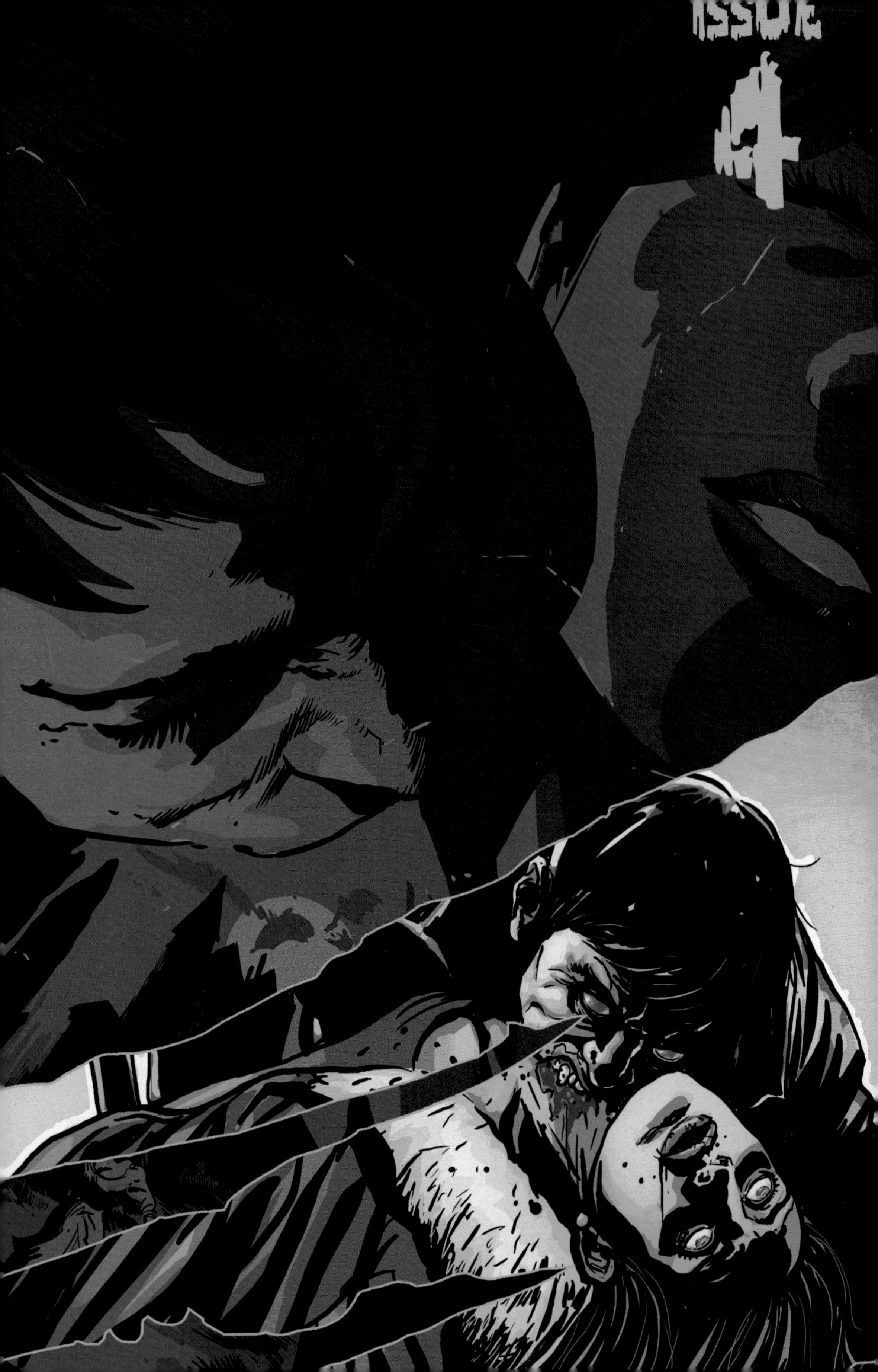
ISSUE
4

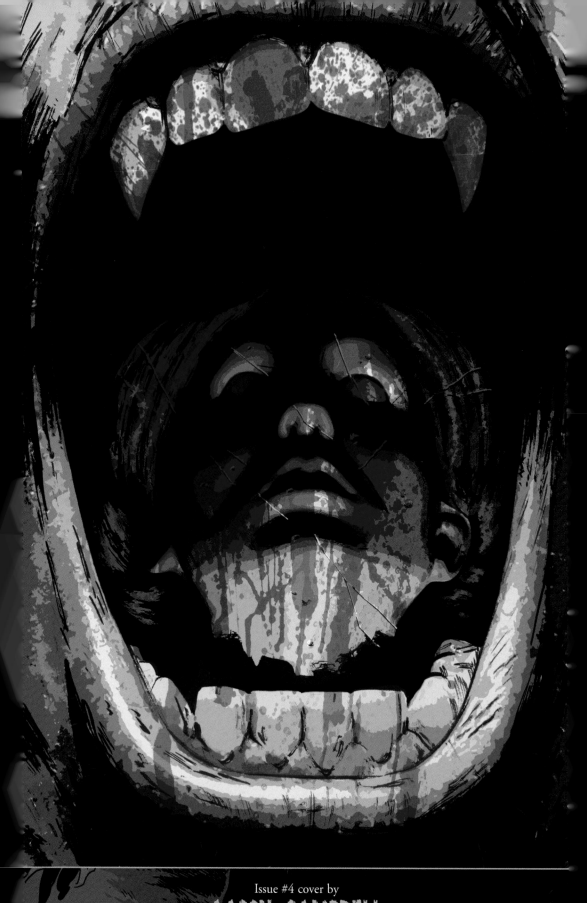

Issue #4 cover by

AARON CAMPBELL

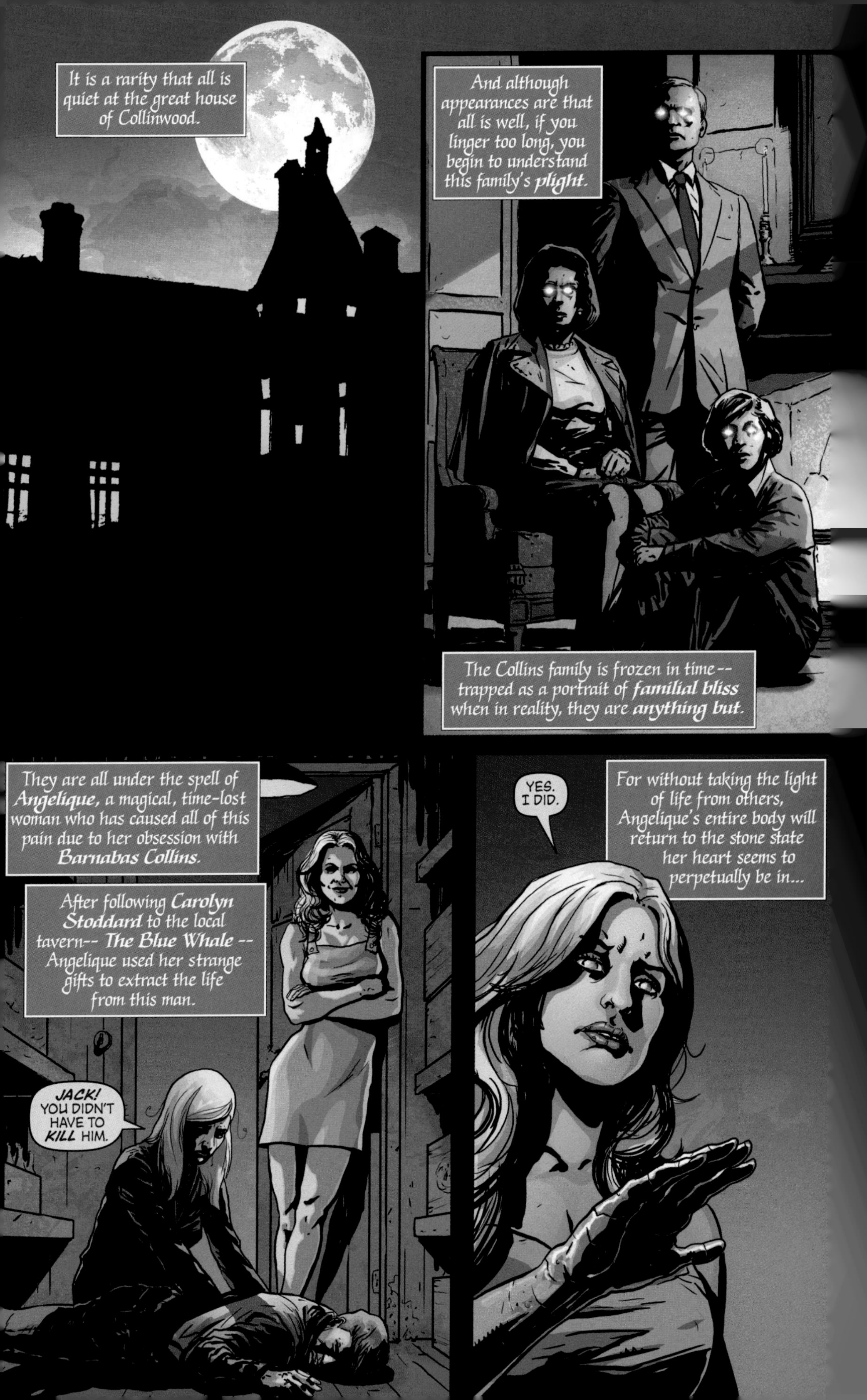
It is a rarity that all is quiet at the great house of Collinwood.
And although appearances are that all is well, if you linger too long, you begin to understand this family's *plight*.
The Collins family is frozen in time-- trapped as a portrait of *familial bliss* when in reality, they are *anything but*.
They are all under the spell of *Angelique*, a magical, time-lost woman who has caused all of this pain due to her obsession with *Barnabas Collins*.
After following *Carolyn Stoddard* to the local tavern-- *The Blue Whale* -- Angelique used her strange gifts to extract the life from this man.
JACK! YOU DIDN'T HAVE TO *KILL* HIM.
YES. I DID.
For without taking the light of life from others, Angelique's entire body will return to the stone state her heart seems to perpetually be in...

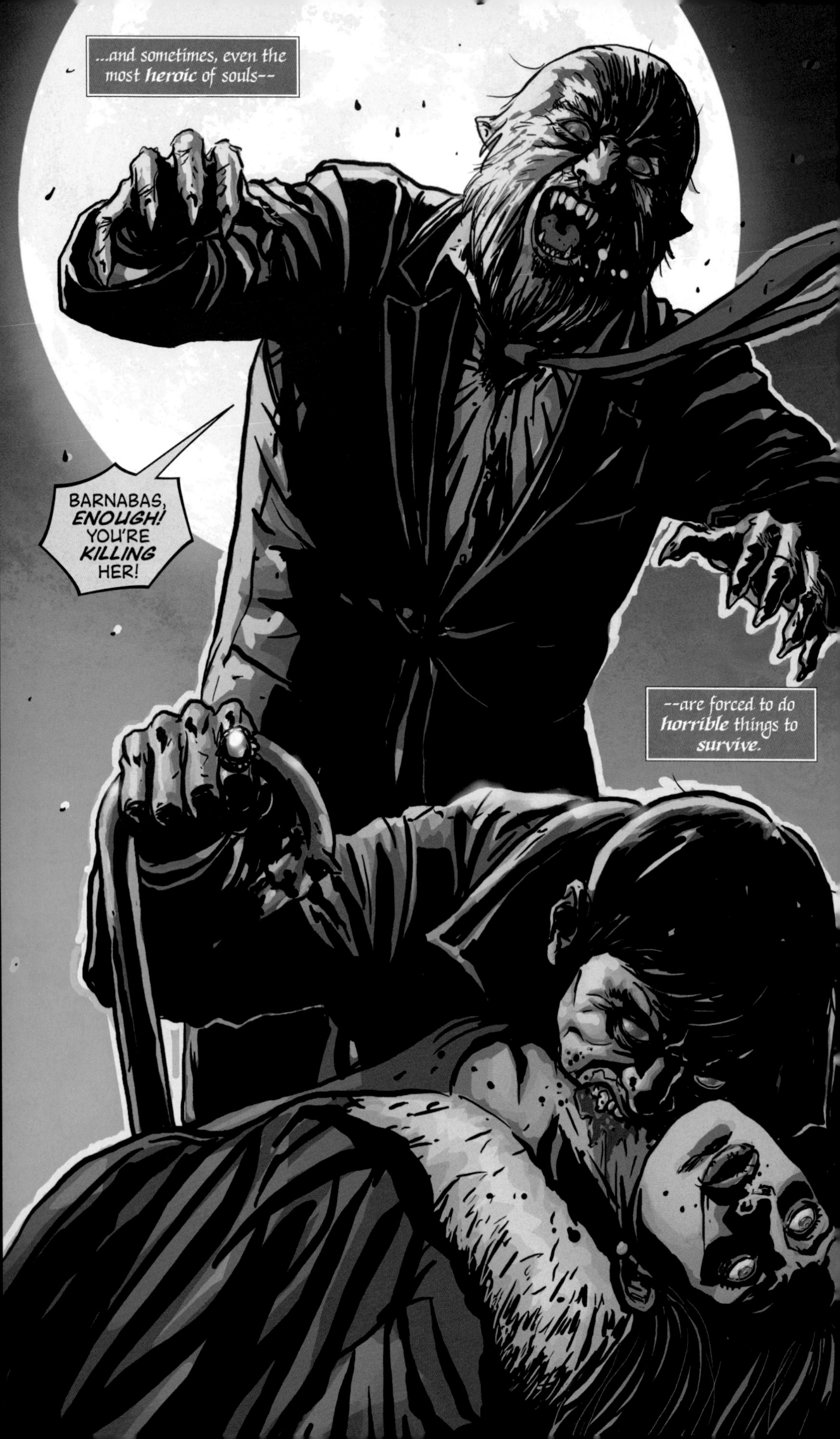

...and sometimes, even the most *heroic* of souls--
BARNABAS, *ENOUGH!* YOU'RE *KILLING* HER!
--are forced to do *horrible* things to *survive.*

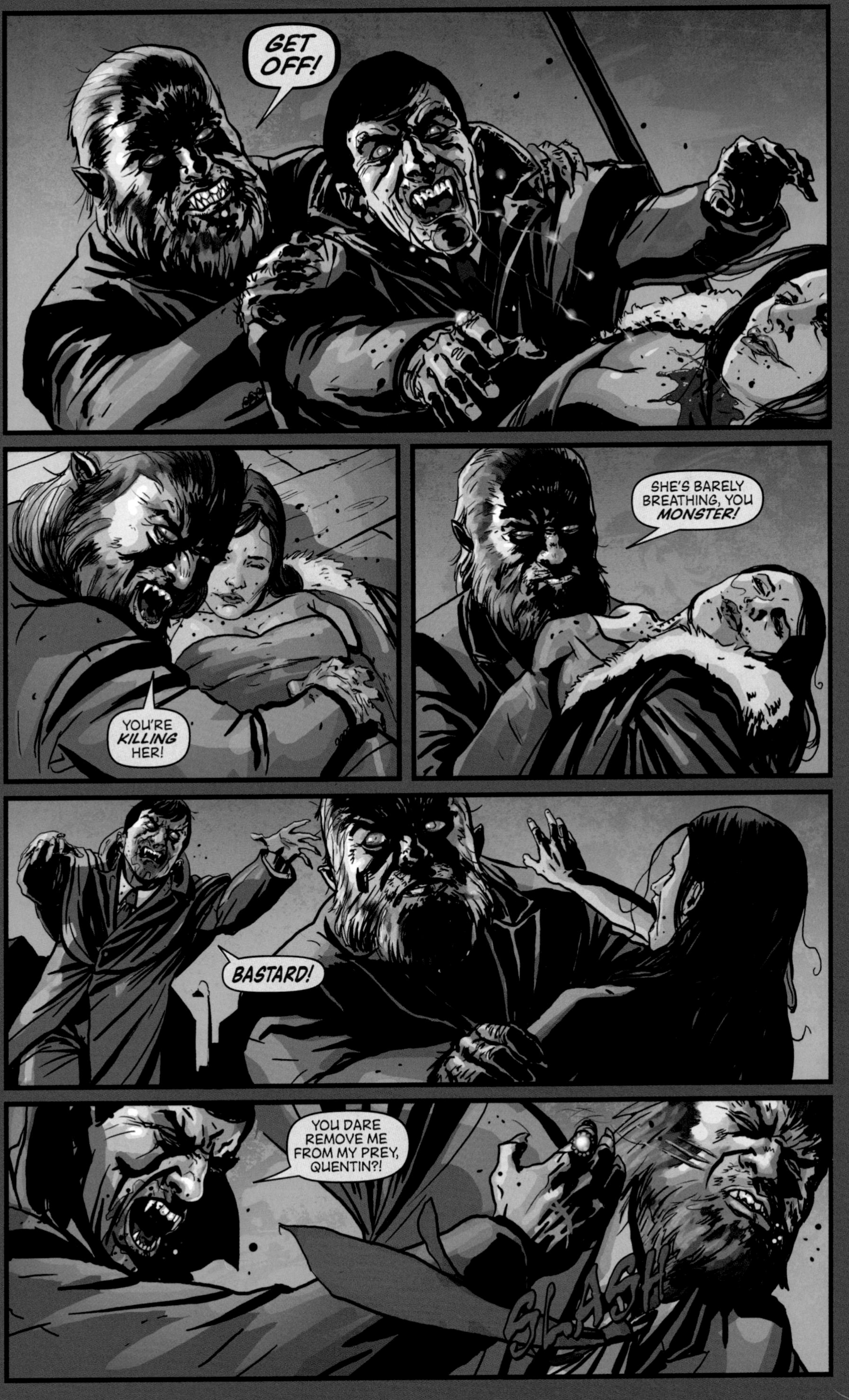
GET OFF!
YOU'RE KILLING HER!
SHE'S BARELY BREATHING, YOU MONSTER!
BASTARD!
YOU DARE REMOVE ME FROM MY PREY, QUENTIN?!
SLASH

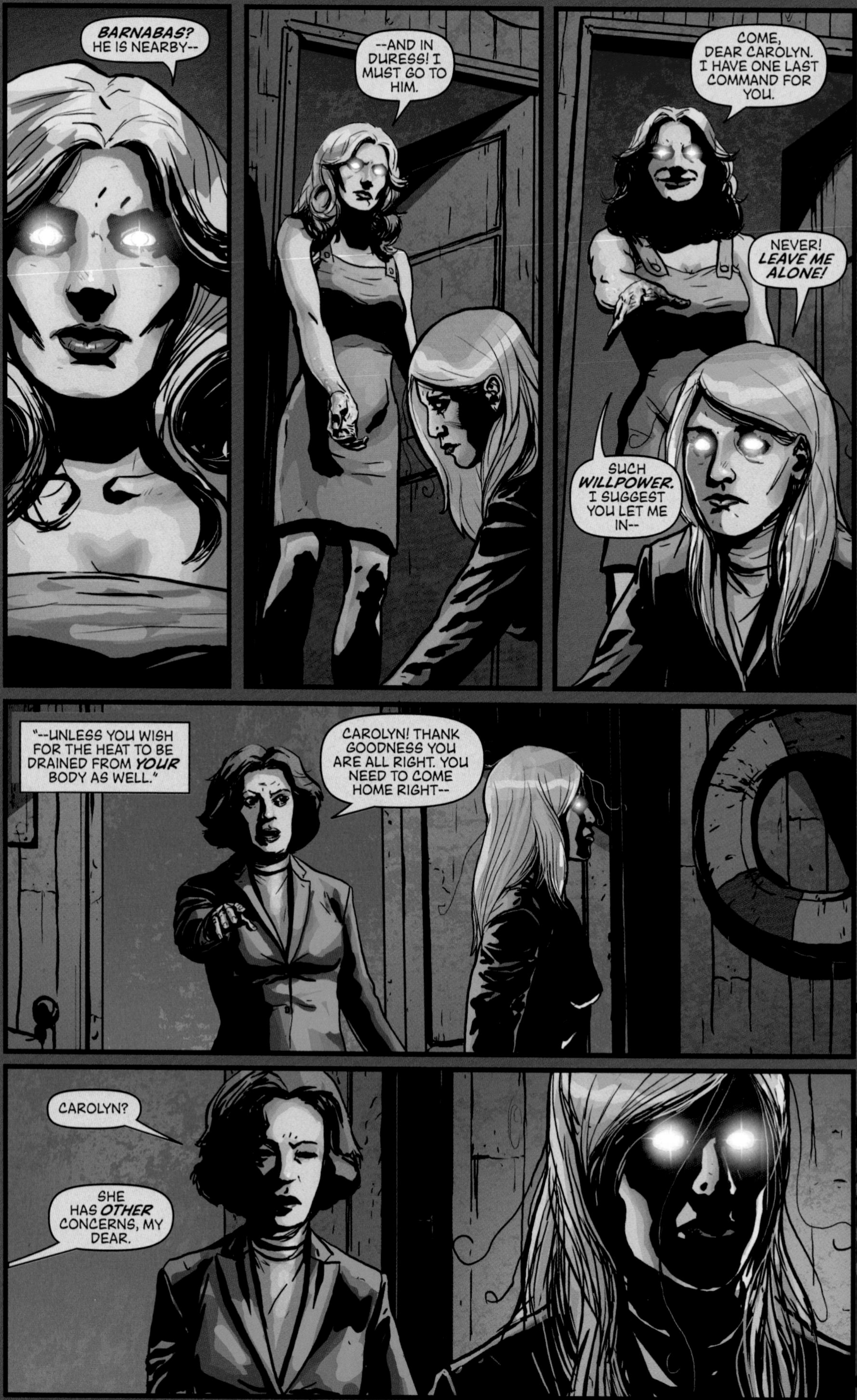
BARNABAS? HE IS NEARBY--
--AND IN DURESS! I MUST GO TO HIM.
COME, DEAR CAROLYN. I HAVE ONE LAST COMMAND FOR YOU.
NEVER! LEAVE ME ALONE!
SUCH WILLPOWER. I SUGGEST YOU LET ME IN--
"--UNLESS YOU WISH FOR THE HEAT TO BE DRAINED FROM YOUR BODY AS WELL."
CAROLYN! THANK GOODNESS YOU ARE ALL RIGHT. YOU NEED TO COME HOME RIGHT--
CAROLYN?
SHE HAS OTHER CONCERNS, MY DEAR.

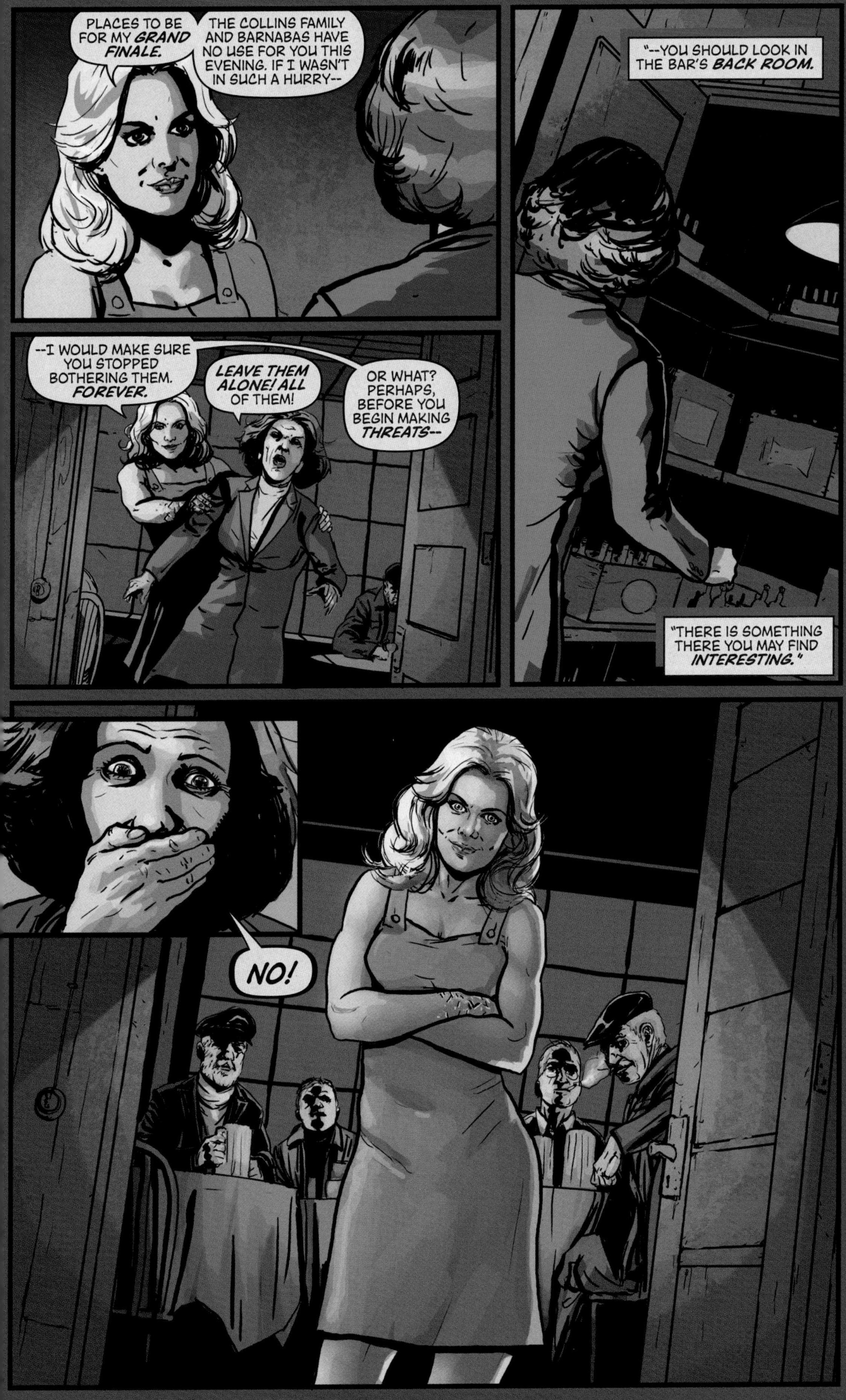
PLACES TO BE FOR MY *GRAND FINALE.*
THE COLLINS FAMILY AND BARNABAS HAVE NO USE FOR YOU THIS EVENING. IF I WASN'T IN SUCH A HURRY--
"--YOU SHOULD LOOK IN THE BAR'S *BACK ROOM.*
--I WOULD MAKE SURE YOU STOPPED BOTHERING THEM. *FOREVER.*
LEAVE THEM ALONE! ALL OF THEM!
OR WHAT? PERHAPS, BEFORE YOU BEGIN MAKING *THREATS--*
"THERE IS SOMETHING THERE YOU MAY FIND *INTERESTING."*
NO!

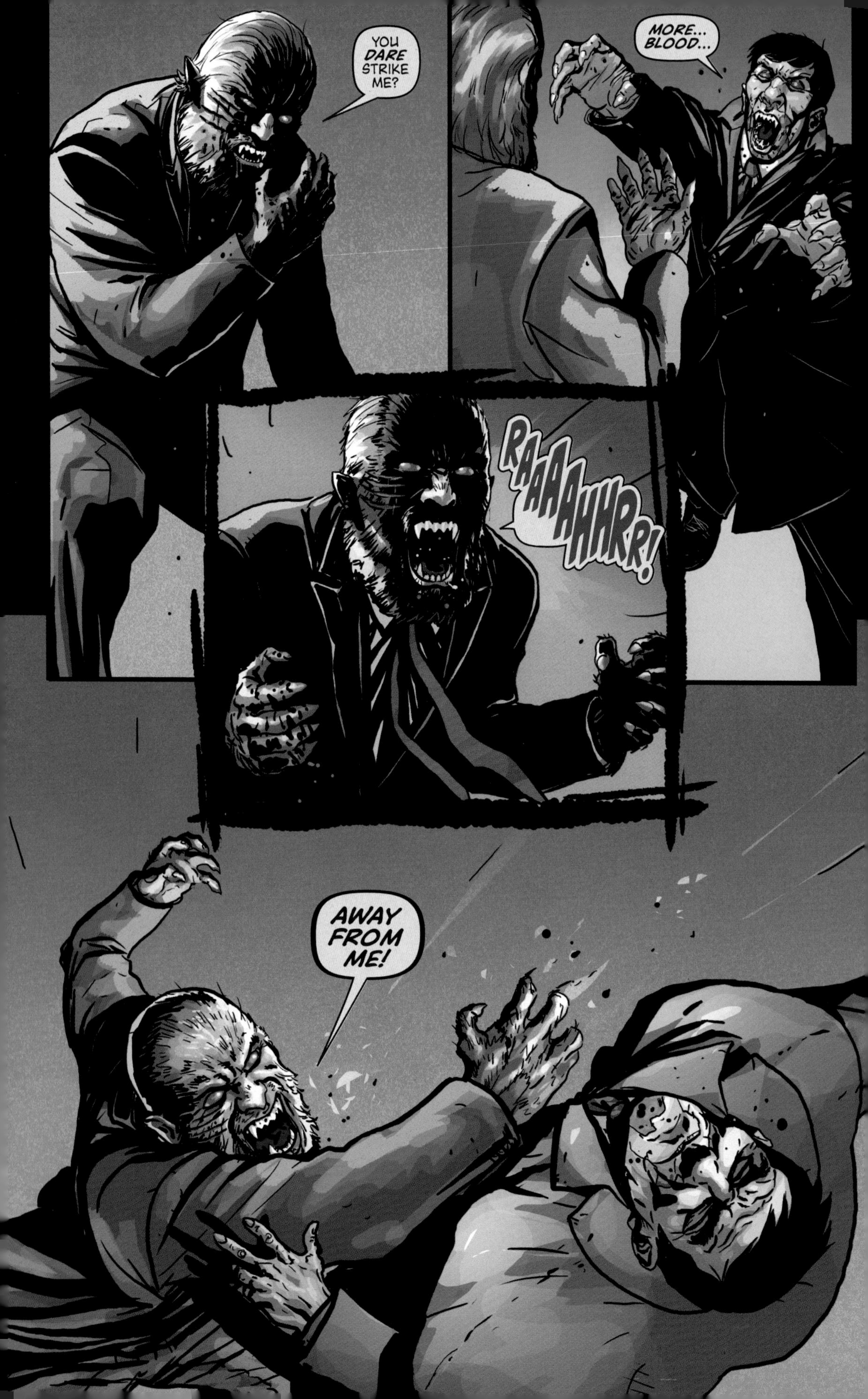
YOU DARE STRIKE ME?
MORE... BLOOD...
RAAAAHHRR!
AWAY FROM ME!

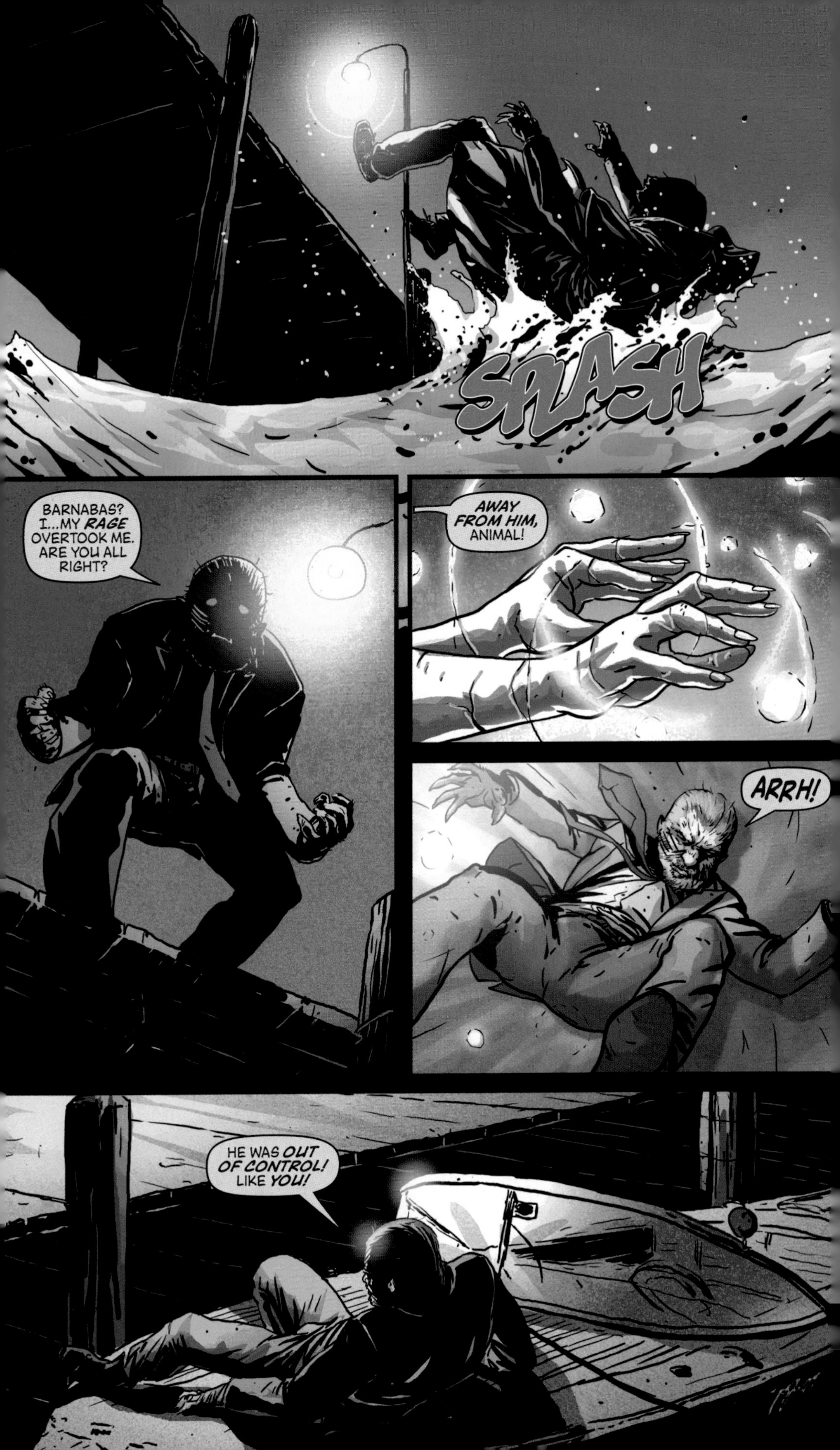
SPLASH
BARNABAS? I...MY RAGE OVERTOOK ME. ARE YOU ALL RIGHT?
AWAY FROM HIM, ANIMAL!
ARRH!
HE WAS OUT OF CONTROL! LIKE YOU!

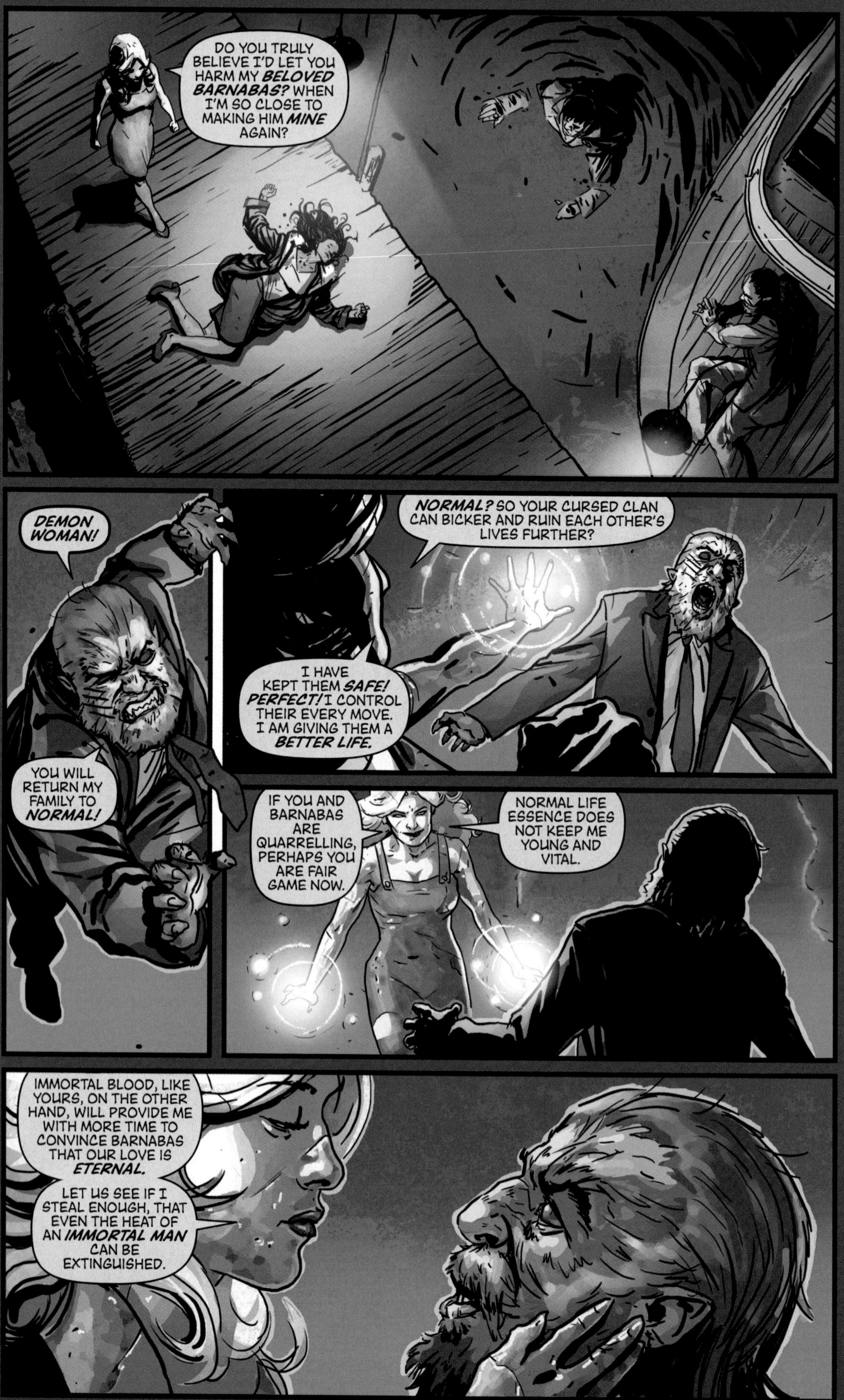
DO YOU TRULY BELIEVE I'D LET YOU HARM MY BELOVED BARNABAS? WHEN I'M SO CLOSE TO MAKING HIM MINE AGAIN?
DEMON WOMAN!
YOU WILL RETURN MY FAMILY TO NORMAL!
NORMAL? SO YOUR CURSED CLAN CAN BICKER AND RUIN EACH OTHER'S LIVES FURTHER?
I HAVE KEPT THEM SAFE! PERFECT! I CONTROL THEIR EVERY MOVE. I AM GIVING THEM A BETTER LIFE.
IF YOU AND BARNABAS ARE QUARRELLING, PERHAPS YOU ARE FAIR GAME NOW.
NORMAL LIFE ESSENCE DOES NOT KEEP ME YOUNG AND VITAL.
IMMORTAL BLOOD, LIKE YOURS, ON THE OTHER HAND, WILL PROVIDE ME WITH MORE TIME TO CONVINCE BARNABAS THAT OUR LOVE IS ETERNAL.
LET US SEE IF I STEAL ENOUGH, THAT EVEN THE HEAT OF AN IMMORTAL MAN CAN BE EXTINGUISHED.

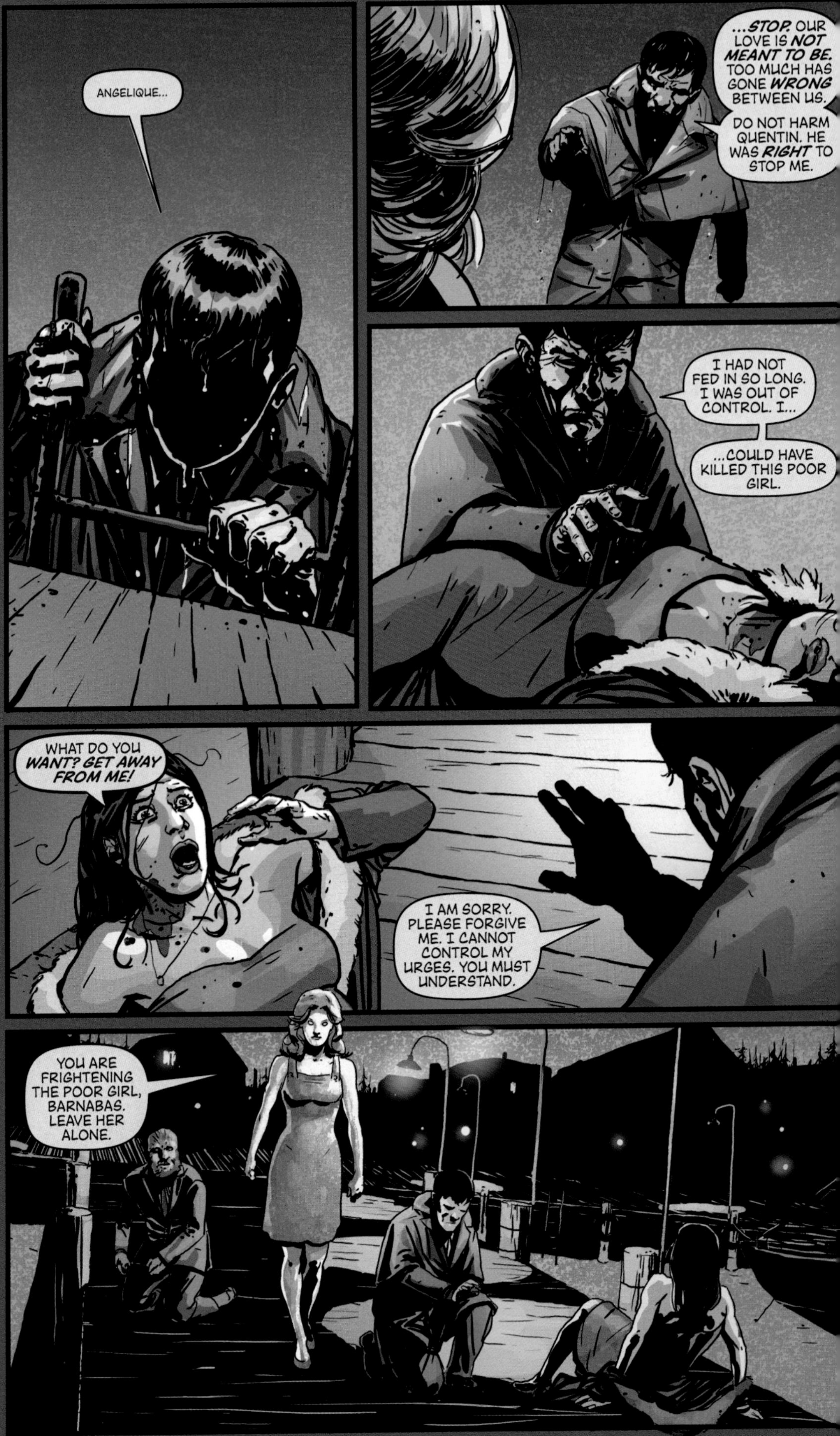
ANGELIQUE...
...STOP. OUR LOVE IS NOT MEANT TO BE. TOO MUCH HAS GONE WRONG BETWEEN US.
DO NOT HARM QUENTIN. HE WAS RIGHT TO STOP ME.
I HAD NOT FED IN SO LONG. I WAS OUT OF CONTROL. I...
...COULD HAVE KILLED THIS POOR GIRL.
WHAT DO YOU WANT? GET AWAY FROM ME!
I AM SORRY. PLEASE FORGIVE ME. I CANNOT CONTROL MY URGES. YOU MUST UNDERSTAND.
YOU ARE FRIGHTENING THE POOR GIRL, BARNABAS. LEAVE HER ALONE.

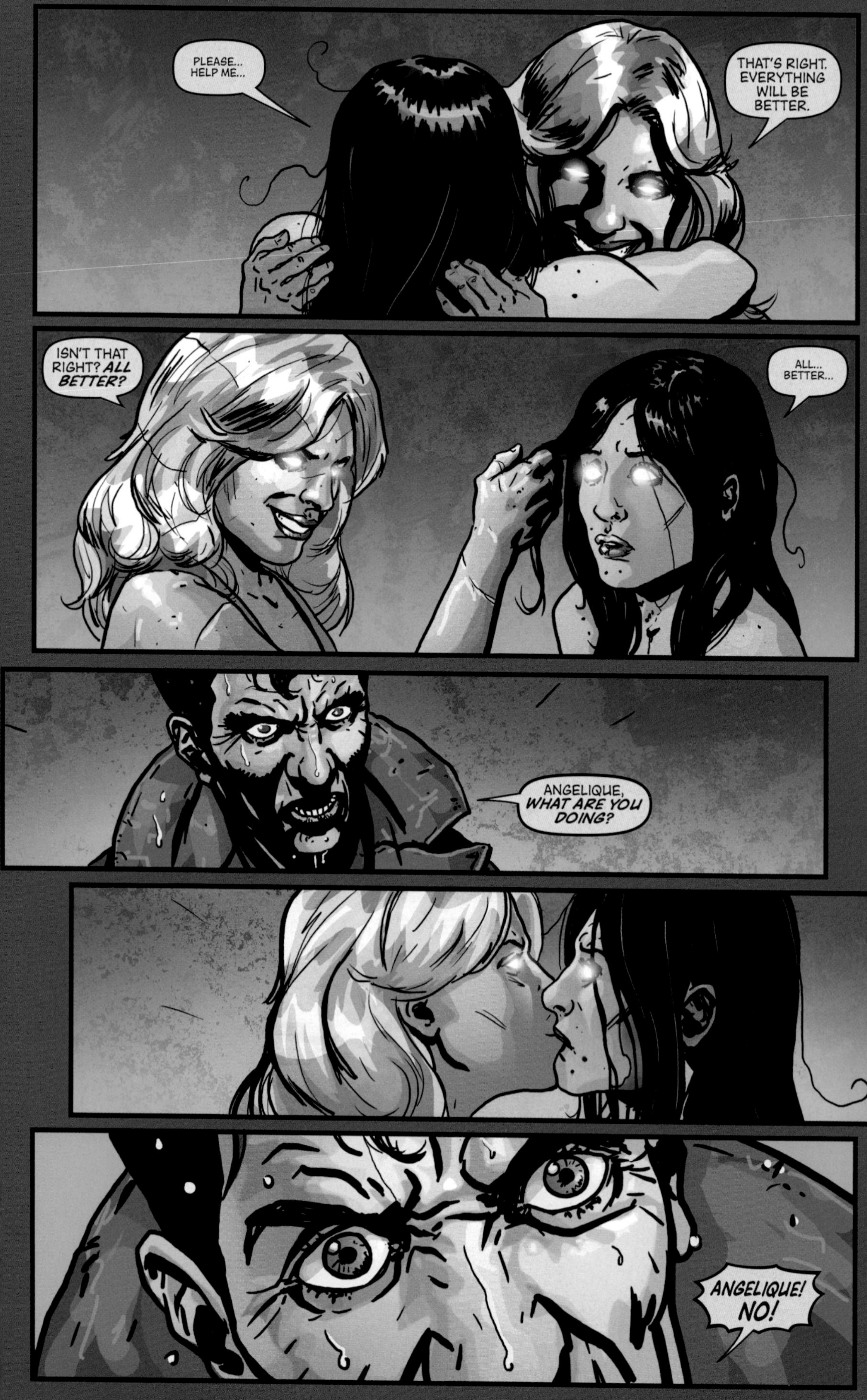
PLEASE... HELP ME...
THAT'S RIGHT. EVERYTHING WILL BE BETTER.
ISN'T THAT RIGHT? ALL BETTER?
ALL... BETTER...
ANGELIQUE, WHAT ARE YOU DOING?
ANGELIQUE! NO!

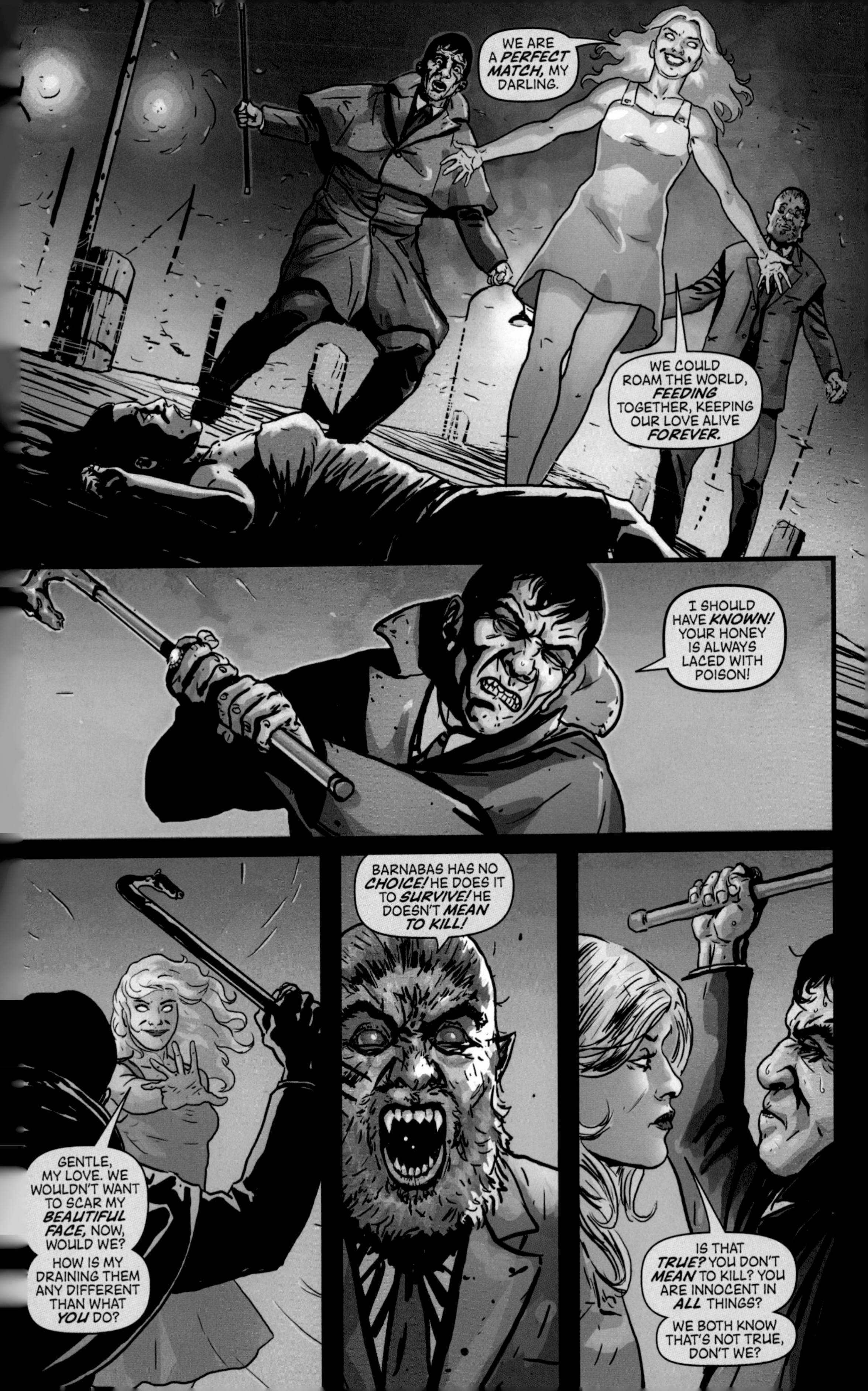
WE ARE A PERFECT MATCH, MY DARLING.
WE COULD ROAM THE WORLD, FEEDING TOGETHER, KEEPING OUR LOVE ALIVE FOREVER.
I SHOULD HAVE KNOWN! YOUR HONEY IS ALWAYS LACED WITH POISON!
GENTLE, MY LOVE. WE WOULDN'T WANT TO SCAR MY BEAUTIFUL FACE, NOW, WOULD WE?
HOW IS MY DRAINING THEM ANY DIFFERENT THAN WHAT YOU DO?
BARNABAS HAS NO CHOICE! HE DOES IT TO SURVIVE! HE DOESN'T MEAN TO KILL!
IS THAT TRUE? YOU DON'T MEAN TO KILL? YOU ARE INNOCENT IN ALL THINGS?
WE BOTH KNOW THAT'S NOT TRUE, DON'T WE?

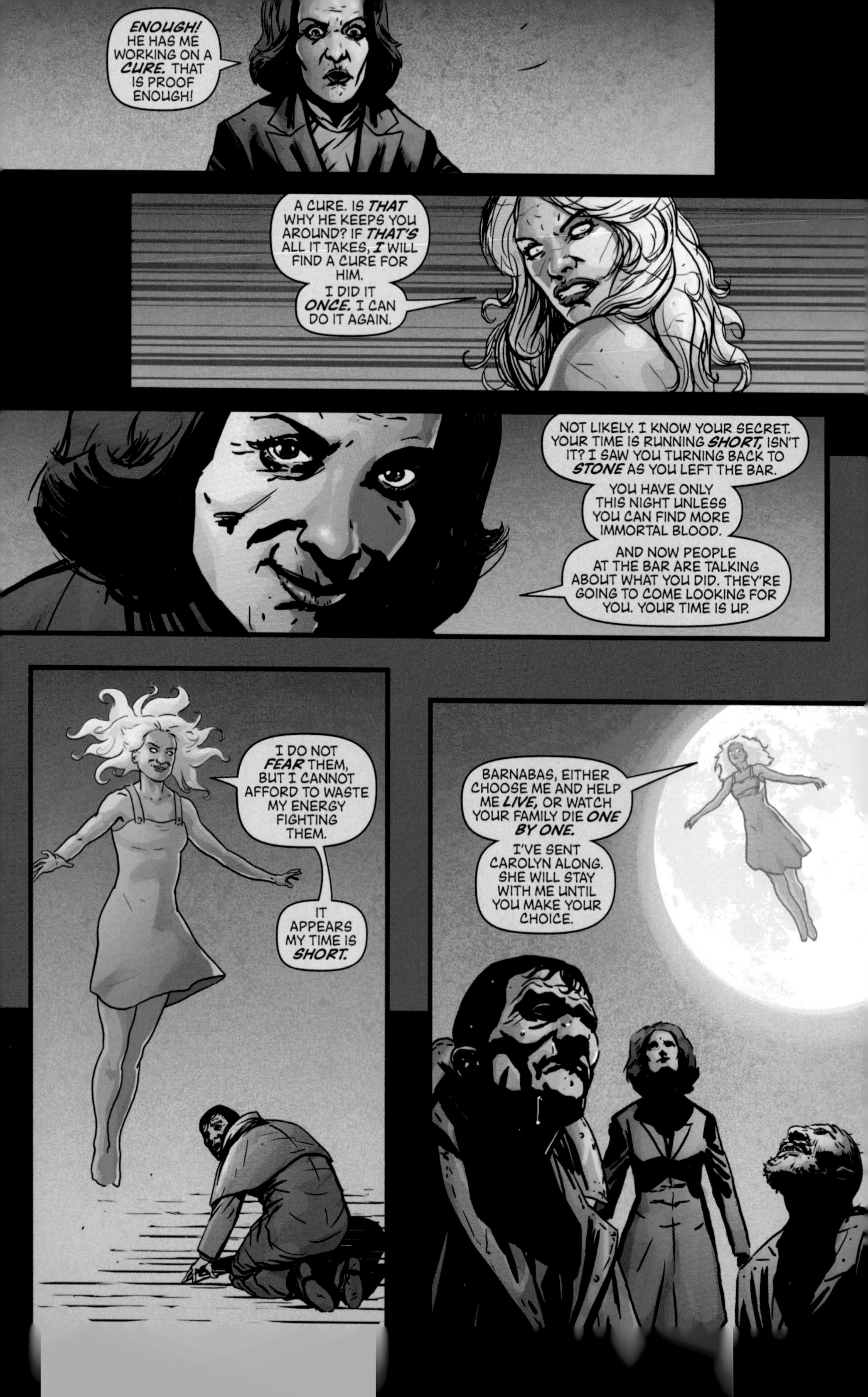
ENOUGH! HE HAS ME WORKING ON A CURE. THAT IS PROOF ENOUGH!
A CURE. IS THAT WHY HE KEEPS YOU AROUND? IF THAT'S ALL IT TAKES, I WILL FIND A CURE FOR HIM.
I DID IT ONCE. I CAN DO IT AGAIN.
NOT LIKELY. I KNOW YOUR SECRET. YOUR TIME IS RUNNING SHORT, ISN'T IT? I SAW YOU TURNING BACK TO STONE AS YOU LEFT THE BAR.
YOU HAVE ONLY THIS NIGHT UNLESS YOU CAN FIND MORE IMMORTAL BLOOD.
AND NOW PEOPLE AT THE BAR ARE TALKING ABOUT WHAT YOU DID. THEY'RE GOING TO COME LOOKING FOR YOU. YOUR TIME IS UP.
I DO NOT FEAR THEM, BUT I CANNOT AFFORD TO WASTE MY ENERGY FIGHTING THEM.
IT APPEARS MY TIME IS SHORT.
BARNABAS, EITHER CHOOSE ME AND HELP ME LIVE, OR WATCH YOUR FAMILY DIE ONE BY ONE.
I'VE SENT CAROLYN ALONG. SHE WILL STAY WITH ME UNTIL YOU MAKE YOUR CHOICE.

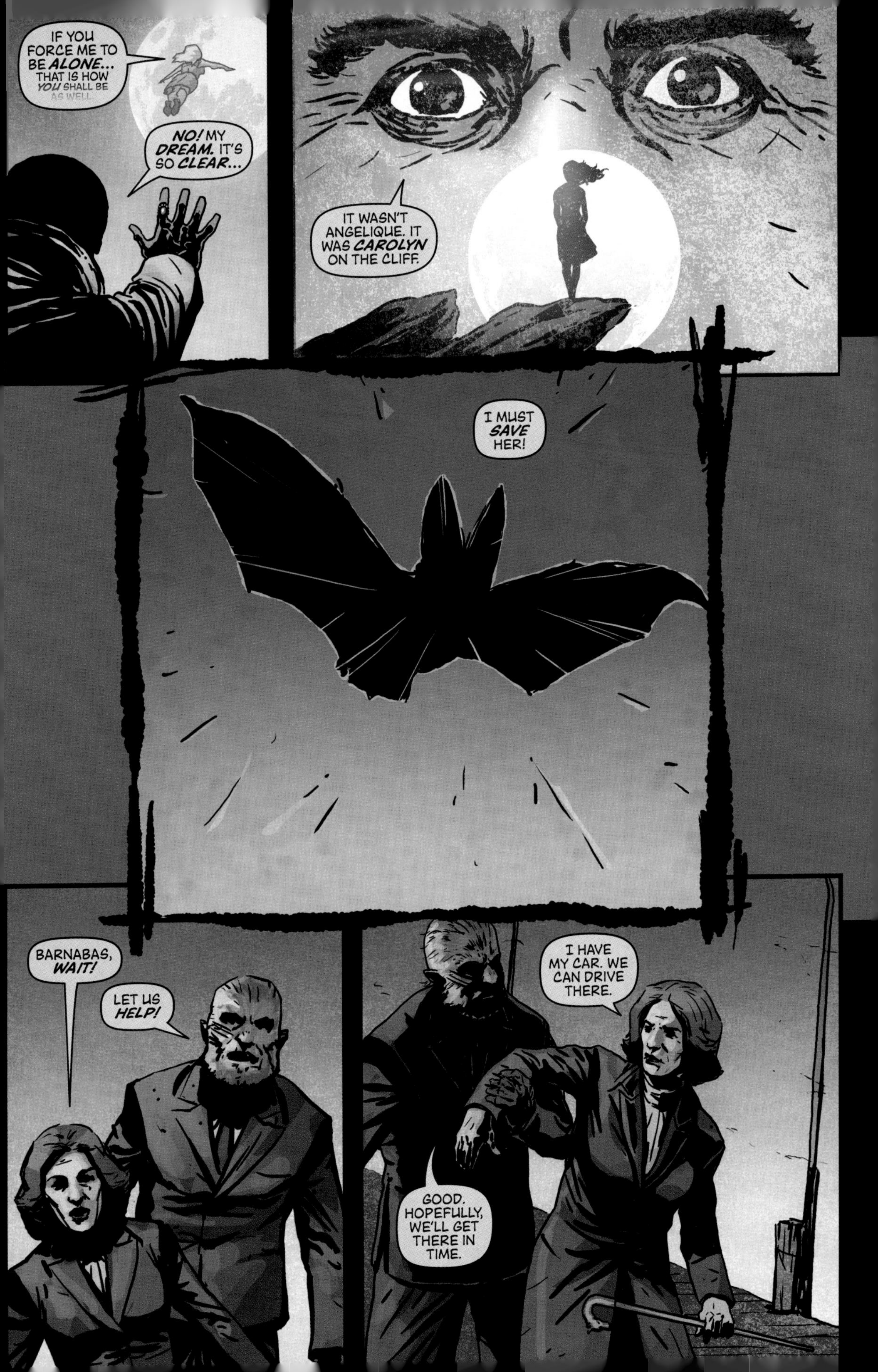
IF YOU FORCE ME TO BE ALONE... THAT IS HOW YOU SHALL BE AS WELL...
NO! MY DREAM. IT'S SO CLEAR...
IT WASN'T ANGELIQUE. IT WAS CAROLYN ON THE CLIFF.
I MUST SAVE HER!
BARNABAS, WAIT!
LET US HELP!
I HAVE MY CAR. WE CAN DRIVE THERE.
GOOD. HOPEFULLY, WE'LL GET THERE IN TIME.

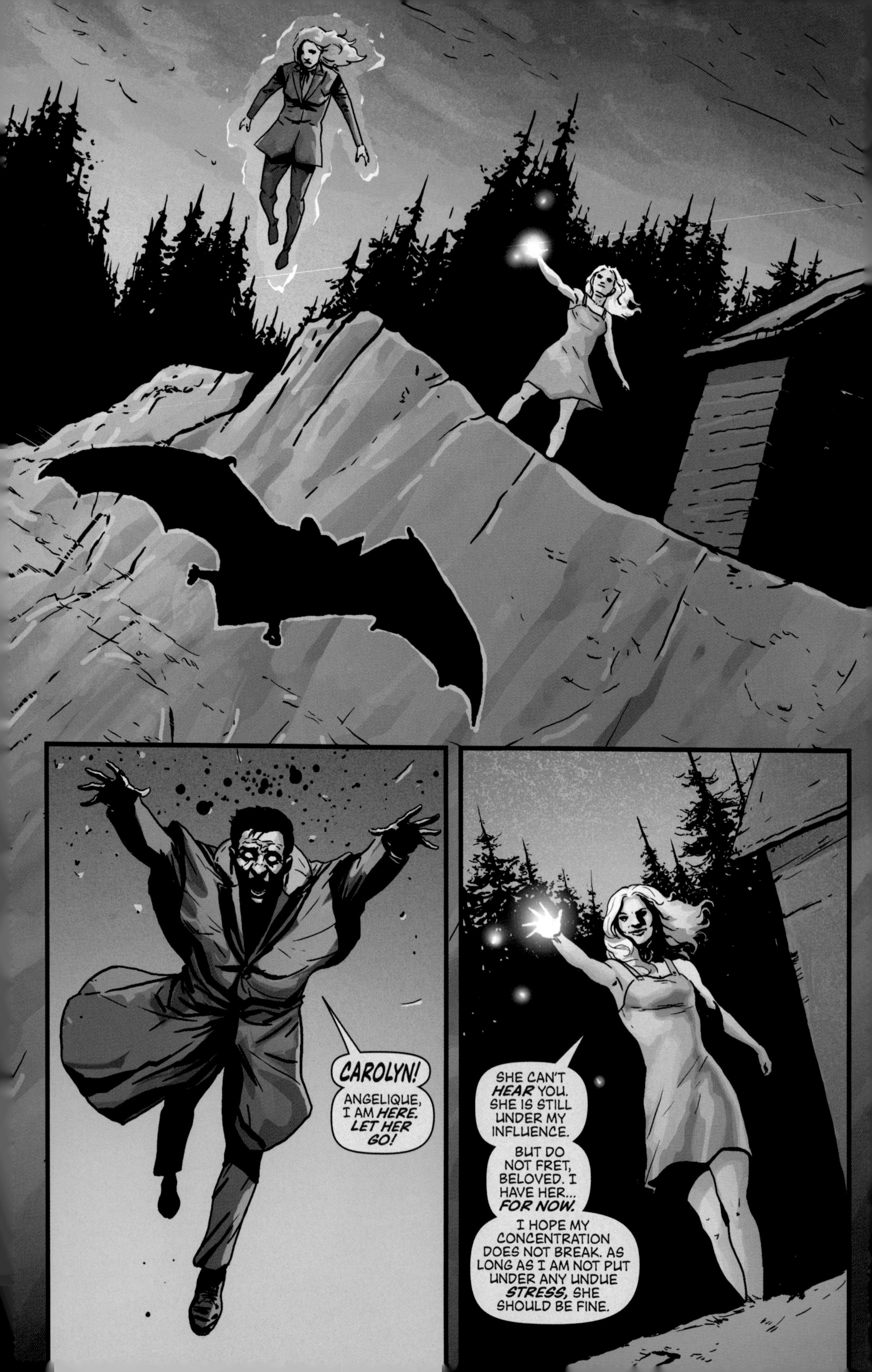
CAROLYN!
ANGELIQUE, I AM HERE. LET HER GO!
SHE CAN'T HEAR YOU. SHE IS STILL UNDER MY INFLUENCE.
BUT DO NOT FRET, BELOVED. I HAVE HER... FOR NOW.
I HOPE MY CONCENTRATION DOES NOT BREAK. AS LONG AS I AM NOT PUT UNDER ANY UNDUE STRESS, SHE SHOULD BE FINE.

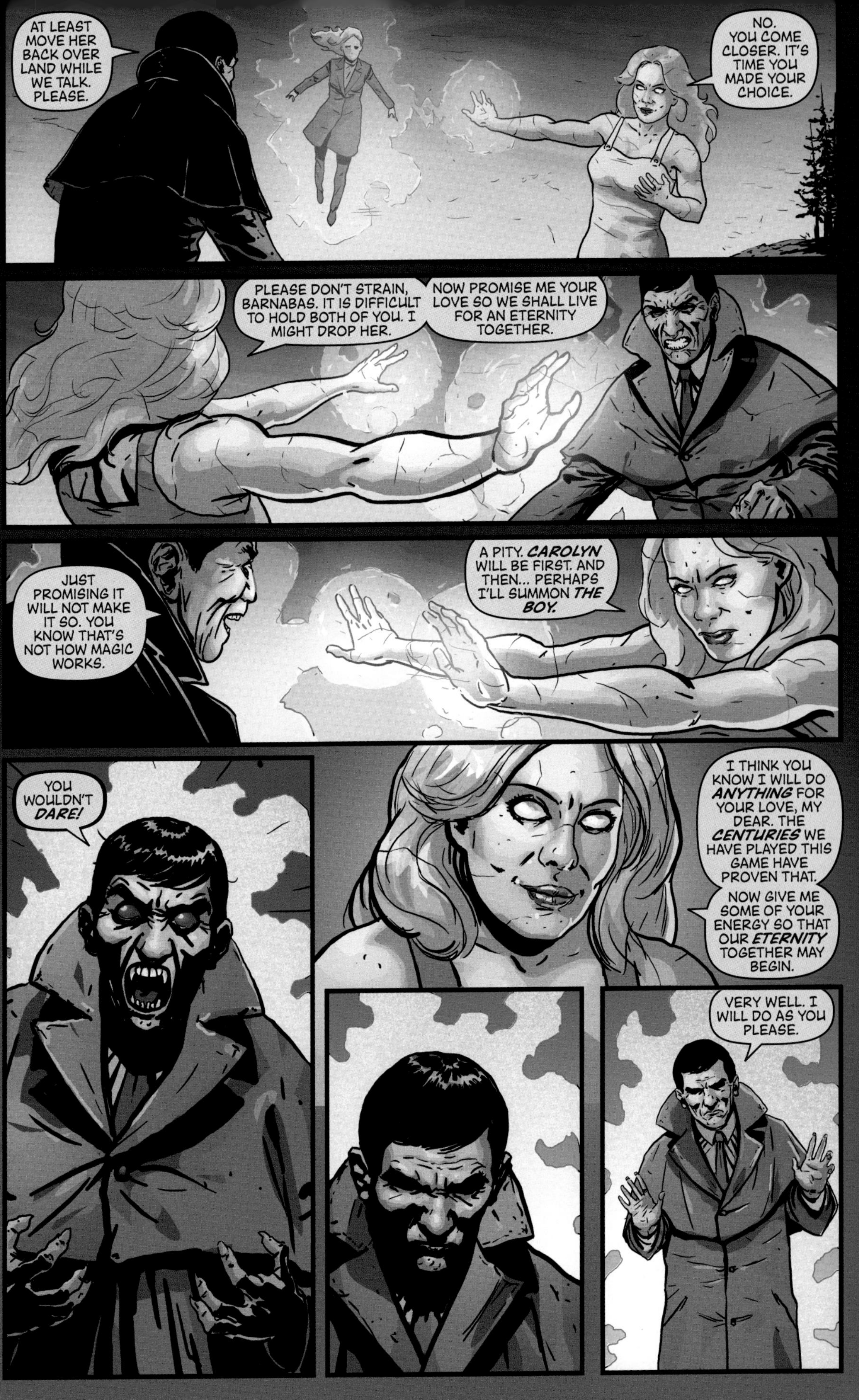
AT LEAST MOVE HER BACK OVER LAND WHILE WE TALK. PLEASE.
NO. YOU COME CLOSER. IT'S TIME YOU MADE YOUR CHOICE.
PLEASE DON'T STRAIN, BARNABAS. IT IS DIFFICULT TO HOLD BOTH OF YOU. I MIGHT DROP HER.
NOW PROMISE ME YOUR LOVE SO WE SHALL LIVE FOR AN ETERNITY TOGETHER.
JUST PROMISING IT WILL NOT MAKE IT SO. YOU KNOW THAT'S NOT HOW MAGIC WORKS.
A PITY. *CAROLYN* WILL BE FIRST. AND THEN... PERHAPS I'LL SUMMON *THE BOY.*
YOU WOULDN'T *DARE!*
I THINK YOU KNOW I WILL DO *ANYTHING* FOR YOUR LOVE, MY DEAR. THE *CENTURIES* WE HAVE PLAYED THIS GAME HAVE PROVEN THAT.
NOW GIVE ME SOME OF YOUR ENERGY SO THAT OUR *ETERNITY* TOGETHER MAY BEGIN.
VERY WELL. I WILL DO AS YOU PLEASE.

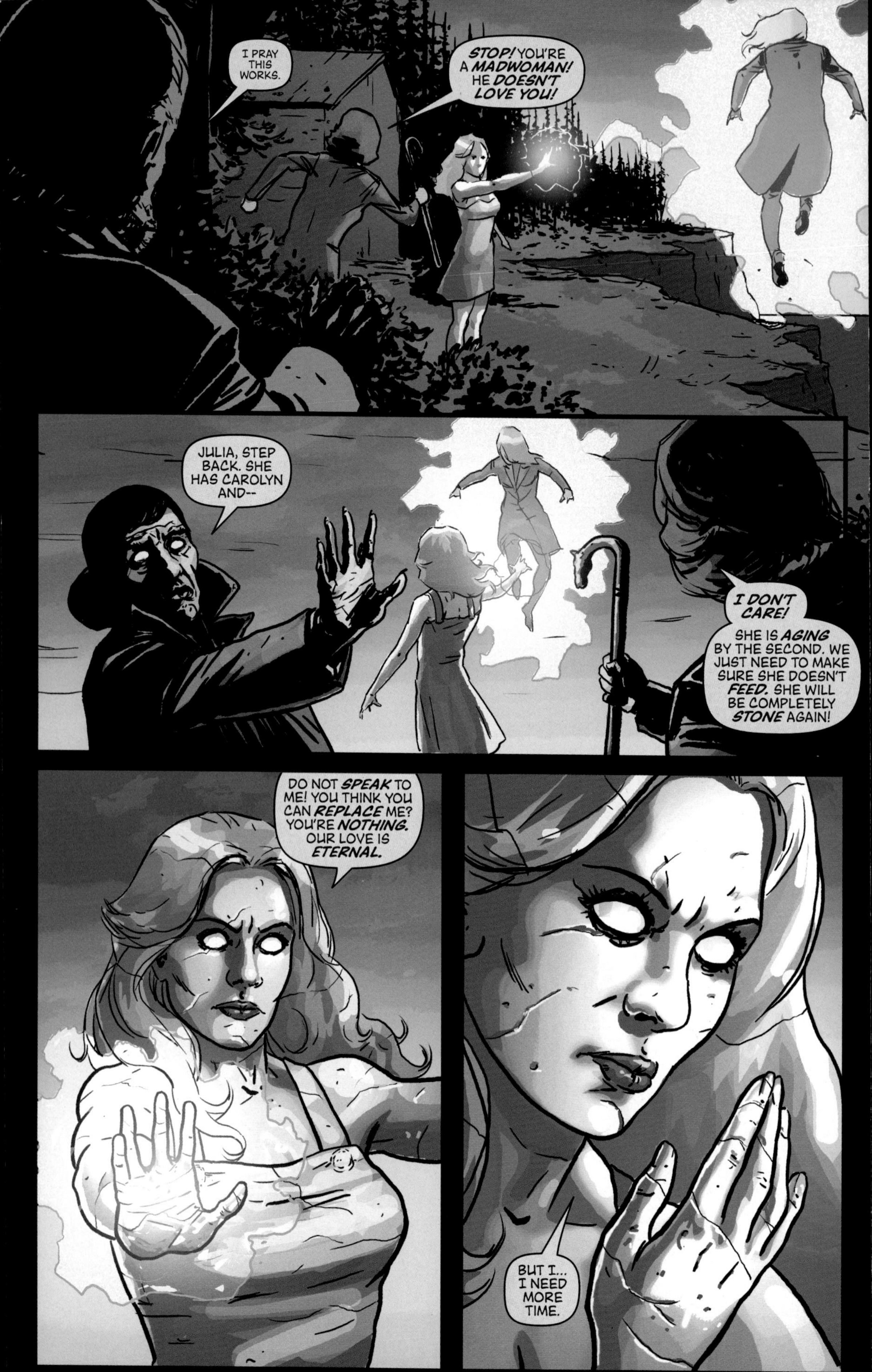
I PRAY THIS WORKS.
STOP! YOU'RE A MADWOMAN! HE DOESN'T LOVE YOU!
JULIA, STEP BACK. SHE HAS CAROLYN AND--
I DON'T CARE!
SHE IS AGING BY THE SECOND. WE JUST NEED TO MAKE SURE SHE DOESN'T FEED. SHE WILL BE COMPLETELY STONE AGAIN!
DO NOT SPEAK TO ME! YOU THINK YOU CAN REPLACE ME? YOU'RE NOTHING. OUR LOVE IS ETERNAL.
BUT I... I NEED MORE TIME.

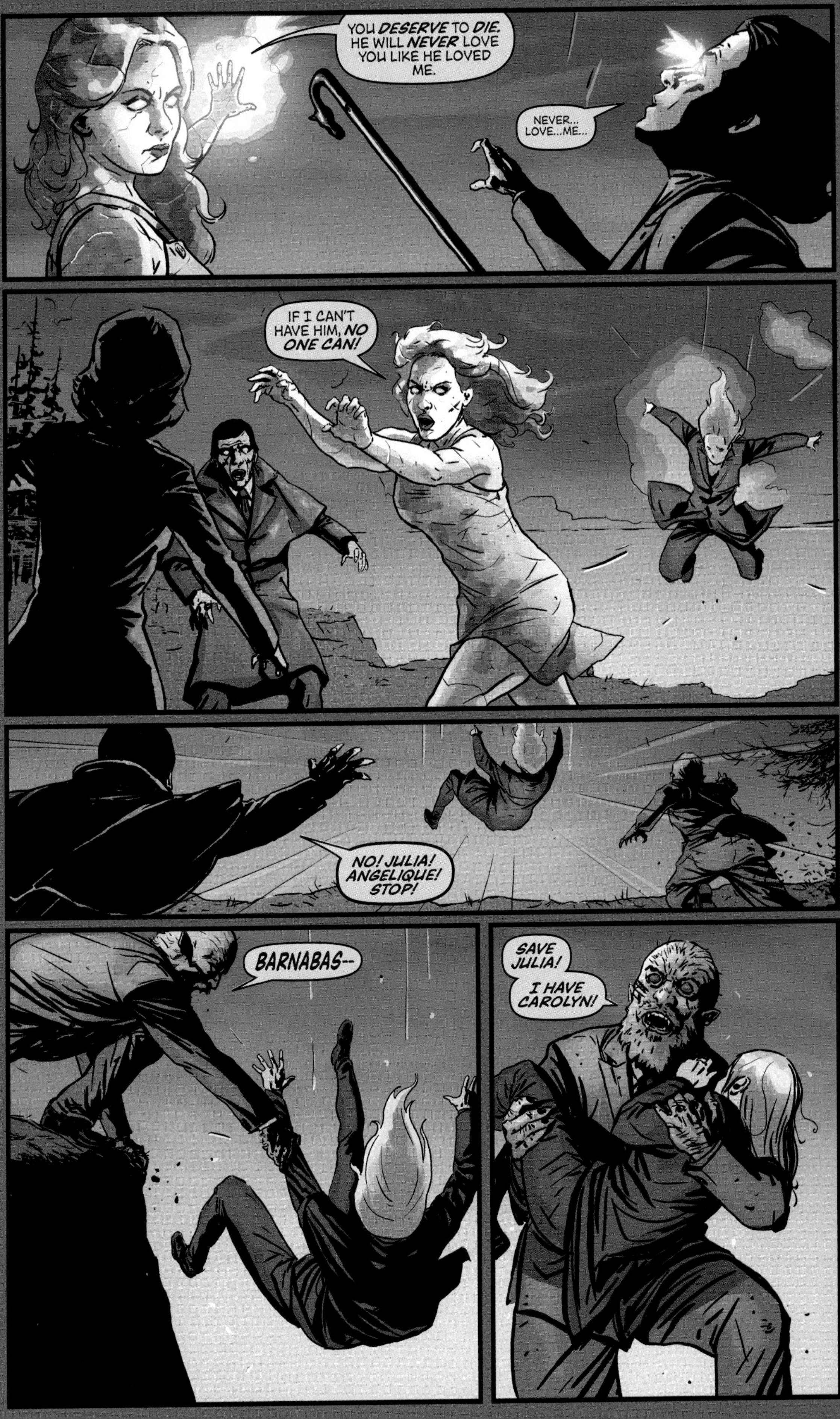
YOU DESERVE TO DIE. HE WILL NEVER LOVE YOU LIKE HE LOVED ME.
NEVER... LOVE...ME...
IF I CAN'T HAVE HIM, NO ONE CAN!
NO! JULIA! ANGELIQUE! STOP!
BARNABAS--
SAVE JULIA!
I HAVE CAROLYN!

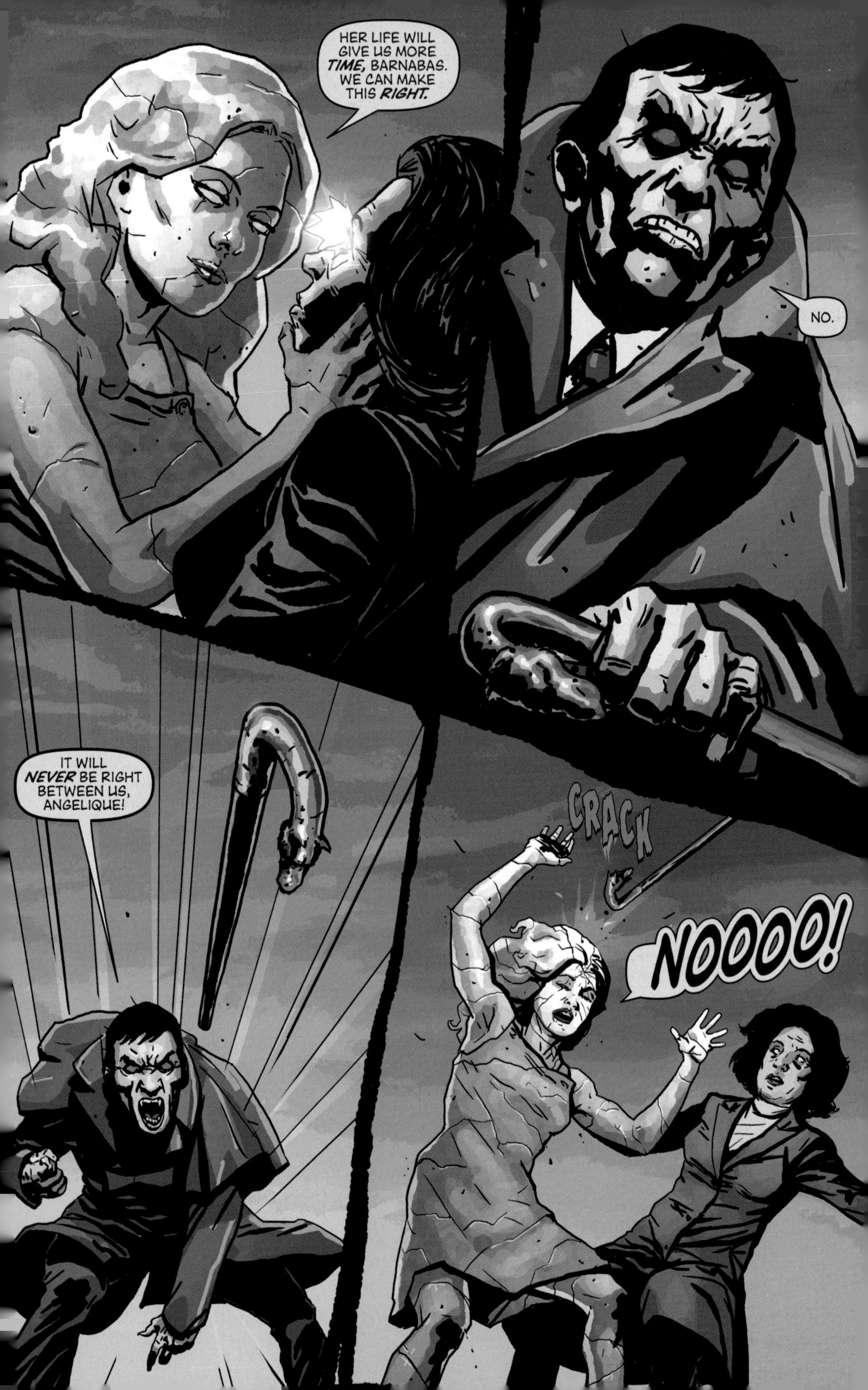
HER LIFE WILL GIVE US MORE TIME, BARNABAS. WE CAN MAKE THIS RIGHT.
NO.
IT WILL NEVER BE RIGHT BETWEEN US, ANGELIQUE!
CRACK
NOOOO!

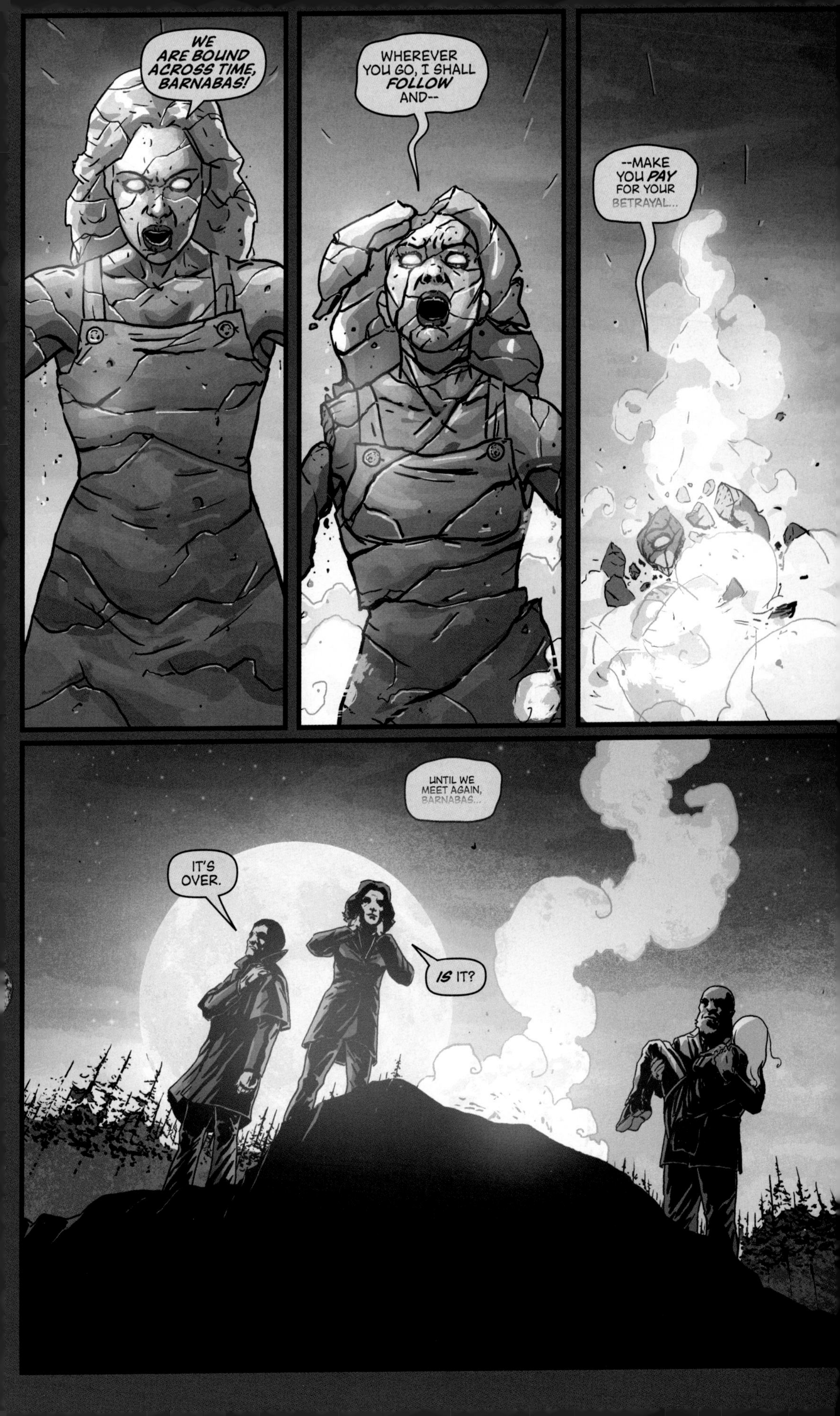
WE ARE BOUND ACROSS TIME, BARNABAS!
WHEREVER YOU GO, I SHALL FOLLOW AND--
--MAKE YOU PAY FOR YOUR BETRAYAL...
UNTIL WE MEET AGAIN, BARNABAS...
IT'S OVER.
IS IT?

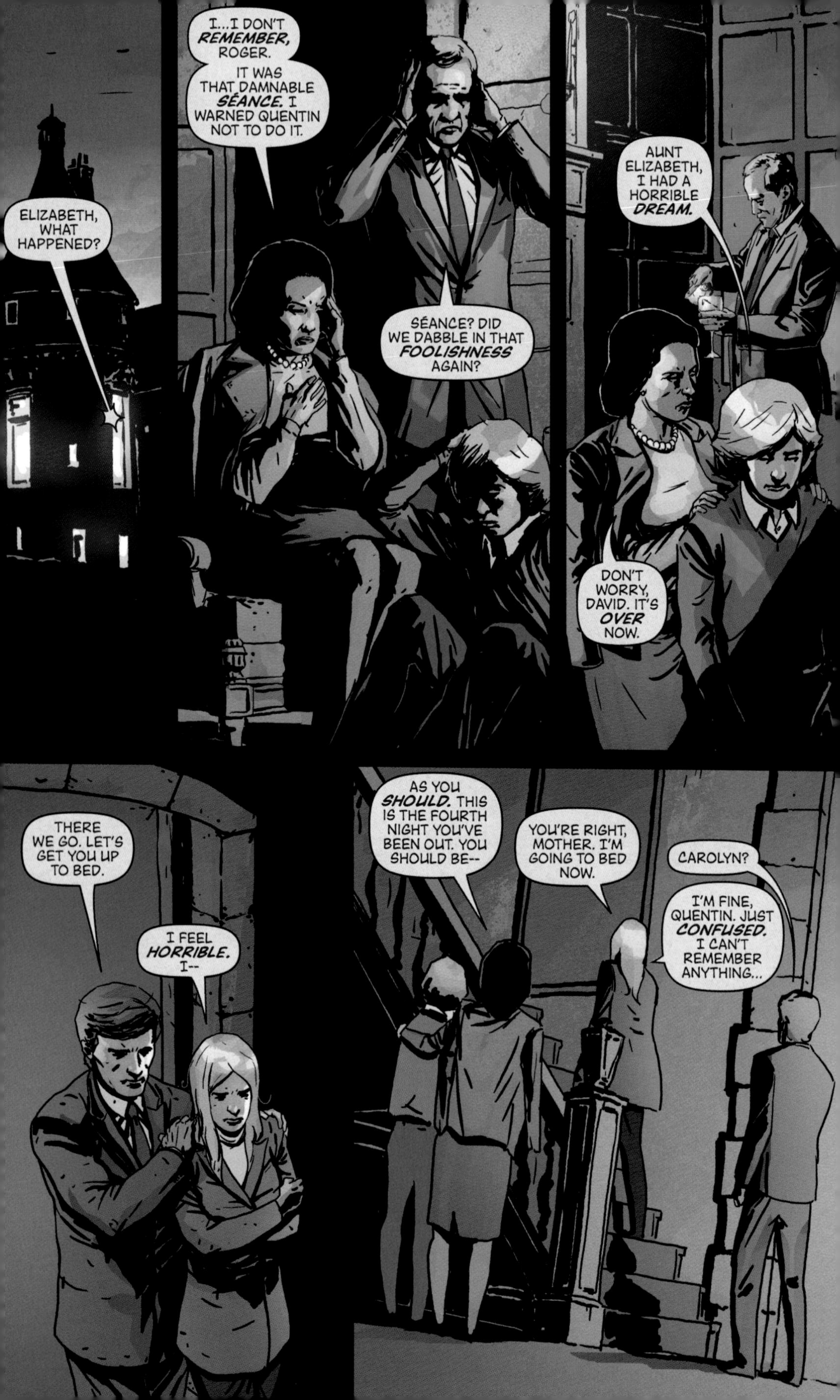
ELIZABETH, WHAT HAPPENED?
I...I DON'T REMEMBER, ROGER.
IT WAS THAT DAMNABLE SÉANCE. I WARNED QUENTIN NOT TO DO IT.
SÉANCE? DID WE DABBLE IN THAT FOOLISHNESS AGAIN?
AUNT ELIZABETH, I HAD A HORRIBLE DREAM.
DON'T WORRY, DAVID. IT'S OVER NOW.
THERE WE GO. LET'S GET YOU UP TO BED.
I FEEL HORRIBLE. I--
AS YOU SHOULD. THIS IS THE FOURTH NIGHT YOU'VE BEEN OUT. YOU SHOULD BE--
YOU'RE RIGHT, MOTHER. I'M GOING TO BED NOW.
CAROLYN?
I'M FINE, QUENTIN. JUST CONFUSED. I CAN'T REMEMBER ANYTHING...

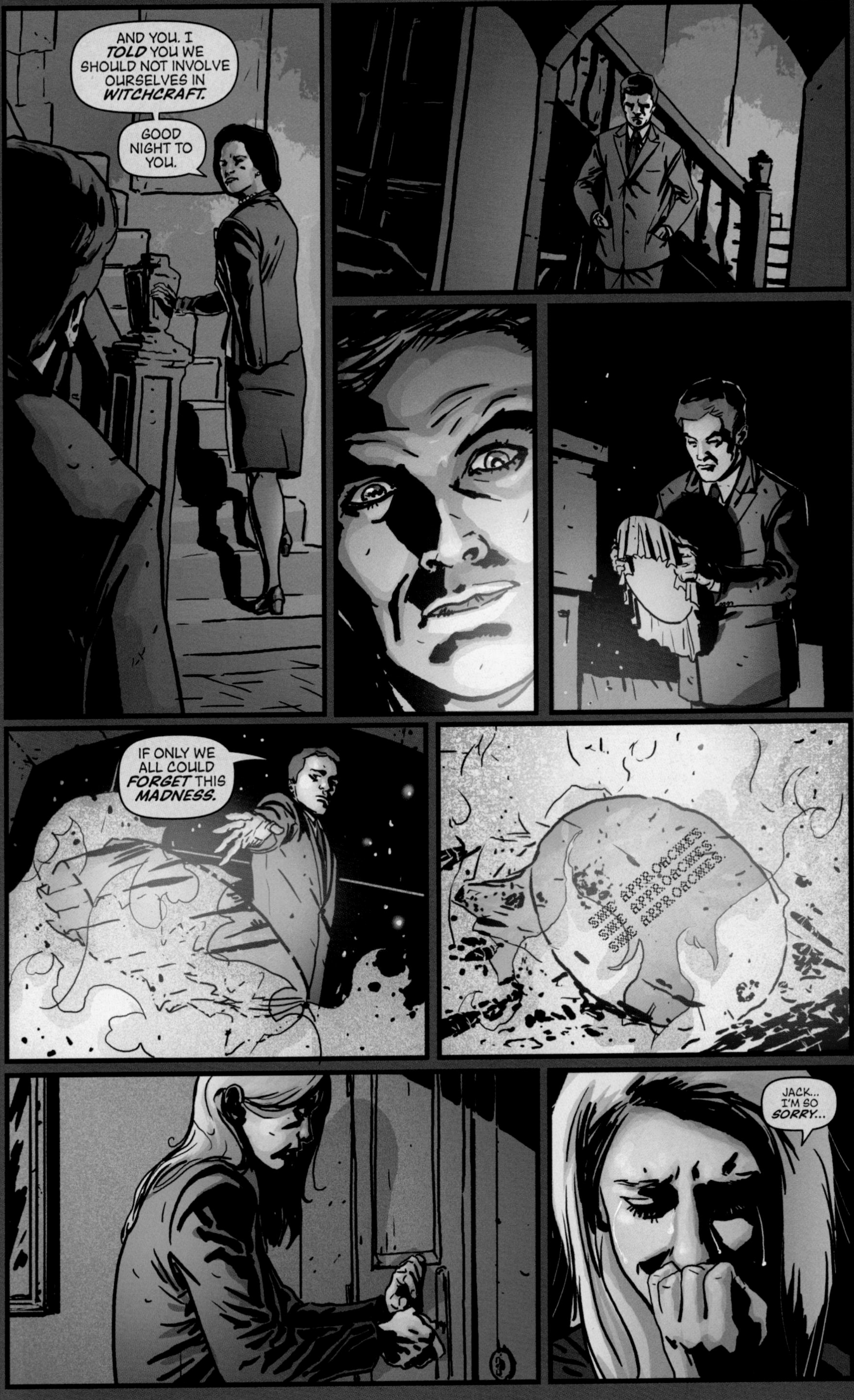
AND YOU. I TOLD YOU WE SHOULD NOT INVOLVE OURSELVES IN WITCHCRAFT.
GOOD NIGHT TO YOU.
IF ONLY WE ALL COULD FORGET THIS MADNESS.
SHE APPROACHES.
SHE APPROACHES.
SHE APPROACHES.
JACK... I'M SO SORRY...

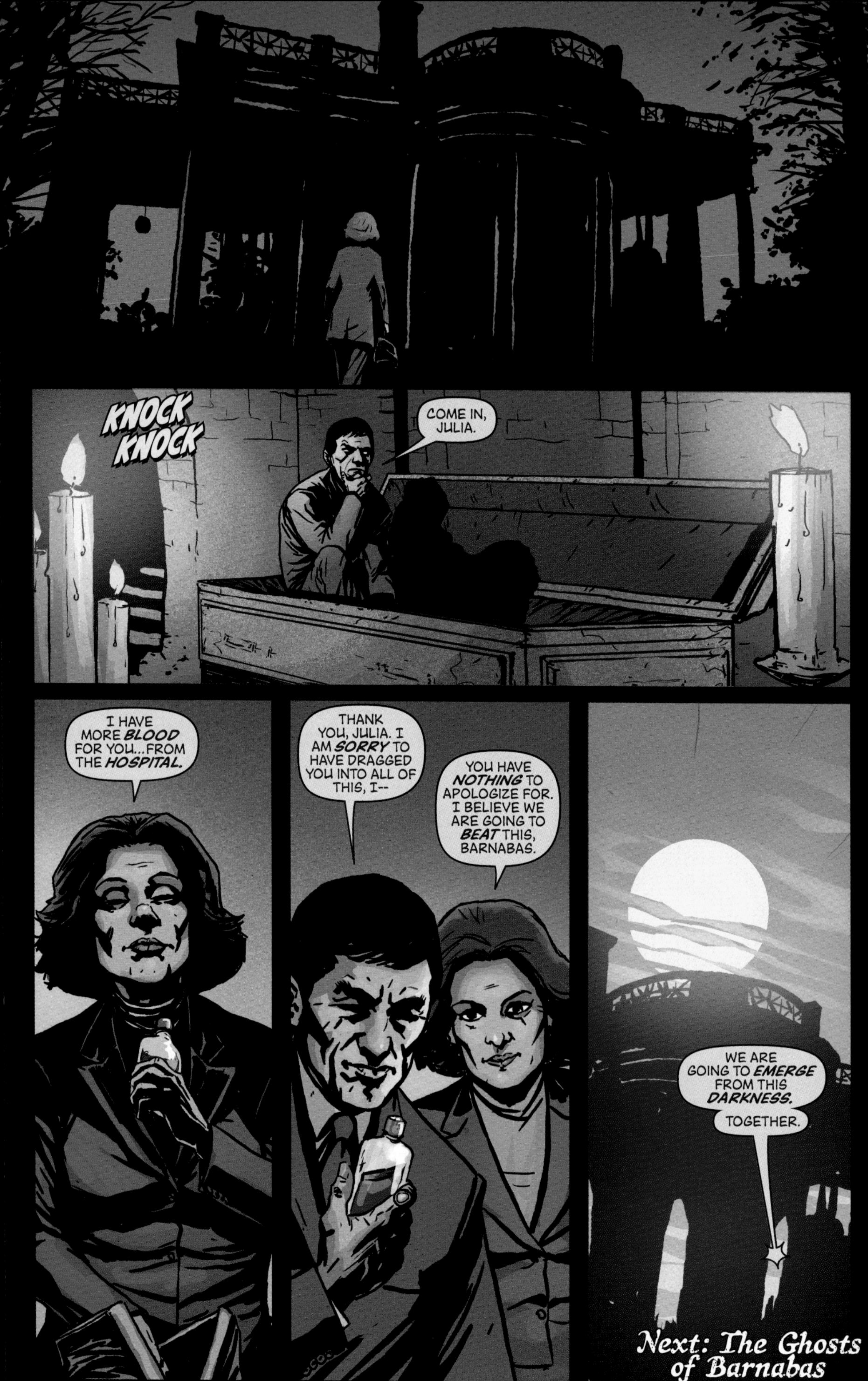
KNOCK KNOCK
COME IN, JULIA.
I HAVE MORE BLOOD FOR YOU...FROM THE HOSPITAL.
THANK YOU, JULIA. I AM SORRY TO HAVE DRAGGED YOU INTO ALL OF THIS, I--
YOU HAVE NOTHING TO APOLOGIZE FOR. I BELIEVE WE ARE GOING TO BEAT THIS, BARNABAS.
WE ARE GOING TO EMERGE FROM THIS DARKNESS.
TOGETHER.
Next: The Ghosts of Barnabas

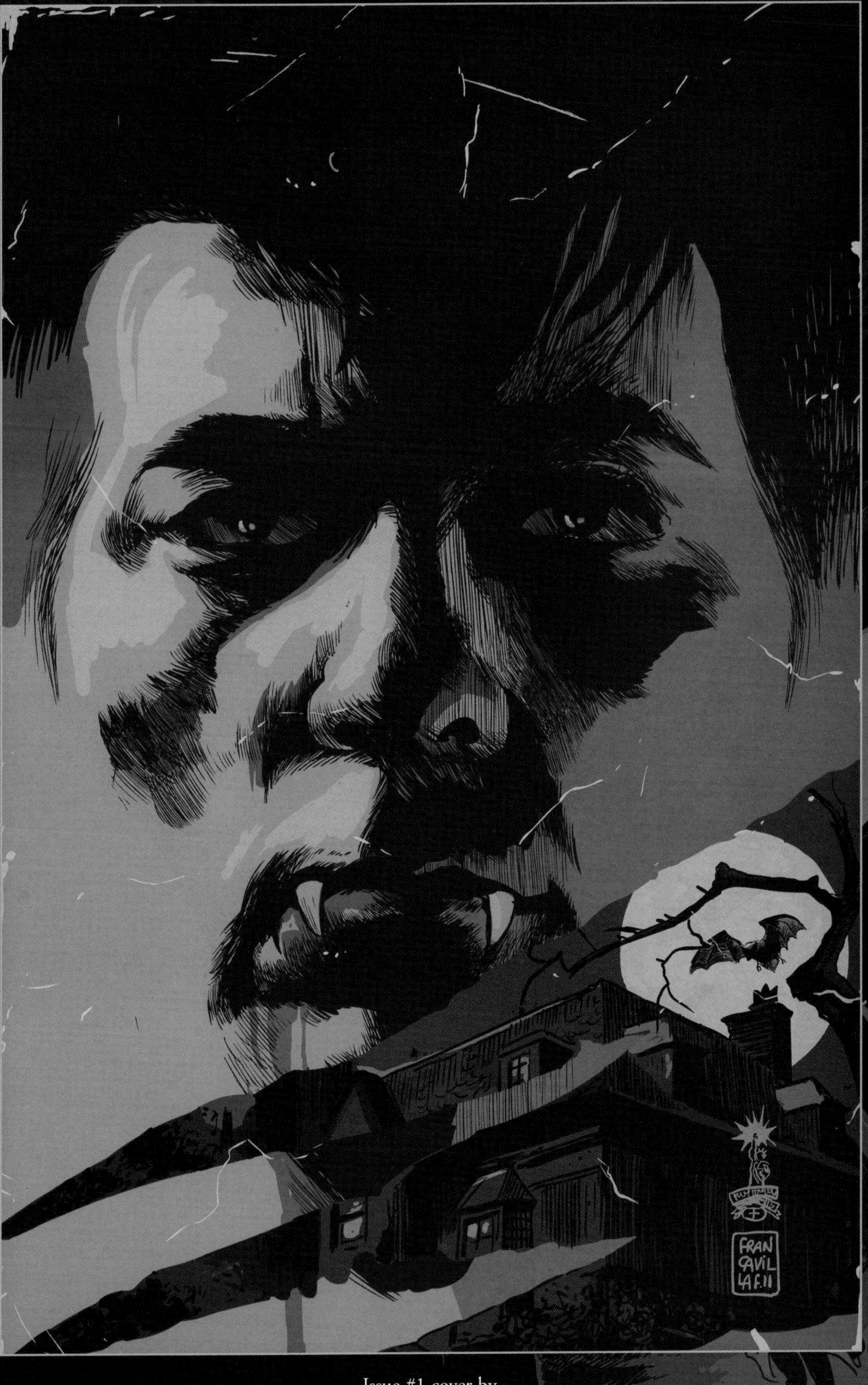
FRAN
CAVIL
LA F.11

Issue #1 cover by

FRANCESCO FRANCAVILLA

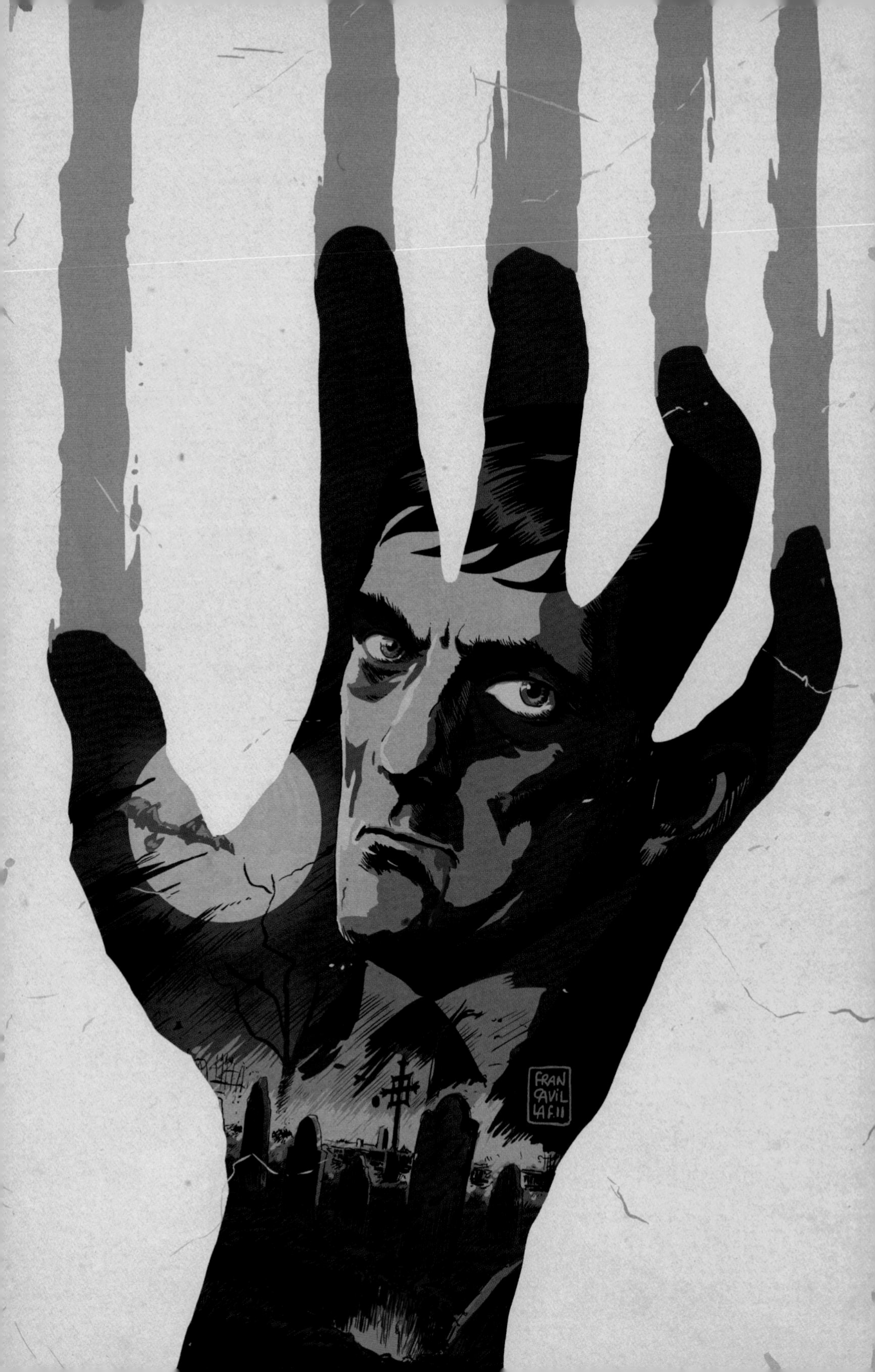
FRAN CAVIL LA F.11

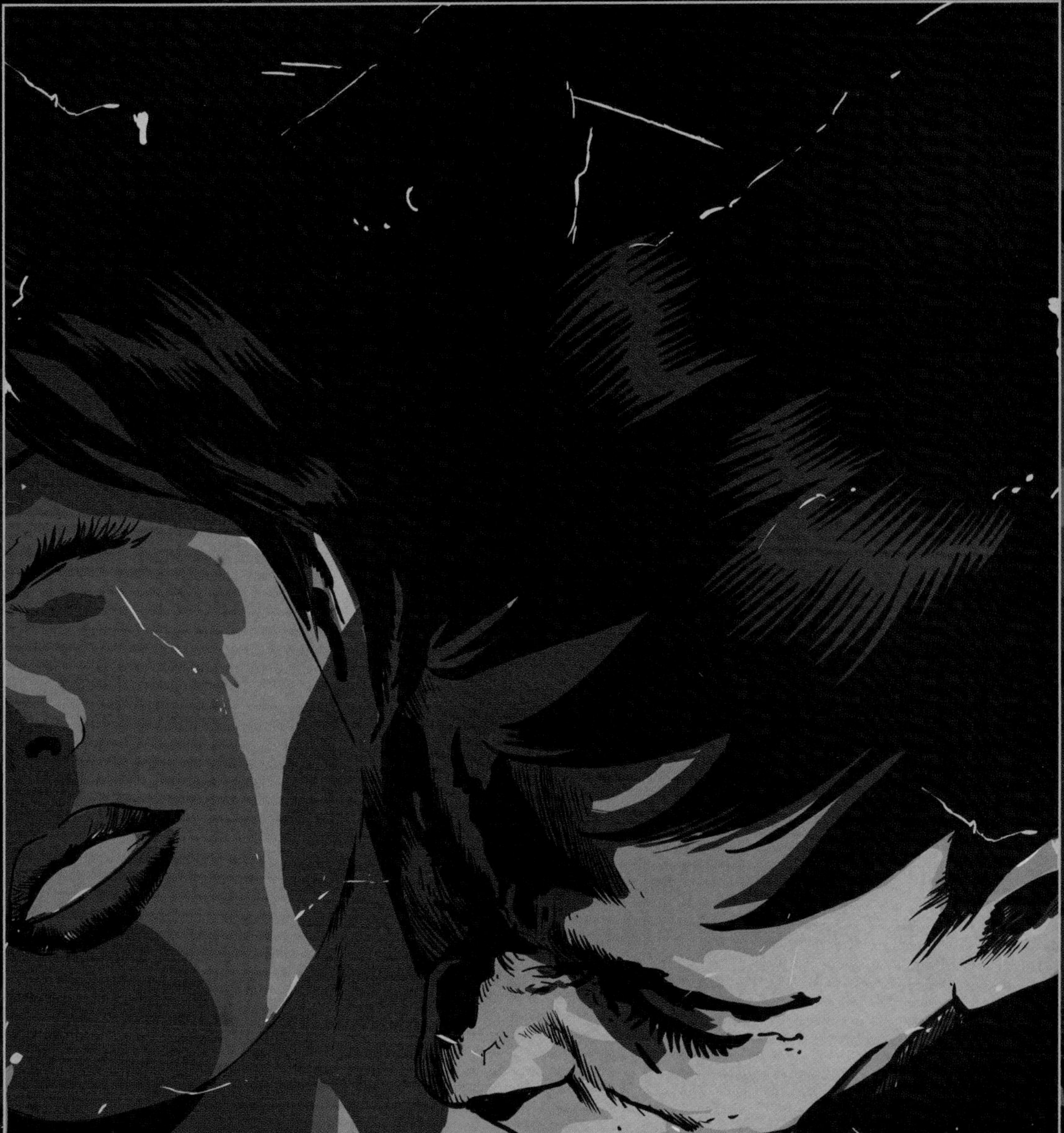

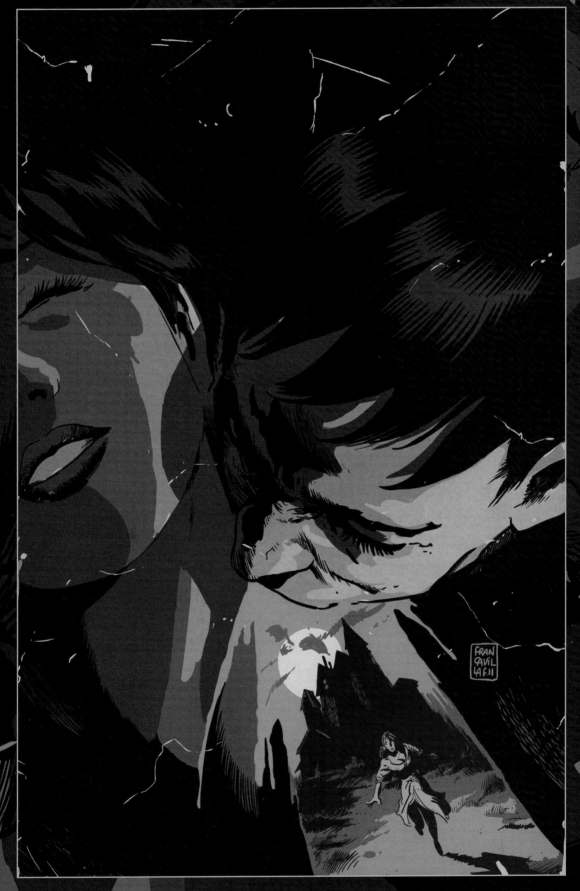

Issue #3 cover by

FRANCESCO FRANCAVILLA

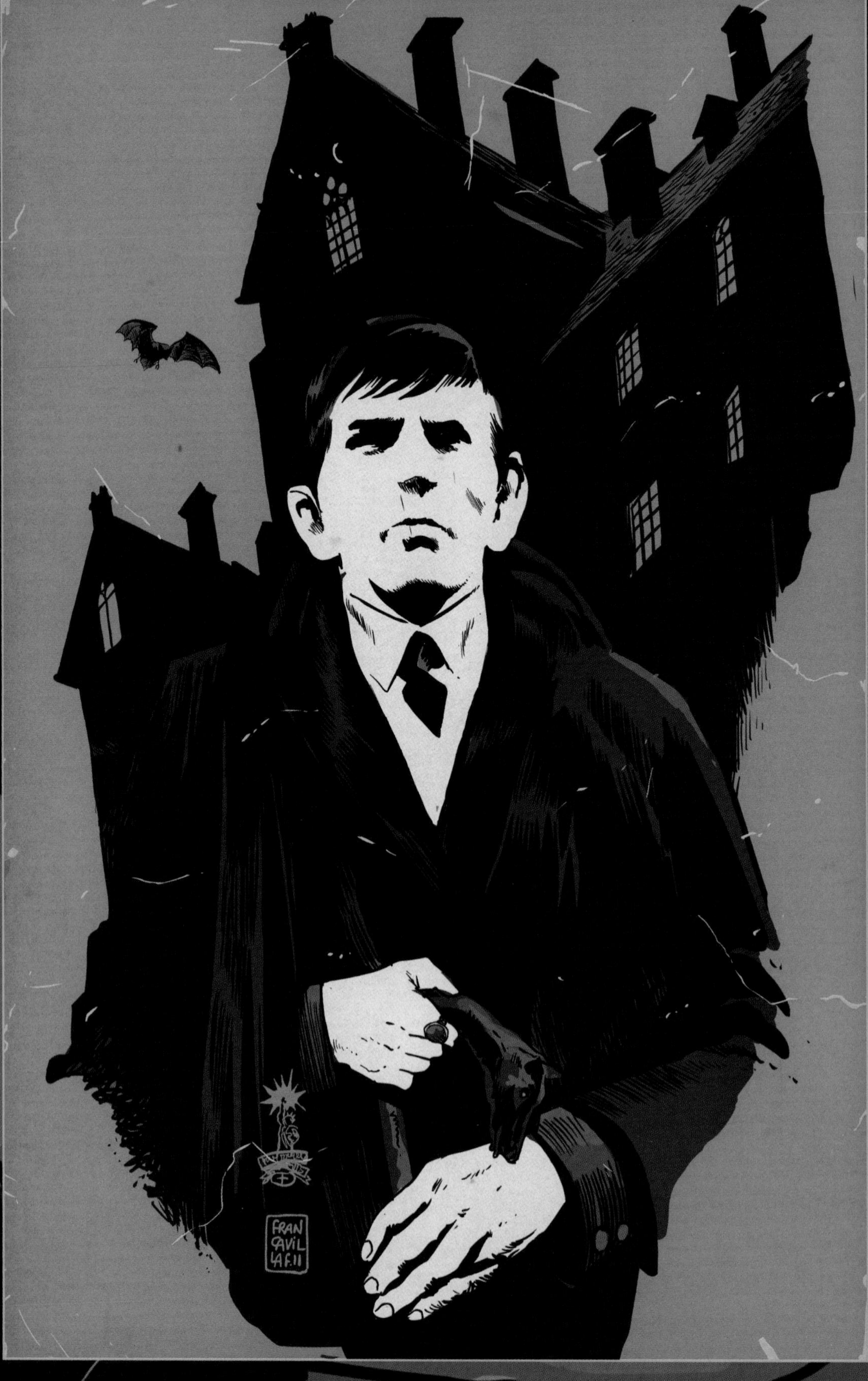
FRAN
CAVIL
LA F.11

Issue #4 cover by

FRANCESCO FRANCAVILLA

CASTING SHADOWS

A BEHIND-THE-SCENES LOOK AT DARK SHADOWS #1 BY ARIST **AARON CAMPBELL**

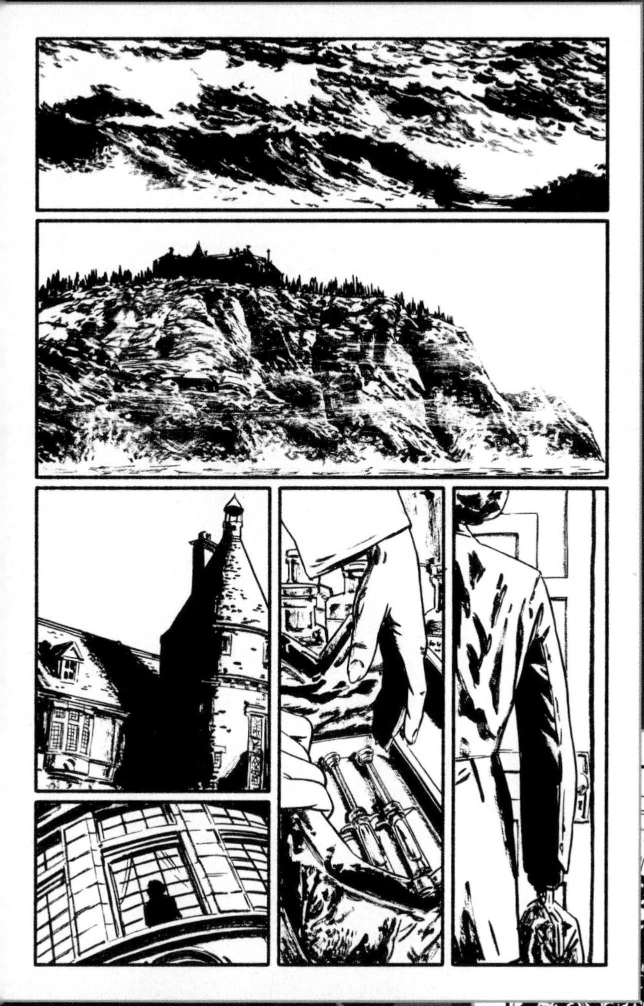

PAGE 1

The craggy, wind swept shore of Collinsport, Maine. In 1991 I was about 14 years old and I have a vague memory of a show called Dark Shadows. I remember that there was a vampire, a creepy old house, and some time traveling, oh and that kid from 3rd Rock from the Sun. What's his name? Joseph Gordon something? I didn't know anything at the time about the original show but that one always stuck with me. So when Dynamite told me about the project I was totally excited.

So here we are at the beginning or the end depending on how you see it. This story is based on the original show from the late 60's and in fact we're picking up where the series left off. Everything is based directly off the tv show right down the sets and actors. We have some good establishing shots of the Seaview mansion and a set up for Dr. Julia Hoffman.

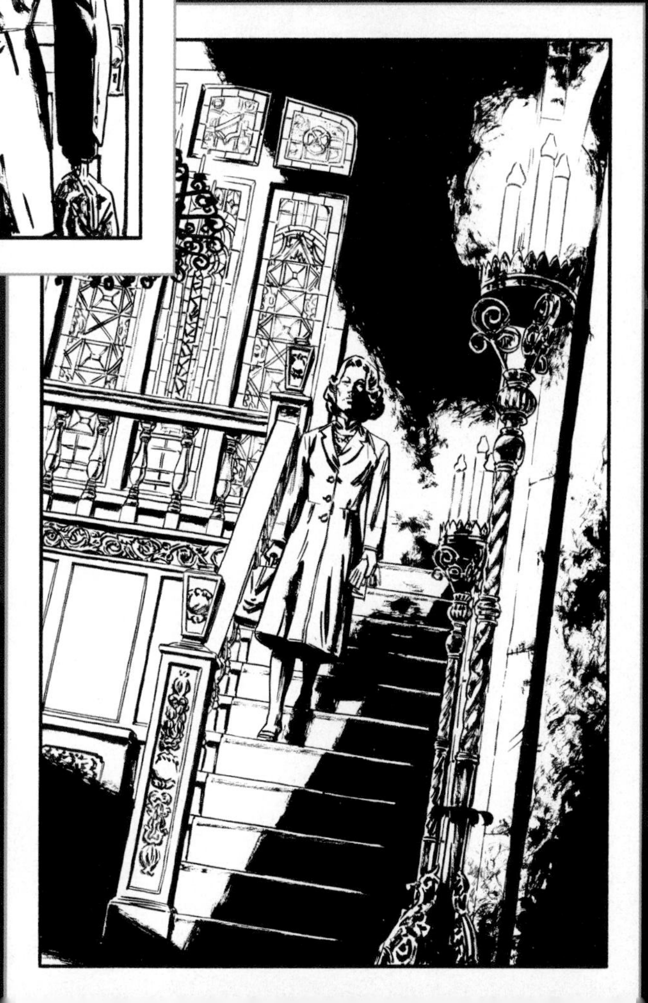

PAGE 2

This is a big establishing shot of the Collinwood Foyer. Typically for reoccurring locations I'll build a 3D model in Google Sketchup. For Dark Shadows, since we're being so faithful to the show, I've made models for all the locations that have appeared in the show. The models allow me to approach every panel the way a cinematographer would on a movie set. I can move around a physical space and find angles and perspectives that would otherwise elude me.

CASTING SHADOWS

A BEHIND-THE-SCENES LOOK AT DARK SHADOWS #1 BY ARIST **AARON CAMPBELL**

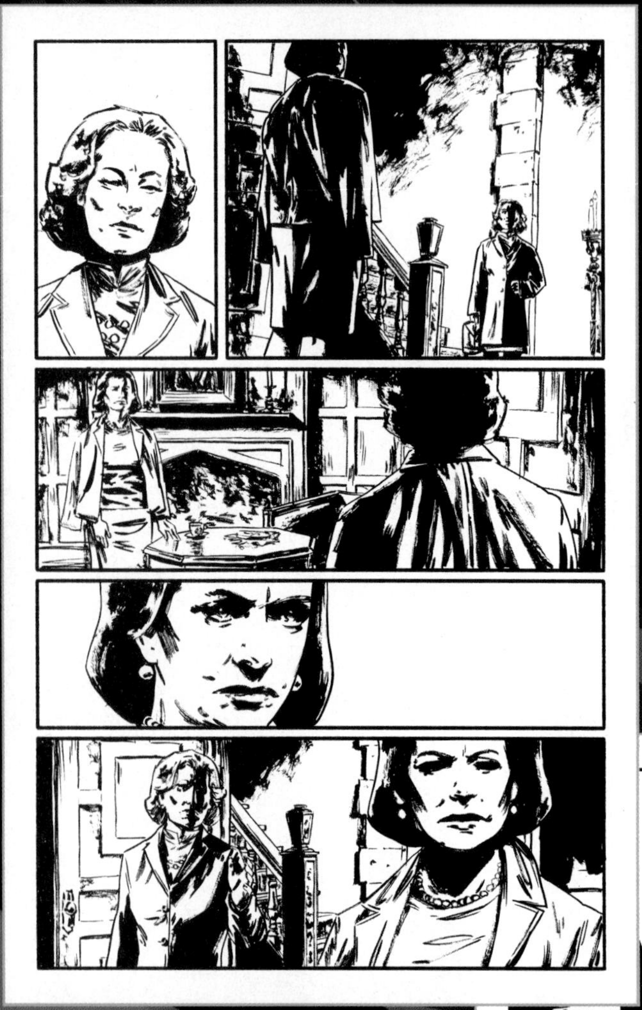

PAGE 3

Here we see Elizabeth for the first time as well as the Collinwood Drawing Room. My 3D models tend to get pretty detailed so one thing I do to help with my workflow is selectively construct them. What this means is that I will only build those parts of the models that I need for the moment. As I require different vantage points I will slowly add to the model piece by piece, area by area.

PAGE 4

Not much to say here, except to ponder what Elizabeth might be needle pointing here. All will be revealed.

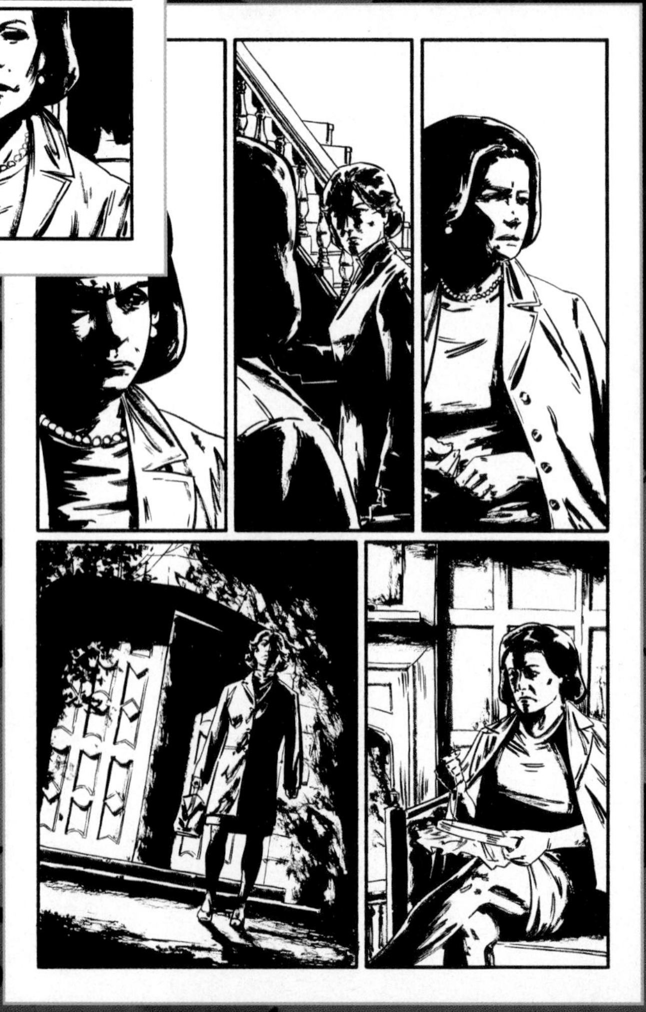

CASTING SHADOWS

A BEHIND-THE-SCENES LOOK AT DARK SHADOWS #1 BY ARIST **AARON CAMPBELL**

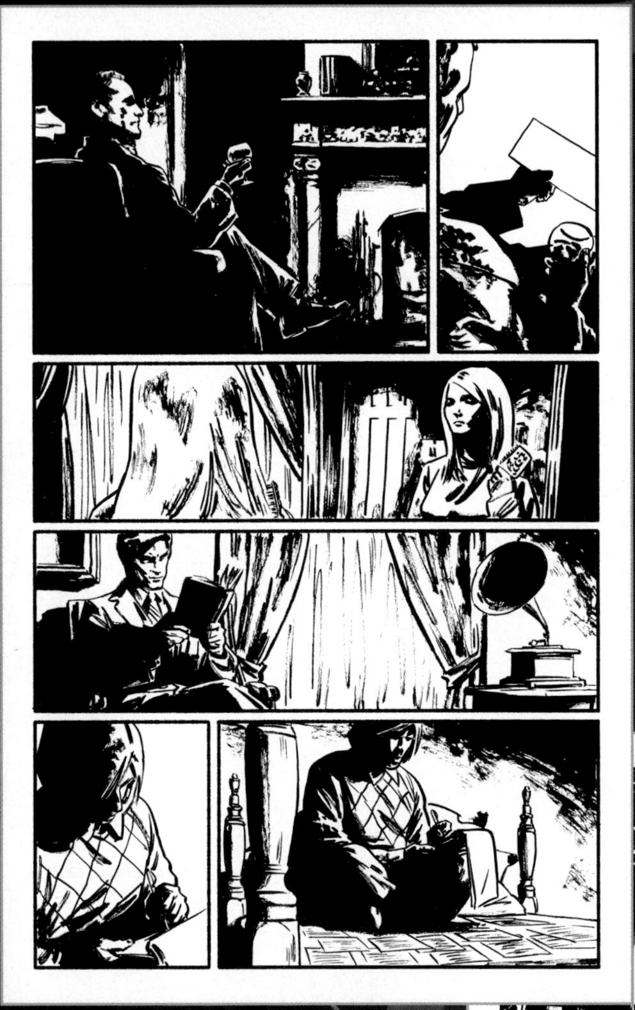

PAGE 5

So here we get to wonder about Collinwood and see what the others are up to. Looks like Roger, enjoying a snifter of brandy, had received a letter. Carolyn is getting ready for the night in her bedroom. A cock-sure Quentin reads by his gramophone, and a young boy is obsessively scribbling something on sheet after sheet of paper.

All the characters need to look like the actors who portrayed them. Needless to say I'm watching lots of Dark Shadows episodes now.

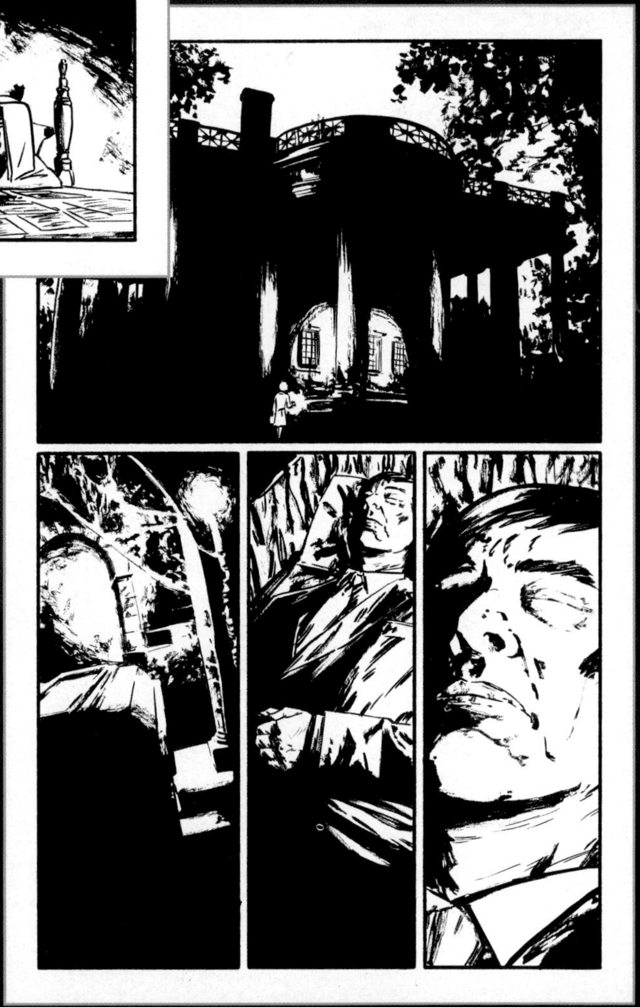

PAGE 6

Here we see the Old House for the first time. I find it funny that the "Old House" is a neo-classical style mansion while the newer Collinwood is an older style Tudor mansion. Just sayin'. Oh there's Barnabas in his coffin the basement.

CASTING SHADOWS

A BEHIND-THE-SCENES LOOK AT DARK SHADOWS #1 BY ARIST **AARON CAMPBELL**

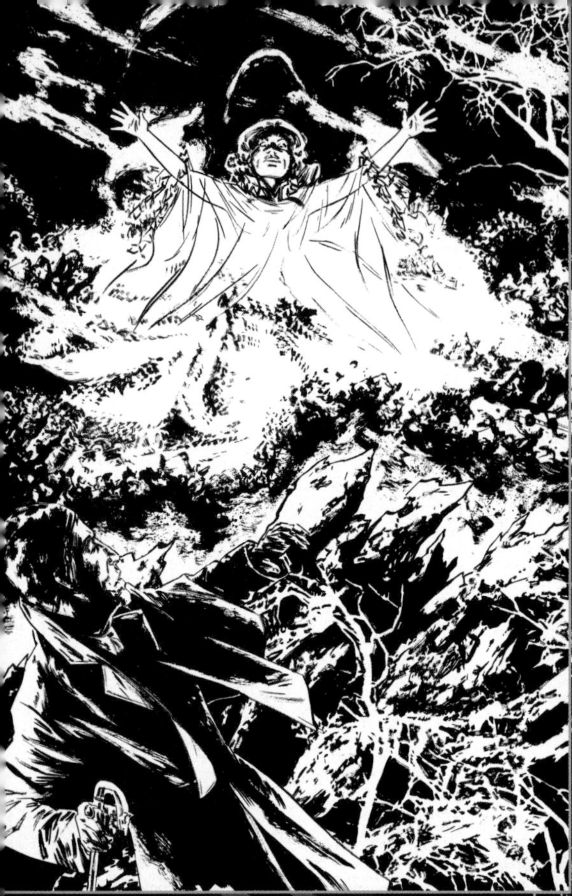

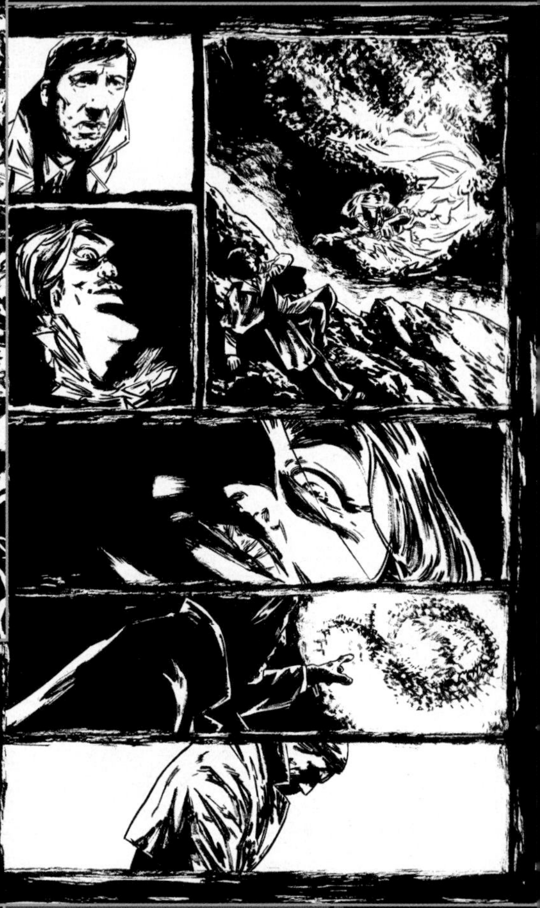

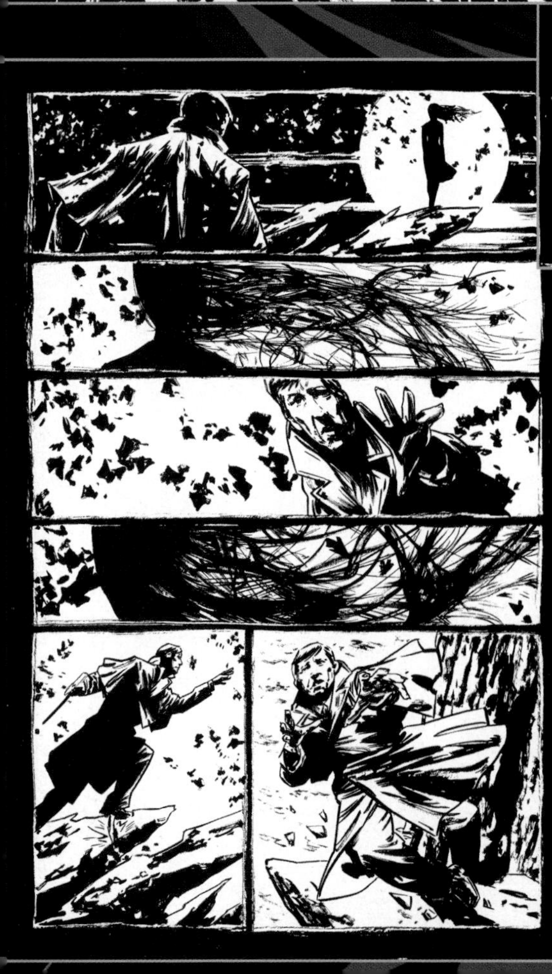

PAGES 7-9

Now we've entered into a nightmare dreamscape that is tormenting Barnabas' sleep. I've done a few things to set the dream world apart from the real world. For one, I've given the panels a loose, brushy border to heighten the sense of anxiety. I'm also distorting the figures, skewing and warping them. A lot of my visual effects are first drawn in Photoshop. For instance, the patterns that dissolve in and out of the spectral female figures were created using a brush form I made in Photoshop. I build these aspects of the image up digitally working back and forth until I get it where I like it. Figures are usually drawn in pencil that I scan and add to the background elements. I then print the pages in non-repro blue and ink over them for the finish.

CASTING SHADOWS

A BEHIND-THE-SCENES LOOK AT DARK SHADOWS #1 BY ARIST **AARON CAMPBELL**

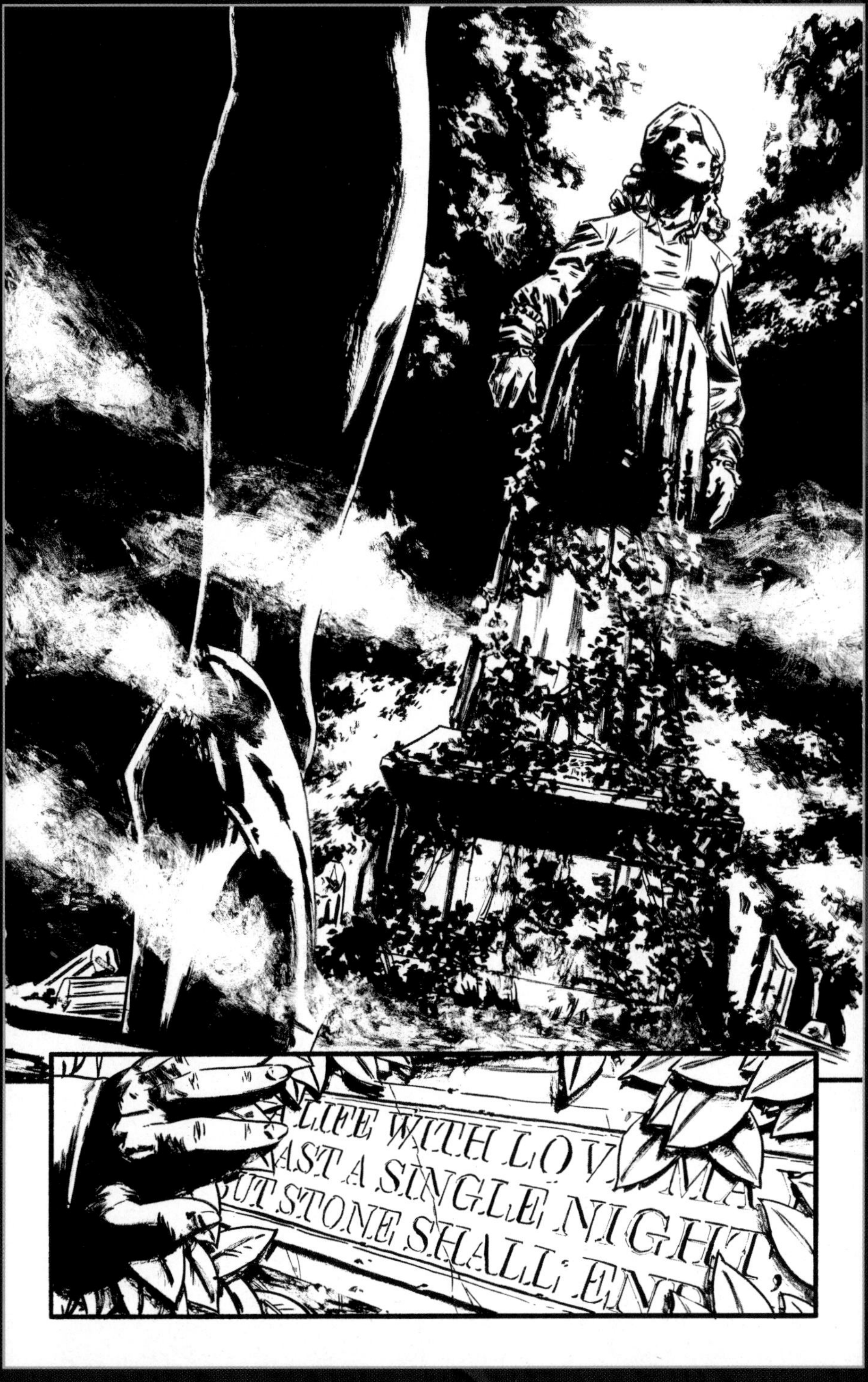
LIFE WITH LOV MA
AST A SINGLE NIGHT,
UT STONE SHALL EN

PAGE 18

I don't have a whole lot to add for the rest of the pages. I will talk briefly about a technique I've been developing that shows up on page 18. If you'll look, there's an interesting texture I'm getting in the smoke circling around the page. I do this with rubber cement. I carefully brush the cement onto the page before I begin inking using it as a resist. When I'm done inking I rub it off and I've got this really cool texture.

Well that's pretty much it. Hope you enjoyed a little view into my process!

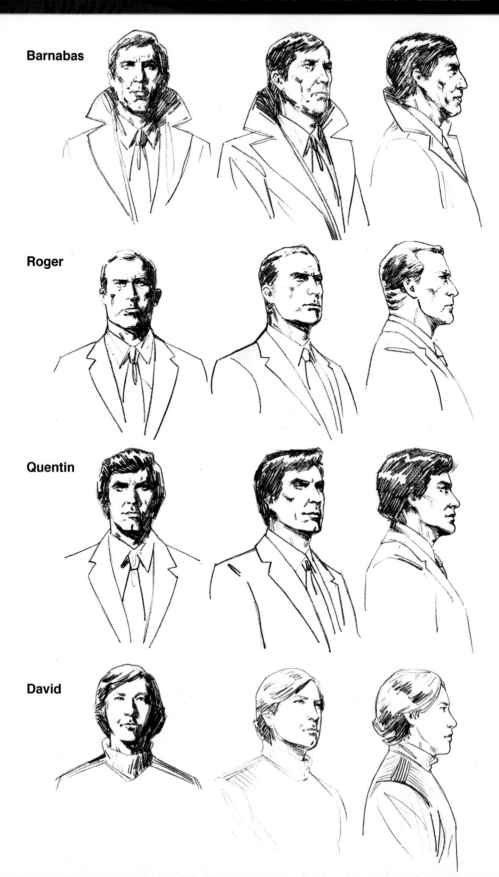

Barnabas

Roger

Quentin

David

CASTING SHADOWS

CHARACTER DESIGNS AND TURN-AROUNDS BY ARTIST **AARON CAMPBELL**

Angelique

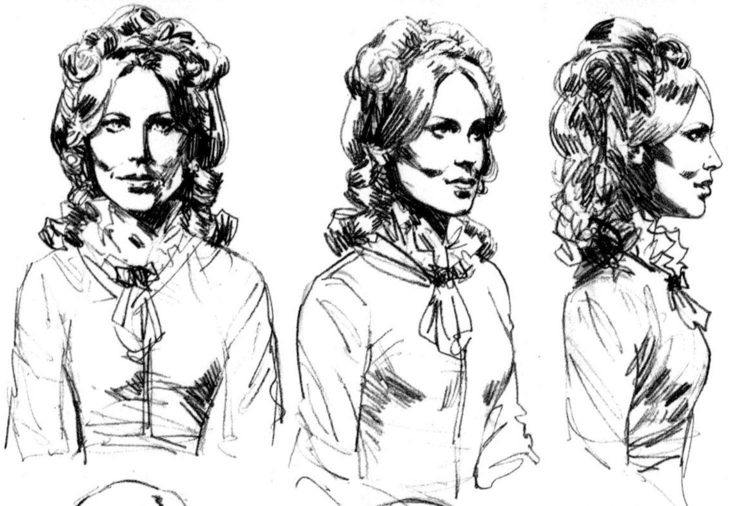

Carolyn

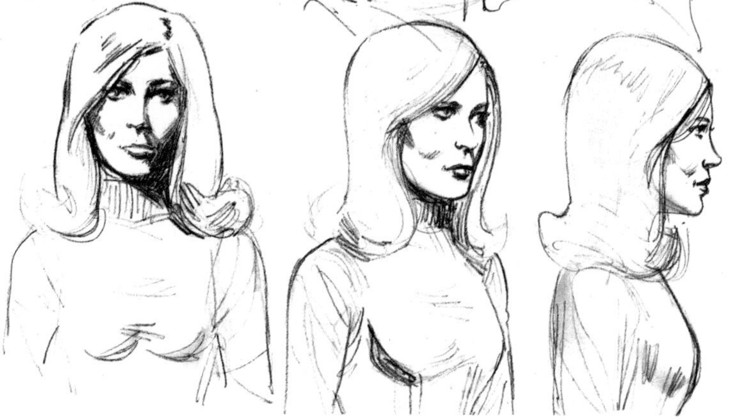

Julia

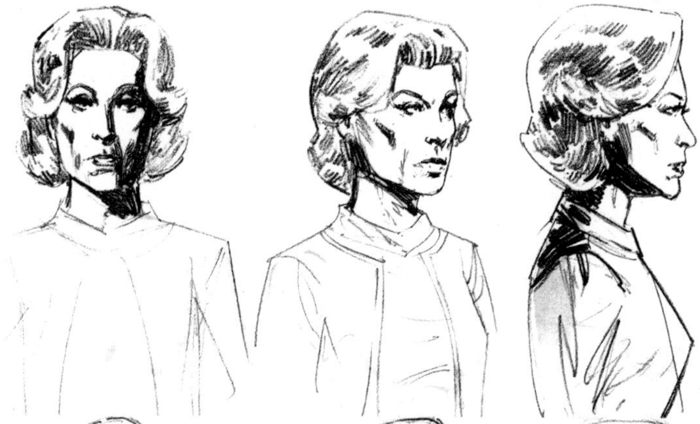

Elizabeth

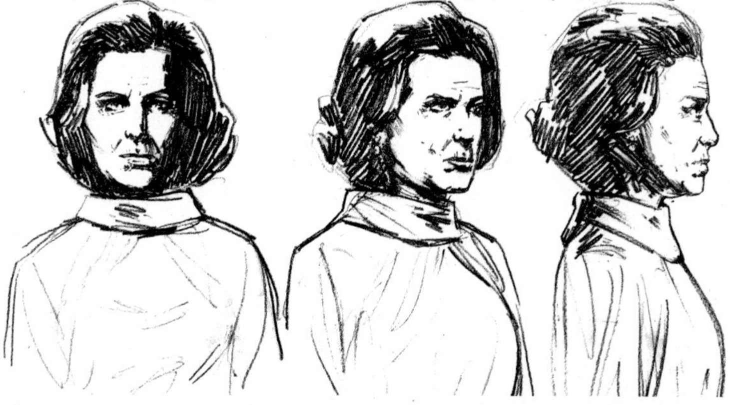